"This is an outstanding book and is must reading for all believers."

"One of the best ways to know somebody is through the testimony of one who has been a close and faithful friend. Bill Bright has spent half of a century in an intimate relationship with God. His devoted study of the attributes of God has prepared him to share with others rare and valuable insights into the character and the personality of Him, whom to know is life eternal."

—Dr. D. James Kennedy, Senior Minister,
Coral Ridge Presbyterian Church

"Dr. Bright, in his compelling and biblically based book, *GOD: Discover His Character*, reminds us that God's power and sovereignty are so awesome that He is eager to have a personal relationship with every person who humbly and sincerely seeks to know Him."

—George Gallup, Jr., Chairman,
George H. Gallup International Institute

"Daniel 11:32 says, '…but the people who know their God shall be strong, and carry out great exploits.' Dr. Bright has written a book that will help believers to know the Lord intimately and to practice courageous Christianity, which is so needed on our day."

—Bill McCartney, Founder & President, Promise Keepers

"I have known God to be a God of love, mercy, and a righteous judge, but Bill Bright's book, *GOD: Discover His Character*, has been a timely reminder to me of His greatness and majesty. A great book to read for even the most mature Christian!"

—Beverly LaHaye, Founder and Chairman,
Concerned Women for America

"Who would not want to know God? And who of us who know God would not want to know Him more personally? This book will help us not only to know about God but to know Him intimately. Every one of us would do well to read these pages carefully and prayerfully."

—Dr. Paul Cedar, Chairman, Mission America

"As we know His power, presence, mercy, and sovereignty, we begin to understand how God deals with us. As we understand His holiness, truth, and righteousness, we again understand His plan and purpose for our life. By understanding the love, mercy, and faithfulness of God, we understand how He forgives all sinners and loves us equally. Bill

Bright has shown us that understanding His attributes helps us to understand God and to live for Him."
—*Elmer L. Towns, Dean, School of Religion, Liberty University*

"Many people know about God, but Bill Bright has written from a personal walk with God, thus it has been a life of discovery that is not his alone, but for all who desire to know God. This is an outstanding book and is must reading for all believers."
—*Thomas E. Trask, General Superintendent, Assemblies of God*

"If we want to make sure our obedience is on target, we first need to make sure that it is grounded in a love relationship with the One to whom we are to be obedient. This book will help you do just that."
—*Robert E. Reccord, President, North American Mission Board, Southern Baptist Convention*

"What an incredible book! Bill Bright eloquently describes what it's like to come into the awesome presence of God. As I read the book, I found myself weeping as I was reminded of His glory, greatness, and majesty!"
—*Dr. Stan Toler, Senior Pastor, Trinity Church of the Nazarene, Oklahoma City*

"In his book, *GOD: Discover His Character*, Bill Bright has captured the heart cry of all sincere Christians…that we may discover the glory of God and His ways toward all mankind."
—*Pat Robertson, Chairman & CEO, The Christian Broadcasting Network, Inc.*

"To know God as He is revealed in Holy Scripture is to love Him and your attitude toward Him will affect almost everything you do in life, particularly the way you feel toward other people. Because he has studied the Scriptures carefully and put God to many tests for over fifty years, no one is better qualified to describe God than Bill Bright. This book will enrich your life!"
—*Tim LaHaye, President, Tim LaHaye Ministries*

"In his new book, *GOD: Discover His Character*, Dr. Bright challenges readers to understand and apply profound truths about the nature and character of God to daily living. The true value of this book lies in its focus on the interaction between understanding the truth about God and the way we are to live in this world. I highly recommend this rich emphasis."
—*Michael D. Cozzens, PhD., Academic Dean, International School of Theology*

GOD

DISCOVER HIS CHARACTER

BILL BRIGHT

GOD: Discover His Character

Published by
NewLife Publications
A ministry of Campus Crusade for Christ
P.O. Box 620877
Orlando, FL 32862-0877

Design and production by Genesis Publications.

Edited by Joette Whims.

Cover by Koechel-Peterson Design.

Printed in the United States of America.

ISBN 1-56399-125-X

Unless otherwise indicated, Scripture quotations are from the *New Living Translation*, © 1996 by Tyndale Charitable Trust.

Scripture quotations designated NIV are from the *New International Version*, © 1973, 1978, 1984 by the International Bible Society. Published by Zondervan Bible Publishers, Grand Rapids, Michigan.

Scripture quotations designated TLB are from *The Living Bible*, © 1971 by Tyndale House Publishers, Wheaton, Illinois.

Scripture quotations designated NKJ are from the *New King James* version, © 1979, 1980, 1982 by Thomas Nelson Inc., Publishers, Nashville, Tennessee.

Scripture quotations designated NASB are from *The New American Standard Bible*, © 1960, 1962, 1963, 1968, 1971, 1972, 1973, 1975, 1977 by the Lockman Foundation, La Habra, California.

For more information, write:
L.I.F.E., Campus Crusade for Christ—P.O. Box 40, Flemington Markets, NSW 2129, Australia
Campus Crusade for Christ of Canada—Box 529, Sumas, WA 98295
Campus Crusade for Christ—Fairgate House, King's Road, Tyseley, Birmingham, B11 2AA, United Kingdom
Lay Institute for Evangelism, Campus Crusade for Christ—P.O. Box 8786, Auckland, 1035, New Zealand
Campus Crusade for Christ—9 Lock Road #3-03, PacCan Centre, Singapore 108937
Great Commission Movement of Nigeria—P.O. Box 500, Jos, Plateau State, Nigeria, West Africa
Campus Crusade for Christ International—P.O. Box 620877, Orlando, FL 32862-0877, USA

DEDICATION

This book is gratefully dedicated to every person who has faithfully prayed for or supported our ministry over the years. In particular, I dedicate this book to the members of History's Handful, a movement of leaders committed to a special strategy to provide resources to help fulfill the Great Commission. These unselfish servants have made possible many, many projects that might not have otherwise been accomplished without their generous sacrifices of personal time and resources.

CONTENTS

PART III: OUR GRACIOUS SAVIOR
(Attributes of Relationship)

PART IV: CONCLUSION

APPENDICES: HELPS FOR SPIRITUAL GROWTH

ACKNOWLEDGMENTS

Remembering and thanking all the people who have influenced me in writing this book over the past fifty years or more would be almost impossible. To the poet's line, "No man is an island," I must add that no author writes a book solely on his or her own efforts and knowledge. Literally hundreds of people have contributed to my journey of seeking and knowing God.

In the early days of my spiritual walk with our Lord, my pastor, Dr. Louis Evans, and our church's Christian Education Director, Dr. Henrietta Mears, nurtured me with their preaching, teaching, and personal friendship. During the five years of my theological studies at Princeton and Fuller Theological Seminaries, I was blessed to learn under spiritual giants such as their presidents, Dr. John A. Mackay and Dr. Harold J. Ockenga. My professors also opened up the Word of God to enrich my life and ministry. A few that I remember the most included Dr. Carl F. H. Henry, Dr. Charles E. Fuller, Dr. Robert Smith, and Dr. Wilbur Smith.

In addition to my formal study in the Word and personal experiences with God, I have learned much from the writings of great biblical scholars and effective ministers of the gospel. I have shared some of their rich insights with you in this book. They include men such as A. W. Tozer, J. I. Packer, Stephen Charnock, Arthur Pink, Charles Stanley, Chuck Colson, Tony Evans, David Jeremiah, D. James Kennedy, Bill Hybels, Jim Cymbala, Norman Geisler, R. C. Sproul, Erwin Lutzer, Ravi Zacharias, Henry Blackaby, and many others. I commend their speaking and writing to anyone who wants to know God more intimately.

I am particularly indebted to my dear friend of more than forty years, Dr. Adrian Rogers, pastor of the famous Bellevue Baptist Church, Memphis, Tennessee, for expressing his thoughts in the Foreword to this book.

My special heartfelt thanks go to researchers and writers Les Stobbe, Helmut Teichert, Nancy Schraeder, and Jim Bramlett. I am indebted to my *NewLife* Publications staff: Dr. Joe Kilpatrick, publisher and general editor; Joette Whims, substantive editing and polishing; John Barber, theological review; Tammy Campbell, editorial assistant; and Michelle Treiber, cover coordination and print brokering. My gratitude also goes to Lynn Copeland of Genesis Publications for her design, typesetting, and copyediting.

Finally, I save my dearest expressions of love and appreciation for my beloved wife of more than fifty years, Vonette. She has walked with me through the good times and the hard times over these years as we have learned to love, trust, obey, and fellowship with our great God and Savior, the mighty Creator of the Universe.

FOREWORD

I guess I should not have been shocked to read recently a national newspaper article titled, "Few TV Dads Give Positive Vibrations." The National Fatherhood Initiative report stated, "For millions of America's children, the primary daily contact they have with the idea of a father is the time they spend watching a father on television." Yet according to a five-week review of prime-time programming on five major networks late last year, only 14.7 percent of these programs featured fatherhood enough to be rated. Of these, only four programs promoted responsible fatherhood positively.

The seriousness of this situation is that 40 percent of the nation's children do not live with their biological fathers, and whole communities exist where single mothers head almost all the households. Is it any wonder that too many children grow up with a distorted, false view of what a good father is really like? Without a healthy view of an earthly father, how can they picture a loving heavenly Father?

Even children who grow up in church often do not reach adulthood with a positive view of God. In an article titled, "When You Think of God, What Do You See?" (*Life*, December 1998), author Frank McCourt expresses the experience of many children and teens:

> We didn't hear much about a loving God. We were told God is good and that was supposed to be enough. Otherwise the God of my memory is one the tribes of Israel would have recognized, an angry God, a vengeful God, a God who will let you have it upside your head if you strayed, transgressed, or coveted. Our God had a stern face…and a message of damnation from the pulpit, scaring us to death. If we didn't understand [some doctrine] and asked questions, we were brushed aside and told it was a matter of faith so [eat your dinner] and shut up."

This article also reported that 96 percent of Americans believe in God and 79 percent pray to God and feel that He has helped them make decisions. McCourt continues:

America's God is vaguely defined. Ours is not a monocultural nation like, say Iran, Italy or Japan, but a proudly diverse one. On the contrary, America makes it society's business to support, protect and nurture minority viewpoints, values, and traditions. Within these are many different views of God (sometimes gods, plural; sometimes "exalted beings" possessing a divine essence). America has become one nation under "gods."

As immigrants bring their religions with them and many Americans experiment with philosophical beliefs based on humanism or secularism, we have indeed become a nation under many gods. The crucial question for all these culturally diverse worshippers and philosophical seekers is, "Who is the one true God who can remove their sins and give them eternal life in heaven after they die?"

There is an answer, and I am so happy that my good friend, Dr. Bill Bright, is addressing this important question of who God is and what He is like. It is a privilege for me to recommend this book, *GOD: Discover His Character*. Having walked with God for almost six decades, Bill's passion, like the apostle Paul's, is to know God and make Him known to others. Here he shares his experiences and the biblical truths he has learned for knowing, loving, serving, and worshipping his God.

As you read this book, you will see the many sides of God's character and nature. These truths, converted into principles of relating to our awesome, majestic God, will help you at every turn in the road of life. In the troubled and uncertain times in which we live, it is comforting to know the God of the holy Bible, the Constitution of the Christian faith. When there are so many gods to choose from, even here in America, we need this solid word of the one true God in this unsure age in which we live.

DR. ADRIAN ROGERS
Senior Pastor, Bellevue Baptist Church
Memphis, Tennessee

CHAPTER 1

CAN ANYONE *REALLY* KNOW GOD?

Have you ever considered one of the most important questions anyone could ask? *Is it possible for a mere human, less than a tiny speck on a pebble of a planet in the midst of a vast galaxy, to know the great God who created everything?* If so, can we know God well enough to trust Him with the most sensitive areas in our lives? Even more, *do* we know God well enough to love and obey Him in whatever He asks of us? The quest to know, love, and serve God is the greatest adventure in life!

Yet the goal of knowing God may seem impossible. We can compare our quest to know God to the story of a microscopic mite that lived on a flea on a little dog in a small yard of a humble home. This house was on the outskirts of Jerusalem in the kingdom of the rich and powerful King Solomon, who reigned centuries ago. The king lived in a mysterious palace in the midst of royal elegance far beyond the microscopic world of the mite. In mite miles, the distance from the mite to the king's palace seemed like light years.

This tiny mite decided that the most important work he could ever do was to write a book about that world-respected king.

13

After reflecting on his book for a long time, the frustrated mite abandoned his project. He just did not know what to write; he had a deep desire, but none of his words seemed adequate to describe such a majestic person.

In a very real sense, that was my predicament as I set forth to write about our glorious and mighty God. He lives in indescribable splendor beyond my wildest imagination. His character is far above the limited scope of my human understanding. The only difference between me and the mite that wanted to write about King Solomon is that, compared to God, I am less than a mite in this universe of more than one hundred billion galaxies.

Have you ever felt like I do about understanding and knowing our great God? How can we as mere human beings fully grasp any facet of our gloriously incomprehensible God? So why would I attempt to undertake such a seemingly impossible task? More importantly, why should any of us try to understand who God is?

Why Is It So Important to Know God?

My desire to write a book about God began many years ago when Dr. James Montgomery Boice of the "Bible Hour" radio program interviewed me. One of the first questions Dr. Boice asked me was, "What is the most important truth to teach any follower of Christ?"

What an incredible question! No one had ever asked me that before, so I was not prepared to answer it. For a brief moment, I was speechless. But then I am convinced that God's Holy Spirit gave me the answer: "The attributes of God."

I have had years to think about that question and my answer. Today I am more convinced than ever that there is nothing more important to teach another believer than who God is, what He is like, and why or how He does what He does. These attributes of God can be referred to as His character, nature, qualities, or personality.

Yet one of the most tragic trends I have noticed in our churches today is the way believers view God. Renowned author A. W. Tozer writes in his book *The Knowledge of the Holy:*

The low view of God entertained almost universally among Christians is the cause of a hundred lesser evils everywhere among us. With our loss of the sense of majesty has come the further loss of religious awe and the consciousness of the divine presence...It is impossible to keep our moral practices sound and our inward attitudes right while our idea of God is erroneous or inadequate. If we would bring back spiritual power to our lives, we must begin to think of God more nearly as He is.[1]

In fact, everything about our lives—our attitudes, motives, desires, actions, and even our words—is influenced by our view of God. Whether our problems are financial, moral, or emotional, whether we are tempted by lust, worry, anger, or insecurity, our behavior reflects our beliefs about God. What we believe to be true about God's character affects our friendships, our work and leisure activities, the types of literature we read, and even the music to which we listen. If the majority of believers do not have the right view of God, how can our society even begin to see Him as He is? Because of the wrong view of God that predominates in all areas of our culture today, our society is in moral turmoil, and we are in danger of losing our moral soul.

We can trace all our human problems to our view of God. A contrast in two lives from history illustrates the different outcomes that result from a wrong and a right view of God.

The first example is Karl Marx, who was born in Trier, Germany, in 1818. Educated in German universities, he became the editor of a Cologne newspaper. Marx denied the existence of God, believing that the individual, not God, is the highest form of being. Instead of God being in control, he felt that people make themselves what they are by their own efforts. Society, therefore, is the supreme agent for achieving success and fulfillment.

In *Economic and Philosophic Manuscripts of 1844,* he wrote, "All that is called history is nothing else than the process of creating man through human labour, the becoming of nature for man. Man has thus evident and irrefutable proof of his own creation by himself...For man, man is the supreme being."[2]

Since Marx believed that man was a god, he concluded that society, composed of the common man, should rule and overthrow the reigning government by force. He and Fredrich Engel collaborated on defining philosophical ideals that eventually formed the basis for communism.

In the 20th century, Vladimir Lenin revived Marx's ideas, accomplishing the overthrow of the czarist rule in Russia. Stalin followed Lenin as Communist leader of the Soviet Union. Under their reigns and the Communist rulers who followed them, tens of millions of Russians were slaughtered by the state. The loss of life resulted because these Communist leaders believed that there was no God, that the individual had no inherent value, and that the state was of supreme importance. Today, Marx's ideas still form the basis for totalitarian government in many countries, including North Korea, Cuba, and China.

HOW WE VIEW GOD WILL CHANGE THE WAY WE LIVE AND RELATE WITH OTHERS.

Contrast the life of Marx with the life of Martin Luther. He too was a revolutionary. He was born in 1483 in Eisleben, Germany, only a couple of hundred miles from where Marx would later begin his life. Martin Luther was also educated in German universities.

Like Marx, the young Luther struggled with ideals of authority, morality, and ethics. Although he tried to serve God as a monk, he grew increasingly terrified of God's wrath. Then he was drawn to Romans 1:17, "The righteous shall live by faith." This simple concept changed his view of God. He wrote:

> At last, meditating day and night and by the mercy of God, I...began to understand that the righteousness of God is that through which the righteous live by a gift of God, namely by faith...Here I felt as if I were entirely born again and had entered paradise itself through gates that had been flung open.[3]

Luther's realization—that God's free gift of forgiveness is available to each person on earth—emphasized the value God gives to each individual created in His image. What a contrast to the beliefs of communism!

Luther's teaching on the life of faith, as opposed to earning salvation by good works, was the beginning of the great Protestant Reformation that reshaped Europe during the next two centuries. Today, the principle of forgiveness by faith is followed by hundreds of millions of people worldwide. In America, we owe much of our historical and religious roots to what Luther began in Germany.

These two examples show that a false view of God leads to sin and corruption—and many times cruelty and great human tragedy. On the other hand, a proper understanding of God leads to a life of blessing for oneself and many generations to follow.

You may dismiss this by thinking, *I am no Karl Marx or Martin Luther. I am not a world leader or a person with great influence.* None of us are. Yet how we view God will change the way we live and relate with others. Consider the couple who takes in a foster child because they know God loves that little one; they may live next door to parents who neglect or abuse their child. One person cheats his customers because he thinks "no one will ever know"; another repays a loan despite severe financial hardships, because he has a reverential respect for a God who notes men's actions and expects honesty.

All of our actions, like Marx's and Luther's, are driven by our views of God and how He interacts with us. Nothing in life could be more important than knowing God accurately.

DOES GOD WANT TO RELATE TO US?

Understanding God is not a simple task. I readily admit that, like all human beings, I am incapable of completely explaining the attributes of our awesome God who reigns in overwhelming majesty. Who am I, a mere man, trying to describe the God of the universe who is all-powerful, holy, and righteous? In fact, while I was writing this book, I was overcome with a sense of my unworthiness. I fell to my knees in tears and confessed, "Oh, Lord, I am not worthy to write about Your character. Forgive me for being so presumptuous." At that moment, the Lord seemed to put His arms around me, assuring me that He had called me to do this.

That's why I am so anxious to share with you, through this book, the truths about God: because I know without a doubt that God wants us to *really know* Him. Let me go back to my analogy of the mite on the flea on the dog. The mite had given up hope that he could ever understand the mighty king. Then it was as though King Solomon searched out that insignificant mite. First, the king found the owner of that small home on the outskirts of Jerusalem. He stepped into the yard, found the dog, then the flea, and finally, with astonishing lovingkindness, told the mite—in the mite's own limited language—all about himself.

This part of the analogy is the most humbling to me. God did not just content Himself with speaking to us through our limited language. Instead, He assumed our limited form—that of a human—setting aside His riches and splendor and honor to become like us! That, of course, was the miraculous day when God was born as a baby in a manger in the small village of Bethlehem. That baby's name is Jesus Christ, the Son of God and Savior of the world. This demonstration of God's love is beyond my comprehension and shows His great desire for us to know Him. God's willingness to become a man changed forever the way I can relate with Him.

HOW CAN KNOWING GOD CHANGE MY LIFE?

What misconceptions do you have about God that are preventing you from getting to know Him better? Are you so unsure about what God is really like that you cannot trust Him completely?

Take heart. Because of God's love, He has provided the way for us to understand more about what He is like, what He is up to, and how He can help us change our lives completely. Keep reading. We will discover many ways He has given us to know Him better.

My prayer is that the Holy Spirit will mightily use this book to reveal to you the amazing and wonderful character of our glorious Creator God and Savior. If you read this book with prayerful sincerity, it will alter your perspective and you will find your life changing in astounding ways.

I can tell you from personal experience that an intimate walk with God never fails to produce an abundance of joy and adventure in people's lives. Let me share an example from one man's life, John Newton. His story demonstrates what a right view of God can do for each of us.

John Newton's mother was a devoted Christian, but she died when he was a child. As a young man, he decided to follow in the footsteps of his father, an English sea captain. He joined the British Royal Navy but was discharged because of unruly behavior. To escape further problems, he moved to the western coast of Africa and worked for a slave trader. He eventually became captain of a slave ship, and he treated the slaves despicably. What a loathsome man he had become!

On one voyage, his ship was severely battered by a fierce storm. Fearing for his life, he surrendered himself to God, setting his life on a new course. Over the next few years as he became convinced that slavery was abhorrent, he gave up his slave trading and later even crusaded against slavery. His life changed so much that he studied to become a minister. When he preached, he was known as the "old converted sea captain." All because he had personally met and come to know God. He wrote one of the most famous hymns in English, *Amazing Grace*. In it, he describes his own transformation:

> Amazing grace, how sweet the sound,
> That saved a wretch like me.
> I once was lost, but now am found,
> Was blind, but now I see.

Who else but almighty God could change a calloused man engaged in the slave trade into a compassionate minister and antislavery crusader?

Have you experienced this change? Has God been intimately involved in your life? For more than fifty years, I have walked and talked with our loving heavenly Father. It has been the greatest adventure of my lifetime. The more I get to know Him, the more peace, joy, love, and excitement I experience. He has proven to be my best friend, someone I can trust in every situation.

My desire is not just to share information about God with you—although that is important. But I trust that the Holy Spirit will help me communicate my heart about God. Hopefully, you will be encouraged to embrace the right view of God and know Him well enough to love, trust, and obey Him as never before.

As we explore the truths of these pages together, discovering who God is and His love and plan for us, I am confident that your life will never be the same. Let us begin by looking more closely at how we can know God intimately.

CHAPTER 2

WE CAN KNOW GOD INTIMATELY!

In 1978 at the height of the Cold War between the Soviet Union and the United States, the Soviet government, at the request of the Russian church, invited me to visit that vast land. During my visit to eight cities, I sensed that millions of people were imprisoned by fear resulting from mental and physical abuse. The KGB, the secret police of the Soviet government, seemed to squeeze every individual to discover information about the activities and views of political dissidents, followers of Christ, and Jews. Under this kind of suspicion and tyranny, no one trusted anyone. Even family members turned against each other in this oppressive uncertainty.

While few of us live under such conditions today, you may have often wondered, *Who can I really trust?* Perhaps you have a friend or two you consider trustworthy. But beyond that, who can you trust with the things that you consider most private and valuable?

I am sure you will agree that trustworthiness is in short supply today. At every level of government, there are officials who feel that dishonesty serves a purpose in politics. Within our financial institutions, businessmen have used the wealth of others to their personal advantage, often depriving those who are most vulnerable, senior citizens, of their retirement funds. People break contracts without remorse under the pretense of smart business practices. Husbands and wives, some who have been married for decades, betray their spouses for their own selfish, lustful desires. Families, especially innocent children, are shattered by broken promises. Good friends become enemies over lapses in honesty.

If a close friend or relative has betrayed your trust, how did that betrayal affect your relationship? Did it influence how much you trust other people today?

In many cases our past experiences, backgrounds, and personalities shape how we view other people and how we form relationships with them. If someone we trusted hurt us, we hesitate to trust anyone else again. If a parent or sibling treated us shamefully, we respond by protecting ourselves from other close relationships. Although trust is an important part of any healthy friendship, for many of us, building trust is one of the most difficult elements of our relationships.

> THE AMOUNT OF TRUST YOU HAVE IN GOD DEPENDS ON HOW YOU VIEW HIM.

But what about God? Can He be trusted? How far are you willing to go in trusting Him? The amount of trust you have in God depends on how you view Him. Some people think of Him as a big bully, a cosmic policeman, or a divine Santa Claus. Others believe He is like their insensitive, selfish parents who do whatever they want because they have the size or power.

Some consider God to be hard to get along with, someone to fear. Others think of Him as a heartless dictator waiting to punish them for doing wrong. Perhaps you see him as a kindly grandfather who just shakes His head over the terrible plight of humankind but does not get involved. Do you see Him as loving, gracious, tender, and compassionate? Or as critical, jealous, vindictive, and haughty?

I hear from many Christians who are discouraged in their quest to know God more fully. They claim to have tried to learn what God is like but have come up short. Maybe they failed on a commitment they made to God and feel the communication lines are down between themselves and heaven. Others believe that God has abandoned them or treated them unfairly. Some simply do not know what God is like and have decided that they probably will never know more than they do now. Millions of people cry out, *"Who are you, God?"*

WE CAN HAVE AN INTIMATE RELATIONSHIP WITH THE GOD OF CREATION

In Chapter 1, we learned how important it is to know God and to have the right view of Him. But how can we develop a relationship with a Being who is beyond our comprehension? The process toward intimacy is similar to getting to know a new neighbor.

Imagine that a new couple moves next door to you. What impression do you get of what they are like? You probably notice the furniture and belongings carried into their house, and the type of car in their driveway. The first time you meet them, you most likely find out what they do for a living. Are they lawyers or construction workers, computer specialists or businessmen, teachers or factory workers? You probably ask questions about their hobbies and interests. Do they enjoy gardening or do they pride themselves in how well they play golf? These facts give you a little insight into what kind of people they are.

As you get to know your neighbors better, you also discover more about their character. Are they kind, generous, amiable, and compassionate? Or do they speak harshly, criticize, and act rudely toward others? Do they have good character?

With time, you may get to know your neighbors more intimately. Are they ambitious or lazy? Do they shade the truth or are they honest? Do they keep their word? Do they practice values similar to yours or do they live by a different set of rules? How do they react under stressful situations? This closer relationship uncovers the deeper qualities of their inner lives.

Of course, God is not like a next-door neighbor. He is so much more than that. His characteristics are far above what we as humans can accomplish or even understand. But because He is loving and gracious toward us, He reveals His character to us so we can relate more intimately with Him. As in any relationship, developing intimacy is a process. Someone has aptly said, "If we take one step toward God, He will take two steps toward us."

GOD HELPS US GET TO KNOW HIM

Through their own ability, human beings cannot advance in their knowledge of God beyond a few biographical facts. But God in His love and mercy has taken steps to make Himself known to us in many ways. Because God is so far above us in every aspect, the process begins with Him as He reveals Himself to those who hunger and thirst to know Him.

The most important place we can turn to find the truth about what God is like is in His holy Word, the Bible. It gives us the most accurate picture of almighty God. Although all facets of God's nature are always present, He reveals Himself in three primary ways:

God reveals Himself as our great Creator. Genesis 1, the first chapter in the Bible, unveils the Creator's mighty works, His unlimited power, and eternal knowledge. In Part I, "Our Great Creator," we will discover that our Creator-God has no limitations.

God reveals the depth of His integrity as our perfect Judge. The remainder of the Old Testament shows how God built a nation of people dedicated to Him and how He led and blessed these people. Throughout this historical account, God gives laws and promises that establish His nature as one of holiness and integrity. If the people obeyed these laws, they would be blessed and happy; if they did not, they would bring God's wrath and judgment upon themselves. In Part II, "Our Perfect Judge," we will look at the holiness, truthfulness, righteousness, and justice of our perfect God.

God reveals Himself as our gracious Savior. In the New Testament, God sent His Son to earth as Savior of the world. Jesus is the flesh-and-blood picture of God with whom we can relate. The life, death, and resurrection of Jesus prove God's love, mercy, and faithfulness. In Part III, "Our Gracious Savior," we will discover the depths of God's compassion through His Son and how we can know that love.

Would you not agree that the most astounding news we can ever hear is that God, the almighty Creator of heaven and earth, invites us to have an intimate relationship with Him? He makes it simple for us to do so. Knowing God intimately can transform your life into one of passion, joy, adventure, and peace. With a clearer understanding of the greatness of our God, we will be able to:

- Learn how to worship and praise God as a part of our daily lives
- Renew our passion, love, and commitment for God
- Clear up misconceptions about God's role in our lives
- Understand the depths of His love
- Learn what it means to "fear" God
- Discover ways to seek God wholeheartedly
- See how His names reflect His character
- Learn how to tell others about God's character in clear and simple terms

Before we begin discovering a right view of God, understanding some truths about what God is like will give us insight into His unique character.

GOD IS A PERSONAL SPIRIT

Someone asked Buddha, the founder of Buddhism, if God existed. He replied, "The question is not relevant. If there were a God, man could not comprehend him anyway. So what good would it be to have such a God?"

Some "religious" people consider God a force, an evil spirit, or something encased in wood or stone. As a result, their concept of God is hazy or impersonal. If God were merely an energy force or a composite of the universe as New Age philosophies teach, knowing Him personally would be impossible. And if God were merely an idol, made by man's hand from wood or some precious metal, our efforts to know Him would be futile. How could a human have a relationship with an inanimate object?

But God's Word reveals God as a personal Spirit; therefore we can know Him personally. This may seem like such a simple concept, but it is the underlying truth on which we base our understanding of God.

The Bible shows that God has a distinct personality. The New Testament book of John says that God is Spirit.[1] Although He does not have a physical body as we do, He possesses all the characteristics of a personality: He thinks, feels, and wills. The Bible gives us several proofs that we can know God personally.

Many Old and New Testament believers knew God and were considered His friends. Let me give you a few examples.

God called Abraham, the "father" of the Hebrew nation, "My friend."[2] Moses met with God "face to face" when he talked to God in the tabernacle. Can you imagine how this personal experience must have changed his life? The Book of Exodus describes this encounter, which occurred just before Moses received the Ten Commandments:

> Whenever Moses went to the Tabernacle, all the people …would rise and stand in their tent doors. As he entered, the pillar of cloud would come down and stand at the door while the Lord spoke with Moses. Then all the people worshiped from their tent doors, bowing low to the pillar of cloud. Inside the tent the Lord spoke to Moses face to face, as a man speaks to his friend.[3]

Both Enoch and Noah were said to have "enjoyed a close relationship with God"; Job talked of a time "when God's intimate friendship blessed my house."[4] And in the New Testament, Jesus, the Son of God, told His disciples, "Now you are My friends."[5]

God has names. Many couples use great care in giving their newborn baby a name that has significance to their family. In the same way, each of God's many names reveals something important about His character. In the Bible, He is called Almighty, Eternal God, Heavenly Father, Lord of Hosts, Living God, Most

High, and Jehovah, along with many other names. In the next chapter, we will see the incredible truth behind God's most important name, Jehovah. (For a complete listing of the names of God with Scripture verses, see Appendix C.)

God is described throughout the Bible by a personal pronoun. He is not described as an "it," but as "He," a word that denotes a definite gender and personality. An impersonal force cannot be described this way.

God acts as a distinct personality. The Bible consistently demonstrates that God is a conscious, self-aware being, someone who thinks and makes decisions. For example, He is the Creator. How could an inanimate object of gold or silver or some impersonal force design the intricacies of the universe? That takes planning, unlimited intelligence, and supernatural power. Also, the Bible tells us that God "speaks," "sees," and

> EACH OF GOD'S
> MANY NAMES
> REVEALS
> SOMETHING
> IMPORTANT ABOUT
> HIS CHARACTER.

"hears."[6] God exhibits a range of emotions from righteous anger to holy jealousy to love and grief.

GOD IS THREE PERSONS IN ONE

As we learn more about God's personality, we will find many areas that are hard to understand. This is because God is so far above our limited understanding that we cannot grasp the fullness of His nature. The fact that God is three-in-one is one of these difficult concepts. Yet this truth is one of the most important aspects of God's relationship with us.

Theologians have called God's triune nature the Trinity. The members of the Trinity are involved with everything together, yet they also have distinct roles. This is hinted at in the first chapter in the Bible. Genesis 1:26 reads, "Let *us* make people in *our* image" (emphasis added). The plural pronouns "us" and "our" mean that more than one person was involved. Who else but God was present during creation? No one. Therefore, the Trinity in its simplest terms means one God manifested in three persons with three distinctive roles.

God the Father is first in the Trinity. In general, He orchestrates action. For example, He sent to earth God the Son, Jesus, and bestowed His authority upon Him.[7]

God the Son is the second person of the Trinity. Jesus Christ is fully God and fully human.[8] He is the cornerstone and head of the worldwide Church.[9] Jesus now sits at the right hand of God the Father interceding for His Church.[10]

God the Holy Spirit, the third person of the Trinity, is our Comforter. As the "active arm" of God on earth, He lives within believers and guides us into all truth.[11] He convicts us of sin and helps us know God and His will.[12]

Yet God is still one. It is difficult for us, with our limited comprehension, to understand how God the Father, God the Son, and God the Holy Spirit are distinct personalities, co-equal, yet one at the same time. Our best efforts to understand this relationship fall far short.

One popular analogy is to compare the Trinity to water. It can be three distinct forms: liquid, ice, or steam. The same chemical formula, H_2O, can assume each form under different temperatures. In a similar way, God assumes three different "forms" to accomplish His purposes.

Here is another analogy. We all play different roles in our lives. I am a husband, father and grandfather, and the head of an international organization. I perform different duties in each role, yet I am the same person. God also performs different roles— heavenly Father, loving Son, and Spirit of Comfort.

Of course, the Trinity is far more complex and profound than any awkward illustration I can give. One of my seminary professors once said, "If you try to understand the Trinity, you will lose your mind…If you deny the Trinity, you will lose your soul."

The reason I take the time to explain the mysterious relationship between the three members of the Trinity is that this truth underlies all the work of God. These are a few examples:

- God the Father orchestrated creation.[13] God the Son performed the work of creation.[14] God the Holy Spirit was also involved.[15]

- All three members agreed upon Christ's birth in human form.[16] Christ's baptism, which marked the beginning of His earthly ministry, was attended and approved by all three members.[17]
- Christ's resurrection was the work of the Trinity: God the Father raised Christ from the dead.[18] Jesus laid down His life and took it up on His own accord.[19] The Holy Spirit was the power in the resurrection.[20]
- All three members of the Trinity participate in the miracle of the new birth when a person becomes a child of God.[21]
- All three members of the Trinity participate in the atonement —when we receive forgiveness of our sins.[22] And then all three persons of the Trinity come to live in the new believer's life.[23]

Each member of the Trinity has His own role to play, but each is fully God. God is not three separate Gods like some might envision, but has complete unity. No Person in the Trinity is less important, less powerful, or less of anything than any other Person. As we discover more about God, we will see how the Trinity works in our behalf.

DEVELOPING A RELATIONSHIP IS AN ADVENTURE

Today, after more than fifty years of getting to know God, I have more joy in the Lord's presence than I have ever had. My communication with Him grows sweeter and sweeter. There is no one in the universe with whom I would rather spend time than my heavenly Father. I do not have adequate words to describe to you the many things He has done for me and the marvelous ways He has guided my life to make it an exciting adventure. My number one priority in life is to maintain my love for Him and to demonstrate my love by my obedience.

To this end, Vonette and I begin every day on our knees reading His holy, inspired Word and surrendering the activities of our day to His guidance. I want to be a suit of clothes for the Lord Jesus. I invite Him to walk around in my body as His temple. My heart's passion is to let Him think with my mind, love with my heart, speak with my lips, and continue to seek and save sinners through me. This is what He came to earth to do 2,000 years ago.

As we explore the amazing attributes of our glorious Lord, I encourage you to walk with Him, talk with Him, worship and praise Him, and give Him your cares and worries. He yearns to be your loving Savior and wrap His strong arms around you. You need never feel lonely or abandoned again. Here is a prayer you might pray as we begin our journey to know God more intimately:

Dear God, I want to know You as You really are, the Creator God of the universe, our Heavenly Father, who holds everything in Your hand. You know my past, present, and future. Help me to love, trust, and obey You with all my heart, soul, mind, and will. Thank You for giving me an opportunity to know You intimately as my heavenly Father and to tell others about You and Your marvelous love. Amen.

CHAPTER 3

OUR AWE-INSPIRING GOD

ow big is your God? Renowned theologian and Bible translator J. B. Phillips once wrote, "Your God is too small."[1] By now, you have probably realized that this is a problem we all face.

Truthfully, none of us can completely grasp the width, depth, complexity, or immensity of any part of God's nature. But if we merely have a human-centered view of God, we limit ourselves to only what we can accomplish through our self-efforts. Or we may think that He is just a little more intelligent, powerful, or wise than we are. Such a view of God robs us of an intimate life-changing relationship with an awe-inspiring God.

God has given us minds that can see farther than our own human limitations. For example, we can discover the intricacies of the DNA molecule, which no one has ever seen. We can study about places we have never visited, such as the underwater world of deep-sea creatures. We use cellular telephones with the knowledge that the signals may be coming to us from as far away as telecommunication satellites orbiting in space. These concepts extend our thinking beyond what we can observe with our eyes.

31

In the following pages, let us put aside our tendency to be superficial in our understanding of God and stretch our minds to get a clearer idea of His magnificent nature.

GOD'S MOST IMPORTANT NAME

One of the biblical concepts that help establish God's unlimited nature is His most important name. When God commanded Moses to lead the Israelites out of Egyptian slavery, Moses wondered what to tell them if they should ask the name of this God. In His short reply, the Lord spoke some of the most profound and revealing words recorded in the entire Bible. He said, "I AM WHO I AM. This is what you are to say to the Israelites: 'I AM has sent me to you.'"[2]

The Israelites immediately understood that the Hebrew word for I AM identified God as the only self-existent, eternal, personal Supreme Being. They clearly realized who had given Moses the message. It was God Himself! In the very next verse, God said to Moses:

> "Say to the Israelites, 'The LORD, the God of your fathers —the God of Abraham, the God of Isaac, and the God of Jacob—has sent me to you.' This is My name forever, the name by which I am to be remembered from generation to generation" (NIV).

The word "LORD" is written in all capital letters in many Bible versions to distinguish this name from other references to God. It is translated from the Hebrew YHWH, which means God's personal name. Other Bible versions translate it as Jehovah. In Isaiah 42:8, God clearly says, "I am the LORD [YHWH]; that is My name!" This name was so sacred and holy that the ancient rabbis would not allow anyone to say it aloud for fear that someone would inadvertently use it wrongly. When reading Scriptures that contained this name, the rabbis substituted Adonai (Lord) instead of reading aloud the most holy name. Consequently, the exact pronunciation of YHWH was lost. Today, scholars believe it was pronounced Yahweh.

Because I AM contains no adjective or qualifier that describes or limits its meaning, it signifies that God is complete. He has no beginning, no end, needs no help, no counsel. Everything He is and does is perfect, not lacking in anything.

THE SPLENDOR OF GOD

As king of Israel, David composed many lyrical psalms expressing God's grandeur. In Psalm 145, he writes:

> I will praise You, my God and King, and bless Your name each day and forever. Great is Jehovah [YHWH]! Greatly praise Him! His greatness is beyond discovery! Let each generation tell its children what glorious things He does. I will meditate about Your glory, splendor, majesty and miracles. Your awe-inspiring deeds will be on every tongue; I will proclaim Your greatness. Everyone will tell about how good You are, and sing about Your righteousness.[3]

Many other biblical writers also wrote of God's splendor. In the New Testament, Paul describes Him as "the King eternal, immortal, invisible, the only wise God, [to whom] be honour and glory for ever and ever."[4] The apostle John described what happened when he glimpsed God the Son during a vision. "When I saw Him, I fell at His feet as though dead. Then He placed His right hand on me and said: 'Do not be afraid. I am the First and the Last. I am the Living One.'"[5]

Our God is so gloriously incomprehensible that our minds just cannot grasp the whole nature of God. Yet we must find some human way to understand God's characteristics—at least in part. Four basic qualities of God are integral to each of His other attributes: His infinity, self-existence, eternal nature, and self-sufficiency.

God is infinite.

One day, Augustine, a leader in the early Church, was walking along the ocean shore pondering God's nature when he noticed a small boy playing in the sand. The child scooped a hole in the sand with a seashell, then ran down to the water's edge and dipped his shell full of seawater. Immediately, he ran back and dumped the water into the hole he had made in the sand. Of course, the water just leaked out through the sand.

Augustine asked the boy, "What are you doing?"

The boy confidently replied, "I am going to pour the sea into that hole."

"Ah," Augustine later reflected, "that is what I have been trying to do. Standing at the ocean of infinity, I have attempted to grasp it with my finite mind."[6]

Who can understand God's infinity? The prophet Isaiah writes, "Who has measured the waters in the hollow of His hand, and marked off the heavens by the span, and calculated the dust of the earth by the measure, and weighed the mountains in a balance, and the hills in a pair of scales? Who has directed the Spirit of the LORD, or as His counselor has informed Him?"[7]

God's infinity means that He has no limits, boundaries, or end. God cannot be compared to any finite standard. Everything within our world is finite; even the universe, as vast as it is, has a limit. God and only God is infinite. Since His infinite nature relates to all of His attributes, God's love, holiness, mercy, and all other qualities are unlimited in their scope and expression.

God is self-existent.

As humans, we use the word "create" differently than God does. When we "create" a work of art, we start with a material, such as sculptor's clay, and mold it into a different shape. Our "creation" is actually something reshaped, rearranged, combined, or invented. Mankind has never made something out of nothing. Not so with God. When He created the world, He made it out of nothing. We cannot really comprehend what that means. We have never seen "nothing."

We cannot even use the word "created" to describe God. God was not created. Everything else in the universe had a beginning, except God. Because He is the Creator, He exists outside of the created order. He is different from and independent of His creation, dwelling in pure existence far above everything He has made.

God is also the force or cosmic glue that holds everything together.[8] Without Him, everything that He created would disintegrate.

God is eternal.

Imagine that you want to discover what is going on in a room filled with people, but the door is locked. You peer through the keyhole, trying to piece together what each person in the room is doing. People move about, coming into view, then disappearing out of sight. What a frustration! If only you could open the door and walk into the room to see what is going on!

That is how time and space are to us. We look at events through a keyhole, and all we know is what we can see happening right now. For us, time defines boundaries. We mark the point in time of our birth and death. We count history by years and ages. As a human being, I cannot even begin to imagine what it must be like to live outside the boundary of time.

But God is not bound by the dimensions of time. Before He spoke the first word of creation, time did not exist. He created time as a temporary context for His creation.

It baffles my mind to realize that God experiences all past, present, and future events simultaneously. Everything that has ever happened or will ever happen has already occurred within His awareness. God sees the beginning of the parade of life; He sees its end. All history is but a little speck within the spectrum of eternity. Our God encompasses all of eternity!

God is self-sufficient.

Every living thing on earth needs food, water, and air. Without a constant supply of these, all living things die.

Although God is a living being, He has no needs. He is dependent upon nothing outside Himself. All creation relies upon God for existence and the maintenance of life. God has no need for anything and is not vulnerable in any way. He does not need our help. Yet He offers us the privilege of being involved with Him in the fulfillment of His purposes as His friends.

We will never be able to fully understand God's magnificence. In fact, His infinity, self-existence, eternal nature, and self-sufficiency are incomprehensible. But are you not glad that God is so far beyond our human abilities? We can have complete confidence in a God who is greater than us and any of our problems.

APPLYING GOD'S QUALITIES TO HIS CHARACTER

One important principle about God's nature is that all the attributes of God are interactive and completely interrelated. With our human limitations, we dissect God's nature into parts or attributes so we can understand them, but that is not how they exist in God's character. Each attribute is perfectly complete and fully a part of God's personality. As we study these attributes, keep in mind that if we exalt one of God's qualities over another, we can get a distorted view of God's character. In fact, overemphasizing any one of God's attributes to the exclusion of others can lead to heresy. For example, teaching only about God's mercy and neglecting His role as a judge will prevent people from understanding God's hatred of sin and the future punishment for wrongdoing. Therefore, as we study each quality individually, we must remember that it is only one aspect of God's magnificent nature.

Since God's attributes are so interlinked, we cannot understand one without the others. The following diagram will help you see how God's attributes relate to each other and how they are all part of the whole of God's nature.

Let me apply the principle of God's unified nature to the four basic qualities we just covered. One of the attributes we will examine is God's love. God is not just a huge bundle of love; His love has all four basic qualities.

God's love is *infinite*. There is no limit to His love; it is beyond measure.

God's love is *self-existent*. It did not come to Him from somewhere else. It has always been a part of His character. God's love did not begin at some point; it has always existed in the heart of God.

God's love is *eternal*. It never had a beginning and will last for-

GOD
IS

One God—Three Persons
Father, Son, and Holy Spirit

ALL-POWERFUL EVER-PRESENT ALL-KNOWING

SOVEREIGN

CREATOR

SAVIOR JUDGE

MERCIFUL FAITHFUL LOVING HOLY RIGHTEOUS JUST

Infinite

Self-Existent UNCHANGING TRUTHFUL *Self-Sufficient* *Eternal*

ever. His love is never less or more. It always exists without the limitations of time or amount.

God's love is *self-sufficient*. He does not need love to make Him what He already is. He is not dependent on love to make Him happy or more fulfilled.

Throughout the rest of this book, keep these four qualities in mind and apply them to each of the attributes we will learn about.

APPLYING NEW INSIGHTS TO YOUR LIFE

Sometimes when I am sharing about God's love and forgiveness with an individual, he will have a questioning look on his face and ask, "But is God real?"

I kindly reply, "Oh, definitely. God is real—very real—and He has made it possible for us to know Him. But this special relationship with God requires a response from us." I often share what Jesus says in John 3:16: "God so loved the world that He gave His only Son, so that everyone who believes in Him will not perish but have eternal life." The only way we can have a relationship with our great Creator is through His Son, Jesus Christ. Knowing Jesus is the first step to knowing God.

Have you made a decision to turn to God by trusting Jesus as your Savior and Lord? If not, turn to Appendix A and read "How to Know God Personally." These few pages will help you get started on your new adventure as a child of God.

Another essential step to growing in our relationship with God is listening to His Spirit. Jesus promises, "When the Spirit of truth comes, He will guide you into all truth."[9] God has given us the Holy Spirit to help us in our relationship with Him. To discover how you can live in the power of the Holy Spirit, turn to Appendix B, "How to Be Filled With the Spirit."

A third response we make as we begin to know and appreciate our marvelous God is to seek Him wholeheartedly. David prayed, "O God, You are my God; I earnestly search for You. My soul thirsts for You; my whole body longs for You."[10] Because of David's desire to seek God wholeheartedly, God called him "a man after My own heart." I urge you to consider what might be keeping you from hungering after God. Ask God to help you resolve any issues and turn away from anything that would prevent you from having an intimate relationship with Him.

In the next chapter, we will embark on our adventure to intimacy with God by looking at God's attributes of ability, beginning with His unlimited power. Then we will see that He is present everywhere and that He knows everything. Together these abilities demonstrate that He is sovereign, ruler over all, and that such a God can do anything!

PART I

OUR GREAT CREATOR

(Attributes of Ability)

Do you not know? Have you not heard?
Has it not been told you from the beginning?
Have you not understood since the earth was
founded?
He sits enthroned above the circle of the earth,
and its people are like grasshoppers.
He stretches out the heavens like a canopy,
and spreads them out like a tent to live in.

ISAIAH 40:21,22, NIV

CHAPTER 4

GOD
IS
ALL-POWERFUL

One of the National Aeronautics and Space Administration's (NASA's) most important projects is the International Space Station that our country is building in cooperation with Russia, Japan, Brazil, and several other European countries. If you visit the Space Center in Houston, you can view a documentary film about the space station. On a huge screen several stories high, space ships carrying materials for the space station are shown blasting into the sky. The power of the rockets can be seen as the huge screen fills with boiling clouds of fire and smoke from the booster engines. The roar thunders throughout the room. What power in those engines!

Then on the screen you see the orbiting space station. Its components are linked to allow astronauts to live in space and perform science experiments. Against the backdrop of the darkness of the universe, the huge space station floats through emptiness. It is thrilling to think about the power that scientists use to put men and women in space miles above the Earth to live and work for months at a time. What remarkable technological progress!

Then the camera turns to show the space station from another angle. Now the Earth is visible behind the steel structure with its many angles and parts. Our blue planet with its swirling clouds looms huge, dwarfing the now fragile-looking space station. The Earth appears so big that only a portion of its surface fills the entire screen.

Suddenly, you get a glimpse of how very close the space station really is to the Earth. Although it has taken thousands of pounds of fuel to blast the astronauts miles into space, they really have not gone far from our planet's surface compared to the expanse of space.

Our human efforts are so minuscule compared to the reaches of outer space. We are like ants trying to scale Mount Everest. After crawling over blades of grass and fallen twigs, the ants think they have traveled a great distance. But when their journey is compared to the distant mountaintop ahead, they have hardly begun.

"THE HEAVENS DECLARE THE GLORY OF GOD; THE SKIES PROCLAIM THE WORK OF HIS HANDS."

PSALM 19:1

Sometimes we as humans become so caught up in our own power that we forget how very limited we are. We are like those ants toiling across a tiny square foot of earth. When was the last time you tried to accomplish something completely beyond your ability? Perhaps you have valiantly concentrated all your energy on the challenge at hand, only to find that it was not enough to do what needed to be done. Afterward, you felt exhausted and defeated.

However, God is capable of doing anything—as long as it does not violate His other attributes. (For example, He cannot lie, change, deny Himself, or be tempted.) Otherwise, no task is too large or too difficult for Him. He never fails or gets tired. Because He is all-powerful, He has the ability and the strength to do whatever He pleases. His power is not restrained or inhibited in any way by His created beings. God generates power within Himself and does what He chooses to do whenever He chooses to do it. His power is not an abstract idea but a force to be reckoned with. Theologians use the term *omnipotence* to describe the awesome, unlimited power of God.

GOD'S POWER IN CREATION

When I tour a historic mansion and scrutinize the building's details—the quality, design, and décor—I can draw some conclusions about its builder. Is the foundation strong? Are the walls and floors plumb and square? How well are the most intricate details constructed? Does the design flow from one room to another?

We live on a grand estate called Earth. As we look at the beauty and intricacies of our residence, we marvel at the genius of the design. When we gaze up into the heavens, we are overcome with awe at the vastness of what our Creator has brought into being. In one of the most beautiful passages in the Bible, King David describes how nature testifies to the power of God:

> The heavens declare the glory of God; the skies proclaim the work of His hands. Day after day they pour forth speech; night after night they display knowledge. There is no speech or language where their voice is not heard. Their voice goes out into all the earth, their words to the ends of the world.[1]

To get just a small idea of God's creative power, let us consider our universe. We live on one of nine planets that revolve around the sun. As the dominant light of our solar system, our sun gives off far more energy in one second than all mankind has produced since creation. With a diameter of approximately 860,000 miles, the sun could hold one million planets the size of the Earth. Yet our sun is only an average-size star.

Our sun is just one among 100 billion stars in our galaxy, the Milky Way. The Pistol Star gives off 10 million times the power generated by our sun, and one million stars the size of our sun can fit easily within its sphere. It takes 100,000 light-years to travel from one side of the Milky Way to the other. (One light-year is 5.88 trillion miles or the distance light travels in one year.) Our galaxy is moving through space at a phenomenal speed of one million miles per hour! If the Milky Way were compared to the size of the North American continent, our solar system would be about the size of a coffee cup!

Yet our Milky Way is not a huge galaxy. One of our neighbors, the Andromeda Spiral galaxy, is 2 million light-years away and contains about 400 billion stars. No one knows how many galaxies there are in the universe, but scientists estimate that there are billions of them.[2]

Isaiah writes, "Look up into the heavens. Who created all the stars? He brings them out one after another, calling each by its name. And He counts them to see that none are lost or have strayed away."[3] Scientists estimate that there are ten billion trillion stars in the universe, or about as many stars as there are grains of sand on all of our planet's seashores. If all the stars were divided equally among the people of the world, each person would receive almost two trillion stars.

Yet, with the unfathomable vastness of our universe, God spoke and the heavens and earth came into being; He laid the foundations of the world.[4] His invisible qualities—His eternal power and divine nature—can be clearly seen and understood from His creation. Even people who have never received a verbal witness about God have no excuse for not knowing Him because of His power displayed in creation.[5] He alone is the Almighty Sovereign of the universe.

Truly, God is omnipotent. Allow me to give you three truths about His infinite power.

GOD IS THE ULTIMATE SOURCE OF ALL POWER

Our homes depend on a central source for electrical power and can be plunged into darkness due to a storm or other disturbance. This power is transmitted into our homes on slender cables, which can break or wear out. But God's power is inherent in His nature. He does not derive His power from any other source; all power has always been His and will continue to be His for eternity. Any power that we have comes ultimately from God. King David acknowledged in one of his prayers, "In Your hands are strength and power to exalt and give strength to all."[6] Paul prayed for the Ephesians that they would "begin to understand the incredible greatness of His power for us who believe Him."[7]

GOD IS MORE POWERFUL THAN ANYTHING IN THE UNIVERSE

God has more power than all the forces of nature. The combined energy of earth's storms, winds, ocean waves, and other natural forces do not equal a fraction of God's omnipotence. He expresses His power through the laws of nature, which He has instituted—although God is not bound by these laws.

I have flown millions of miles, but I remember the most violent storm I ever encountered. Vonette and I were on our way from New York City to Washington, D.C., when suddenly the airplane began to buck like a wild mustang throwing its first rider. It felt as though the plane was out of control, like a leaf blown about in the wind. The sky seemed to explode with brilliant flashes of lightning.

As we rode through the storm, Vonette and I were reminded of when Jesus calmed the wind and waves. The disciples shouted to the Lord, "Save us, we're sinking!" Vonette and I began to pray, "Oh, Lord, You have not lost Your power over nature. We ask You to still the storm and to save us, though we're ready to meet You now if it is Your will. But if You have something yet for us to do in this life, we ask You not to allow the enemy to destroy us and all these other passengers."

Almost immediately, the turbulence stopped. The plane was stabilized and we continued on our course. Our petitions to God turned into praise and thanksgiving. Later we discovered that the plane had been severely damaged—lightning had knocked a hole in the fuselage—and that our lives were truly in danger. Yes, our God is more powerful than the greatest storm.

God is also more powerful than all the rulers on earth. Do the nuclear capabilities, chemical weapons, and military strength of other countries frighten you? We do not need to fear. The prophet Isaiah writes, "All the nations of the world are nothing in comparison with Him. They are but a drop in the bucket, dust on the scales."[8] After learning firsthand of God's power, King Nebuchadnezzar acknowledges, "He does as He pleases with the powers of heaven and the peoples of the earth. No one can hold back His hand or say to Him: What have You done?"[9]

We need not fear that any one person or nation will put God to the test. He is so far above our earthly governments that they can do nothing outside His power. No ruler or army can change any plan that God has made.

God is also infinitely more powerful than Satan and his evil legions. God is not intimidated by the devil's rebellious hatred. God is the Creator; Satan is a created being who can operate only within the prescribed limits God places on him. Satan is nothing compared to God.

Jesus told His disciples that "the prince of this world [Satan] now stands condemned."[10] Demons screamed in fear when they saw Jesus. The Book of Matthew records Jesus' encounter with two men who were demon-possessed. The demons immediately recognized the Son of God's power over them by saying, "Have you come here to torture us before the appointed time?" They requested that He let them go into a nearby herd of pigs. He said one powerful word—"Go." And they did. In response, the pigs ran over a cliff to their deaths.[11]

As Christians, sometimes we feel that Satan has the upper hand. But our almighty God fights for us. Romans 16:20 gives this promise: "The God of peace will soon crush Satan under your feet." How encouraging that promise is when we are battling the evil forces that confront us every day!

GOD HAS THE POWER TO DO ANYTHING

Whatever God chooses will come to pass because He has the omnipotent ability to make it happen. God told Isaiah, "Everything I plan will come to pass, for I will do whatever I wish."[12] Speaking to God, Job acknowledged, "I know that You can do all things; no plan of Yours can be thwarted."[13] Consider some of the things our almighty God can do without any effort.

God has the power to create anything from nothing.

The psalmist writes, "The LORD merely spoke, and the heavens were created. He breathed the word, and all the stars were born... Let everyone stand in awe of Him. For when He spoke, the world began! It appeared at His command."[14] When God spoke, the sky was filled with stars. Pastor Tony Evans writes, "It takes no more effort for God to create a universe than it does for Him to create an ant."[15] God's power is so unlimited that He could speak a few trillion more universes into existence, then the next day a few trillion more, then the same every day for a trillion years. It would not lessen His power one bit!

God has the power to sustain everything He has created.

Deists believe that God created the world then withdrew, letting His creation run automatically like a watch with a battery. It is up to us to maintain what is in the world, they say. Yet that is not how God is depicted in the Bible. The ongoing existence of all creation depends on our all-powerful God every second of every day. The writer of Hebrews affirms: "The Son...sustains the universe by the mighty power of His command."[16]

God has the power to judge sin and rebellion.

One of the great mysteries of life is why God allows evil on the earth. We will never find a complete answer to this puzzle. At the same time, we can know for sure that God will use His mighty power for the destruction of evil. He has given us examples in His Word: the great flood in Noah's time and God's judgment of Sodom and Gomorrah. Every injustice will be righted; every act of sin and rebellion will be accounted for.

OUR RESPONSE

As we discover the character of our heavenly Father, we will want to do more than file away facts; we will want to seek His presence and fellowship. Worship is our response to God that shows our gratitude for who He is. But what does it mean to worship God? Picture a huge, ornate room with an immense throne at one end.

The room is filled with people and angels praising God. The throng opens up to reveal a carpeted aisle that leads right to the throne.

Suddenly, you realize that you must walk up that aisle and stand before the elevated throne. Your eyes look up to catch sight of the Person who sits in the honored seat. That Being is so full of light and power and righteousness that your eyes cannot bear to look at Him.

What can you say that will mean anything to this glorious King? Your mouth is dry and you cannot speak. There are no words adequate for the moment. All you can do is bow down before Him in humble adoration, servitude, and worship.

Throughout this book, we will learn the importance and the simple truths about worshipping our great Creator. The most basic element of worship is attitude. Our worship should begin with an attitude of awe for who God is and what He can do. We must realize how weak we are compared to the infinite power of God.

Once we have a right view of God, we will begin to praise Him. King David expressed this attitude when he was gathering materials to build a glorious temple to almighty God:

> O LORD, the God of our ancestor Israel, may you be praised forever and ever! Yours, O LORD, is the greatness, the power, the glory, the victory, and the majesty. Everything in the heavens and on earth is yours, O LORD, and this is your kingdom. We adore you as the one who is over all things… O our God, we thank you and praise your glorious name![17]

Do his words reflect your awe of God's power? Take a few moments right now to praise God. The following "Life Application" will help you focus your attention on Him and address any attitude problems hindering you from worshipping Him.

As believers, we have access to the greatest force in the universe—the awesome power of God. In our next chapter, we will examine how God uses His unlimited power in our behalf.

LIFE APPLICATION

EXALT YOUR GOD—An important part of worshipping God is praising Him. Make the following Scripture prayers your songs of praise. As you repeat the words, meditate on the character of God:

> Ah, Sovereign LORD, you have made the heavens and the earth by Your great power and outstretched arm. Nothing is too hard for You...O great and powerful God, whose name is the LORD Almighty, great are your purposes and mighty are your deeds (Jeremiah 32:17–19, NIV).

> The LORD merely spoke, and the heavens were created. He breathed the word, and all the stars were born. He gave the sea its boundaries and locked the oceans in vast reservoirs. Let everyone in the world fear the LORD, and let everyone stand in awe of Him. For when He spoke, the world began! It appeared at His command. The LORD shatters the plans of the nations and thwarts all their schemes. But the LORD'S plans stand firm forever; his intentions can never be shaken (Psalm 33:6–11).

REFLECT HIS IMAGE—Prayerfully answer these questions about your life and put them into practice: How do you think God wants to display His power in your life? What areas in your life need to be transformed by His power? How can you draw on His power to make a difference in the lives of those around you?

SHARE HIS MAJESTY—Think of one person you know who needs to be reminded that our Creator is all-powerful. Share the truths of this chapter with them; encourage them that nothing is too difficult for God.

CHAPTER 5

GOD USES HIS POWER IN OUR BEHALF

S ome time ago, I had to fly from Los Angeles to New York for a mere three-hour stop, then fly to Portland, Oregon, to speak to several hundred pastors at a conference. When I reached Portland, I was bone tired. Every fiber of my being ached with fatigue. As I stood in the terminal, I felt impressed to pray, "Lord, do You have something that You would like to share with me?"

Immediately, I felt another impression to turn to the 40th chapter of Isaiah. I began to read a familiar passage, which took on new meaning for me. "Don't you know by now that the ever-lasting God, the Creator of the farthest parts of the earth, never grows faint or weary?...He gives power to the tired and worn out, and strength to the weak."[1] I could identify with the writer, for I was absolutely worn out.

I continued to read: "Even the youths shall be exhausted, and the young men will all give up. But they that wait upon the Lord shall renew their strength. They shall mount up with wings like eagles; they shall run and not be weary; they shall walk and not faint."[2]

At that moment, it was as though a great infusion of power

flooded my very being. I was so excited as I thought about who God is and what He had said to me. I felt I could have thrown my luggage over the airport terminal and run to the meeting some miles away. Suddenly, I could hardly wait to stand before those pastors and proclaim to them the glory and power of our great and faithful God and Savior. Within thirty minutes or so, I did have that privilege, and God empowered and anointed me for the occasion in a marvelous way.

In all my years as a believer, I have found God faithful to use His power in the behalf of those who seek Him. A right understanding of who God is will revolutionize the life of every believer. It will launch him or her into the exciting adventure of supernatural living in the power of this mighty God.

But perhaps you have asked yourself: How much can I expect God to do through me? How involved is He in what I see going on around me? What is He willing to accomplish in my life?

GOD USES HIS POWER PURPOSEFULLY

When we look at the cosmic universe, we see order and design. Everything is in its place; everything has its purpose. If creation has so much purpose and design, then human history must also have purpose and design.

Many people are skeptical about God's willingness to get intimately involved in their affairs. They may agree that God has a general purpose for everything, but they wonder: *Do we live by luck or the breaks produced by our own hard work and cleverness?* They question if God even knows or cares about the details in their lives.

In His Word, however, God shows that He has a plan for this world and every person in it: "I have a plan for the whole earth, for My mighty power reaches throughout the world."[3]

No matter what happens anywhere in the world at any moment, God is always in control. This is a comforting truth. How would you like to live in a world where everyone could do whatever he wanted? Can you imagine the chaos? For example, I have visited countries that seem to have no traffic laws. Taxi drivers go at breakneck speed, in and out of lanes, often colliding with each other. Fortunately, I have not been in a collision although I have ridden in thousands of taxis. I certainly would not want to drive to work each day in heavy traffic where drivers do not follow traffic laws.

Sometimes this world seems just as chaotic and out-of-control, yet God knows what is in the future. He is not the author of evil and suffering, nor is He responsible for the consequences of mankind's sins. He does place authorities in their positions to help bring order to our world. The apostle Paul tells us, "Obey the government, for God is the one who put it there. All governments have been placed in power by God. So those who refuse to obey the laws of the land are refusing to obey God."[4]

God has unlimited power within Himself and does what He wants with it. This would be terrifying if God were a tyrant who meted out His power indiscriminately. Fortunately, the Bible says God acts out of love and righteousness (attributes that we will examine later). Some of us may question why God does not answer our prayers when and how we ask. But God is not a "genie" or Santa Claus who gives us everything we ask for just the way we want it. He uses His power to fulfill His purposes, plans, and will for us and everyone involved in our situations. He knows what we need far better than we do. Can you think of at least one prayer request for which you are now thankful God did not answer the way you wanted? Often we pray selfishly or from our fleshly natures. But as we align our ways and desires with His perfect will, and pray in faith, we will see His power demonstrated more frequently in answered prayer.

> GOD KNOWS THE BEGINNING FROM THE END, AND HAS US IN THE PALM OF HIS HAND.

When we study God's Word from Genesis to Revelation, we get a glimpse into how He directs history and nations. The psalmist writes: "Come and see what our God has done, what awesome miracles He does for His people!…By His great power He rules forever. He watches every movement of the nations."[5] Although events at times make no sense to us, God knows the end from the beginning, and has us in the palm of His hand.

Man is at best a microbe on the "grain of sand" we call earth, yet God created us for a purpose. We feel most fulfilled when we respond to that purpose.

GOD'S POWER IS SHOWN THROUGH HIS SON

First Corinthians 1:24 tells us that God demonstrates His power through His Son. We can see evidence of this in His virgin birth. God planned before the foundation of the world to send His Son to die for us.

God's ultimate display of power was raising Jesus Christ from the dead. After Jesus' death by crucifixion, His enemies put a Roman seal on the tomb and set guards to make sure no one disturbed His body. Yet their efforts meant nothing to God. When He was ready to display His power, He simply rolled the stone away from the tomb and Jesus walked out alive and well.

Paul writes that the power available to us as believers is "the same mighty power that raised Christ from the dead and seated Him in the place of honor at God's right hand in the heavenly realms."[6] Does that not thrill you? The amount of power available to us through God's Spirit is equal to the power God used to raise Christ from the dead! Like Paul, we can honestly say, "I can do everything through Him who gives me strength."[7]

REFLECTING GOD'S POWER

In the midst of the barren desert between Los Angeles and Las Vegas stands a 300-foot tower. On top of this tower rests a black receiver that is 45 feet high and 23 feet wide, surrounded by 70 heat-conducting tubes. Tens of thousands of people who drive across the desert during the daylight hours see what looks like a brilliant ball of fire glowing from the top of the tower. This is the world's largest solar-powered electricity-generating station: Solar One.

How can a receiver turn into a glowing ball with a temperature exceeding 1,175° F? The secret is on the ground. On the desert floor surrounding the tower are 1,818 computer-controlled frames, each holding 12 giant mirrors that track the sun daily from the time it rises until it sets.

When sunlight strikes these mirrors, it is reflected onto the receiver at the top of the tower. The heat generated at the receiver is then transformed into electrical energy through a system of thermal storage and a turbine generator. When the network of mirrors is working in harmony, tremendous power is generated from the sun.

Note that the tower itself does not have the ability to generate power. This process is possible only because light from the sun—the real source of the power—is reflected onto a helpless receiver.

Have you considered that God wants us to reflect His power on earth? As we begin to understand our God's vast and magnificent power, our lives cannot help but be transformed. Everything about us will change—our attitudes, actions, motives, desires, our lifestyle, and even our view of God. As we are transformed, we light up the world around us. Our society which was once darkened by fear, ignorance, and hopelessness will become lightened with our witness of God's power, care, and intervention in our lives.

GOD WANTS US TO BE VESSELS FOR HIS POWER

Just because God has the power to do anything should not cause us to assume that we can use that power for selfish purposes. His power is dedicated to the accomplishment of His purposes, not ours. He will bring about the future that He desires. As our all-powerful God and loving Father, His ways are infinitely better than ours.

God is seeking faithful servants to be channels of His incredible power. Paul was one of countless servants of Christ who was available for God's mighty power. Acts 19:11 records that "God did extraordinary miracles through Paul" (NIV). Through Paul's prayers, other Christians also understood what it means to be "strengthened with all power according to His glorious might."[8] The ways God desires to use us are beyond counting, but let me mention five that will help us reflect God's glory.

God gives us power to conquer evil forces.

We have already seen that God's power is infinitely greater than the forces of evil. We can apply that truth to our own battle with Satan and his helpers—no matter what they throw at us.

When God instructed Moses to lead the Israelite people out of Egypt, conflict developed between God's servants (Moses and his brother, Aaron) and Pharaoh's magicians. These accomplished sorcerers could have intimidated Moses and Aaron. Their demonic power was clearly evident when they threw their rods to the floor and the rods became serpents. But God demonstrated His superior power when Aaron's rod devoured the other serpents. This was a graphic illustration of how much greater God's power is than any other.

> GOD'S POWER IS INFINITELY GREATER THAN THE FORCES OF EVIL.

Satan's power is most clearly demonstrated through false religious systems. Millions have followed him to disastrous endings. From the 900 followers of Jim Jones who tragically died in Jonestown, Guyana, to Heaven's Gate cult members who committed suicide in recent years at the command of their leader, many have been deluded by Satan's wiles. But when we walk with God, we need not be afraid. The devil and his forces are no match for God. God's Word promises that we can have victory in our spiritual battles. James 4:7,8 says: "Resist the devil, and he will flee from you. Draw close to God, and God will draw close to you."

Although we are weak at times, we can stand firm and say "no"; we can quit any habit or addiction; and we can speak up to tell the truth at any time. How do we do these difficult feats? In the power of the name of Jesus Christ and faith in our almighty and powerful God.

God gives us power to live a holy life.

I like to compare the Christian battle against sin to an individual swimming upstream against a surging current. His progress is slow and tortuous; he is constantly swept backward by powerful undercurrents. Hovering near the swimmer is a speedboat with a powerful motor. He can continue to try to swim upstream or he can choose to climb aboard the speedboat, which can easily whisk him up the river. Staying in the water means he must trust in his own efforts. Accepting a ride in the speedboat allows him to take advantage of a power far greater than his own.

We have a similar choice. When battling evil spiritual forces, worldly influences, and our own fleshly temptations, we can either fail miserably by fighting temptation in our own efforts or defeat that sin-current that drags us down by living in the unlimited power of the Holy Spirit.[9]

Peter explains, "As we know Jesus better, His divine power gives us everything we need for living a godly life. He has called us to receive His own glory and goodness!"[10] We do not have to make our own lives holy or clean up our messy lives before we invite God in; we can appropriate God's holiness through His Holy Spirit living His life within us.[11]

The Scriptures assure us "that if we ask anything according to His will, He hears us. And if we know that He hears us—whatever we ask—we know that we have what we asked of Him."[12] We can become holy vessels of the all-powerful God by committing to live holy lives and being filled with the power of the Holy Spirit.

God gives us power in our weakness.

Since nothing is too hard for God, we do not have a need too great for Him to meet nor a problem too complicated for Him to solve. We can never face a foe too strong for Him to conquer. We can never pray a prayer too difficult for Him to answer.

His ways are always above our ways, and when we submit to His will, we experience peace and He builds patience into our lives. Our frailties in His hands become strengths. When Paul repeatedly asked God to remove a physical ailment that was tormenting him, God responded, "My gracious favor is all you need. My power works best in your weakness."[13] God uses our weakness to highlight His magnificent power. Just as He helped me speak to those hundreds of pastors in Portland, He will enable you to do more than you could ever imagine.

God gives us power to proclaim the gospel.

One important aspect of living a holy life is spreading the good news of God's love and forgiveness to everyone we meet. Paul writes, "Everywhere we go, we tell everyone about Christ...I work very hard at this, as I depend on Christ's mighty power that works within me."[14]

Each time I am with someone for five minutes or more, I consider it a God-given opportunity to testify of God's mercy and grace in my life. Whether in an airport, a taxi, or a restaurant, I am prepared to share with others my excitement about my Lord and my love for Him. How can I do this? Because God through His Holy Spirit gives me the power to represent Him.[15]

You may be thinking: *Bill Bright is the president of a worldwide organization dedicated to introducing people to Christ. Surely, proclaiming the gospel is easier for him than for me. I could never witness like that.*

I am naturally a shy and reserved person, so sharing my faith is sometimes difficult for me. I must continually rely on the power of the Holy Spirit to be a fruitful witness. When I obey God's command to tell others of Jesus, God makes the experience joyful and meaningful. He reminds me that I am not responsible for convicting the sinner or drawing others to Him. He is. I am just to follow His command in love, concern, and the power of His Holy Spirit.

At Campus Crusade for Christ we have trained millions of believers around the world to share their faith in Christ. We have learned that successful witnessing is simply taking the initiative to share Christ with everyone who will listen, in the power of the Holy Spirit, and leaving the results to God.

God gives us power to fulfill His plan for our lives.

God wants to strengthen us so we can serve Him in the fulfillment of His purposes. That plan includes allowing us the privilege of making an eternal difference in the lives of others. But that is possible only as we come to know God as He really is. He is our God who can do anything through us that He chooses to do: "By His mighty power at work within us, He is able to accomplish infinitely more than we would ever dare to ask or hope."[16]

If we really believe that God is all-powerful, we will no longer walk in fear and unbelief. We will place our faith in God—not necessarily *great faith* in God, but rather faith in a *great God* who is omnipotent. In turn, He will lead us into a life full of adventure and purpose. I have found no better way to live!

Pastor David Jeremiah explains that the unlimited power that raised Jesus Christ from the grave is available to us today:

> Most believers give lip service to God but live their lives in their own strength. They operate in their own energy about 80% of the time. Then they have a power outage. You know what a power outage is? It's going to the doctor and finding out there is something wrong with you that they can't fix. And realizing that you don't have control. It's going into an office where you have been going for 25 years where you feel secure, and getting a pink slip saying that you have been laid off from your job. Now you don't know what to do. Most of us as believers don't really touch the power of God until we have our own power outage. Then we discover that when we are weak, God is strong. I tell you that the power of God that was in Jesus Christ is the power that is available to you today. So we, too, can say with the Apostle Paul, "I can do all things through Christ who strengthens me" (Philippians 4:13).[17]

God's power is something we can trust. Yet God's character involves much more than power. His strength is used in conjunction with His many other qualities. One of these is the unlimited nature of His knowledge. In the next two chapters, we will learn more about God's incredible knowledge—and how it affects our lives.

LIFE APPLICATION

WRITE IT ON YOUR HEART—Commit the following statement and verses to memory. Then as you encounter situations during this week where you are in need of strength, claim these promises by faith.

- Because God is all-powerful, He can help me with anything.
- Philippians 4:13—"I can do everything with the help of Christ who gives me the strength I need."
- Isaiah 40:29—"[God] gives power to those who are tired and worn out; He offers strength to the weak."
- 2 Chronicles 16:9—"The eyes of the LORD search the whole earth in order to strengthen those whose hearts are fully committed to Him."

COUNT ON GOD—What difference can God's power make in a situation you currently face that is beyond your control? Commit your circumstances to Him in prayer and by faith depend on Him to give you strength and to work changes through His mighty power.

OBEY GOD—Do you feel incapable of doing something that God wants you to do? Rather than concentrating on your inadequacies, focus on God who "by His mighty power at work within us...is able to accomplish infinitely more than we would ever dare to ask or hope" (Ephesians 3:20). By faith, take the steps necessary to do what God is asking of you.

CHAPTER 6

GOD
IS PRESENT
EVERYWHERE

In 1985 during the week between Christmas and New Year's Day, my fellow staff members and I were involved in a conference televised simultaneously on every continent via 97 down-link locations. Using the newest satellite technology, I spoke from Seoul, South Korea, in the early morning hours while audiences around the world watched in their corresponding time zones. The following day, I traveled to Manila to speak at the televised conference. The third day I was in Berlin, and the fourth night in Mexico City. I traveled more than 40,000 miles in five days and spoke more than twenty times.

Although physically present in only one city at a time, I was present on television sets around the world. In every part of the globe, people saw my face in full color. Those who had met me personally could say, "Yes, that's Bill Bright, because that's a perfect picture of him." Viewers also heard my voice, and those who had previously heard me in person could say, "It's Bill Bright, all right! I recognize the inflections in his voice and the way he pronounces words."

In a narrow sense, I was "present" through my face on the screen and the voice that came out of the speakers, but I was not really present. Viewers could not touch me. I could not see the people in the worldwide audience. I did not know if they were standing or sitting, and I was not aware of what they were thinking, planning, or doing.

But God is present everywhere at the same time. It's not that He is physically present in one city and present by voice and picture in another city, as I was by the technology of electronics; He is present in the fullest sense everywhere at once. How does He do it? This is how God explains His presence when speaking to Jeremiah: "'Am I only a God nearby,' declares the LORD, 'and not a God far away?...Do not I fill heaven and earth?'"[1]

God's ability to be present everywhere is called *omnipresence*. It means that there is not a sliver of space anywhere in the universe where He is not dynamically and powerfully present with all of His wonderful personal attributes. Everywhere throughout the world, to the utmost reaches of the universe and in heaven, God is always and immediately present with all of who He is!

GOD'S SPIRIT-PRESENCE

Can you imagine being completely free of all the limitations of time and space? We cannot, of course. But God can, and is! He is not limited by a body, but is a Spirit who moves wherever He wishes.

How can we explain His Spirit-presence? Many writers have compared it to the wind. No one can see the wind; it comes and goes as it pleases. No one can box it in or stop it from blowing. Yet we can see the results of wind. We see its massive strength in roiling tornadoes, hurricanes, and typhoons. The wind can also be gentle, like the whisper of a breeze off the ocean. It can bring the smell of soft rain on the leaves or the freshness of spring through an open window. Is this not like the wonderful contrast of our God who can both topple rulers and calm the fears of a little child?

Meteorologists try to predict the wind, yet with only partial success. Recently, the meeting of hot and cold air masses spawned deadly tornadoes in Central Florida, which took weather forecasters by surprise. The devastation caused the loss of more than forty lives and millions of dollars in property. In a similar way, God's presence and work cannot be predicted for He does what He wills (of course, He will not contradict His nature). Jesus also used the wind analogy to describe the work of the Holy Spirit: "Just as you can hear the wind but can't tell where it comes from or where it is going, so you can't explain how people are born of the Spirit."[2]

Yet a wind analogy is inadequate to completely describe the awesome presence of our infinite Creator who lives outside the time-space dimension in which we find ourselves bound. Unlike the wind, He is literally in every place in the entire universe at the same time! Not a single atom in any galaxy is hidden from His sight.

Solomon, the famous biblical king who was given unparalleled wisdom from God, built a temple for our majestic God. Awed by the holy task, Solomon asks, "Will God really live on earth? Why, even the highest heavens cannot contain you. How much less this Temple I have built!"[3] Truly, a temple of gold could never contain God, since even the heavens cannot hold him.

GOD'S SPIRIT IS DIFFERENT THAN HIS CREATION

Many religions believe that God's existence is somehow bound up with His creation. A. W. Tozer writes of one such scene:

> Canon W. G. H. Holmes of India told of seeing Hindu worshipers tapping on trees and stones and whispering, "Are you there? Are you there?" to the god they hoped might reside within.[4]

The belief that God is everything and everything is God is called *pantheism*. Like these Hindus, if you touch a tree, you touch God. To carry it further, this belief leads to the conclusion that since everything is god, we are gods. These fallacies take away God's majesty and make Him common and ordinary. But pantheism is not what the Bible means when it describes God's omnipresence. Author Bill Hybels explains the difference this way:

The Bible says that God is Spirit, so technically, He doesn't dwell in three-dimensional space as we do (John 15:15). His *presence* is everywhere, but not His *essence* (that would be the heresy known as pantheism). God is no less present in one portion of the universe than any other. And He is no more present anywhere than where you are right now. In other words, anyone, anywhere in the universe might say, "The Lord is in this place." Wherever you are, God is right there, right now.[5]

Think of the difference this way. Earlier we described God's creative power as a potter who forms a pot out of clay. We would never confuse the pot and the potter. They are distinct in nature and substance. So it is with God. He is distinct from His creation, so far above it in every way that we cannot equate His essence with His creation. Yet because He has no limitations, God is also present in every corner of His universe. This means that He is present in the mountains and the stars, but He is not these things.

> WHEREVER YOU ARE, GOD IS RIGHT THERE, RIGHT NOW.

In this chapter, we will consider three truths that provide the basis for an understanding of the omnipresence of God. These truths are promises on which we can base our lives.

GOD'S PRESENCE SUSTAINS THE UNIVERSE

There is no place within all of creation that is not supported by the divine presence of God. Acts 17:28 records, "In Him we live and move and exist." Let me use an example that is very personal to each of us. God was present when you and I were fashioned in the womb. Psalm 139:13–16 says:

> You created my inmost being; You knit me together in my mother's womb. I praise You because I am fearfully and wonderfully made; Your works are wonderful, I know that full well. My frame was not hidden from You when I was

made in the secret place. When I was woven together in the depths of the earth, Your eyes saw my unformed body. All the days ordained for me were written in Your book before one of them came to be (NIV).

We are the result of God's marvelous workmanship. He designed us. He made our bodies wonderfully complex. He was present from the moment of conception, is present every moment we live, and will be present when we die.

Let us think for a moment about what God sustains for each of us. It is estimated that as adults our bodies contain sixty trillion cells that have all been carefully organized to perform life's various functions in harmony. Consider these other facts about the human body:

- Our nose can recognize up to 10,000 different aromas.
- Our tongue has about 6,000 taste buds.
- Our brain contains ten billion nerve cells. Each brain nerve cell is connected to as many as 10,000 other nerve cells throughout the body.
- Our body has so many blood vessels that their combined length could circle the planet two-and-a-half times.

God also customized each of us with our own special DNA blueprint, which is contained within every single cell. It has been estimated that if our individual blueprint were written out in a book, it would require 200,000 pages.[6] And God knows every word on every page!

Can you imagine if factories all over our country were manufacturing intricate human bodies? With our human record, what a mess it would turn out to be! The assembly line would grind to a halt because of back-orders on hands and feet. Hearts would malfunction due to system design defects; recalls would bring back hundreds of thousands of misassembled brains.

Now think of the millions of living organisms, from viruses to elephants, and the trillions of systems, from galaxies to earth's numerous ecosystems. It all works. It runs without tune-ups or teardowns and rebuilds. We hire experts to keep sophisticated computers functioning at maximum capacity, yet many people believe that our amazing universe has no Designer and no Sustainer! But it does—our loving, creative, ever-present God.

GOD REVEALS HIS PRESENCE IN DIFFERENT WAYS

God reveals His presence to us, which allows us to have an intimate relationship with Him. Let us consider several ways in which God manifests His presence to us.

God's "illuminating presence" affects every person.

Like turning on a light in a dark room, the light of God's presence opens our eyes to truth. Paul explains that God "made His light shine in our hearts to give us the light of the knowledge of the glory of God in the face of Christ."[7]

We begin to know God when the light of His presence exposes our sin. Paul writes, "It is shameful even to talk about the things that ungodly people do in secret. But when the light shines on them, it becomes clear how evil these things are."[8] Once we recognize our sinfulness and turn from it, God in His grace can reconcile us to Him through the death of His Son, Jesus, on the cross.

GOD CHOOSES THE TIME AND PLACE TO REVEAL HIMSELF TO US IN SPECIAL WAYS.

King David was well aware that God is present everywhere at once, and what that meant for him. At times, he may not have wanted God's presence—for example, during his adulterous affair with Bathsheba. In Psalm 139:7, he asks, "Where can I go from your Spirit? Where can I flee from your presence?" (NIV). But after he was forgiven and for the rest of his life, he reflected on God's companionship. He realized that at any given moment, God was present in Israel, in all of the nations around it, even in the distant regions. David also counted on God's presence during troubling times.[9] This affirmation of God's help came from the heart of a man who had walked in God's illuminating presence and found Him faithful—even during his disobedience.

We can have this same assurance. Hebrews 13:5 says, "Never will I leave you; never will I forsake you" (NIV). This promise gives us hope for the future and confidence in our gracious God.

God's "inspirational presence" is revealed in special places and at special times.

God has revealed Himself to men in unique ways. God spoke to Moses on Mount Horeb through a burning bush. Later on Mount Sinai, God came down in a pillar of cloud and passed in front of Moses. God's glorious presence so filled Solomon's temple that the people fell face down on the ground and worshipped the magnificent God of Israel. Paul saw the Lord in a blinding light on the road to Damascus.

On countless other occasions, God makes His presence especially known to ordinary believers. The setting may be a devotional time, church service, or during a revival. God chooses the time and place to reveal Himself to us in special ways, and when He does, we never forget the joy of being in His inspirational presence.

I have experienced God's special presence many times since surrendering my life to Him in 1945, although I have never seen Him or heard His audible voice. One dramatic experience happened early in my ministry when He gave me a vision for Campus Crusade for Christ. One evening at about midnight during my senior year in seminary, I was studying for a Greek exam. Vonette was asleep in a nearby room. Without warning, I sensed the presence of God in a way I had never known before. Within moments, I had the overwhelming impression that the Lord had flashed His instructions for my life on the screen of my mind.

This was the greatest moment of my Christian life. In a very definite way, God commanded me to invest my life in helping to fulfill the Great Commission in this generation.[10] I was to begin by helping to win and disciple students of the world for Christ. How I would do this was not spelled out in detail. That came later to my fellow staff and me as the Lord has given additional insights for the implementation of the original vision.

I awakened Vonette, and together we praised God for His direction and promised that through His grace and strength we would obey Him.

God's "incarnate presence" is manifested in Jesus Christ.

Perhaps you have heard the story of the little girl who was afraid of the dark and whose mother kept insisting, "God is watching over you. He will take care of you." But the little girl insisted, "Mommy, I want a God with skin on." And that, of course, is the reason God visited this planet. God became a man, the God-man Jesus. The God with skin on.

John tells us, "The Word [Jesus] became human and lived here on earth among us...No one has ever seen God. But His only Son, who is Himself God, is near to the Father's heart; He has told us about Him."[11] Our awesome God was willing to restrict Himself to a physical body so He could live among us and teach us about Himself. This is the most tangible way God has revealed His presence to us.

God's "indwelling presence" resides within every believer.

How would Jesus' followers continue to have fellowship with Him once He left this earth to return to His Father's side? Just before Jesus returned to heaven, He told His disciples, "I will ask the Father, and He will give you another Counselor [the Holy Spirit] to be with you forever—the Spirit of truth...He lives with you and will be in you."[12] Paul wrote, "Don't you know that you yourselves are God's temple and that God's Spirit lives in you?"[13]

Unbelievers cannot begin to comprehend why we are so confident that God is filling us with His presence. Though God is omnipresent in their universe just like He is in ours, they cannot sense His presence, so they deny He is there. Jesus explained this to His disciples: "The world cannot accept Him [the Holy Spirit], because it neither sees Him nor knows Him. But you know Him."[14]

Do we deny that the wind does not exist because we cannot see it? Of course not, for we can feel it. The God who is present everywhere is felt by those sensitive to the Spirit of God.

GOD WANTS US TO CONSCIOUSLY
LIVE IN HIS PRESENCE

Indeed, our confidence is in the ever-present nature of God. We can be sure that He sees us, walks with us, and loves us no matter where we are. That fact leads us to our third truth: God wants us to "consciously" live in His presence every day.

A classic little book, *The Practice of the Presence of God*, gives the essence of living moment by moment in God's presence. Its author was a humble monk named Brother Lawrence, who served his Lord by washing pots and pans in a monastery during the 16th century. Joseph de Beaufort, his close friend, says of Brother Lawrence, "The worst trial he could imagine was losing his sense of God's presence, which had been with him for so long a time."[15]

Brother Lawrence spoke openly about his practice of living in the presence of God:

> All we have to do is to recognize God as being intimately present within us. Then we may speak directly to Him every time we need to ask for help, to know His will in moments of uncertainty, and to do whatever He wants us to do in a way that pleases Him. We should offer our work to Him before we begin, and thank Him afterwards for the privilege of having done them for His sake. This continuous conversation would also include praising and loving God incessantly for His infinite goodness and perfection.[16]

Every morning, I make it a practice to fall to my knees in prayer beside my bed. I ask my Lord to live His life in and through me throughout the day. My request is that He will walk around in my body, speak with my lips, use my hands and feet for His glory, and control my thoughts so they honor Him.

I encourage you to begin a daily practice of praising God during all your activities. The following Life Application will help you get started. But praise is just the beginning of a lifestyle of practicing the presence of God. Remember, wherever you go, He is already there. In our next chapter, we will see how God's omnipresence means that He will always help us.

LIFE APPLICATION

EXALT YOUR GOD—Praising God is one way to consciously live in the presence of God. This week, pay special attention to how God is at work in your life and in the world around you. Make a list of one of these areas. Then praise Him for the special ways He is present in your life.

REFLECT HIS IMAGE—Contemplate the following questions:

- How does knowing that God is everywhere influence what I think, say, and do?

- Are there "hidden" areas of my life that I need to turn over to my all-seeing God?

- If I fully understand that our ever-present Lord is *in* me, how will I live my life differently?

- How can having the Creator of the universe live His life through me impact my life and the lives of others?

SHARE HIS MAJESTY—Who can you encourage today with the great news that our God is always with us? Share the following verses with that person:

- Deuteronomy 31:6—"The LORD your God will go ahead of you. He will neither fail you nor forsake you."

- Psalm 139:12—"Even in darkness I cannot hide from You. To You the night shines as bright as day. Darkness and light are both alike to You."

CHAPTER 7

GOD IS ALWAYS WITH US

When I awaken in the morning, God is with me. When I kneel to worship Him, He is with me. When I arrive at the office or at the airport for one of my many trips, He is still with me.

God is with me while I am on the airplane, and He is with me when I arrive at my destination, whether in California, Pakistan, or Brazil. He is with me as I turn out the lights at night anywhere in the world. We can be confident that Christ is present with us and all believers in the United States, Canada, Germany, Russia, Indonesia, Egypt, and every other country—at the same time.

God is not limited by time or space or height or depth—or even our level of faith. He is always with us whether we are taking giant steps of faith or we are taking the first baby steps of faith. He lives inside of every person who puts his trust in God through faith in Jesus Christ.

GOD IS PRESENT WITH US IN ALL PLACES

Let us apply this attribute to the events of our lives. First, God's omnipresence means that we cannot go anywhere that God is not beside us. The psalmist writes, "If I go up to the heavens, You are there; if I make my bed in the depths, You are there. If I rise on the wings of the dawn, if I settle on the far side of the sea, even there Your hand will guide me, Your right hand will hold me fast."[1] God sees us, walks with us, and cares for us no matter where we are.

During NASA's Apollo 13 flight, Jim Lovell, Jack Swaggart, and Fred Haise were scheduled to walk on the moon. Just after they blasted off, an explosion on their ship endangered their lives. Not only did they have to abort their plans to make a moon landing, but it also looked as if they would not have enough engine power and cabin oxygen to return to Earth alive. One of the tensest times during the flight was when the space ship orbited behind the moon. For agonizing hours, the astronauts were sailing through the darkness on the far side of the moon, out of reach of radio contact with Mission Control in Houston. All over our country, Americans prayed for the safety of the astronauts. The country breathed a sigh of relief when radio contact was reestablished and when Apollo 13 was successfully brought back home.

How could God hear all the prayers for the astronauts? Because God is no less present behind the shadow of the moon than right beside you right now. In fact, without God's omnipresence, prayer would be ineffective. God promises His people, "Before they call I will answer; while they are still speaking, I will hear."[2] When I am in Orlando and pray for a fellow staff member in Thailand, God is with both of us. He is fully present in Orlando to hear my prayer, and at the same time fully present in Thailand to act in behalf of the one for whom I am praying! The basis for all prayer rests on the fact that God is omnipresent.

GOD IS PRESENT IN ALL OUR CIRCUMSTANCES

Have you had an experience that left you wondering where God is? Sometimes we do not feel God's presence, but emotions can be misleading. No matter what we feel, God is still there.

David often felt abandoned by God. In Psalm 22, he implores, "My God, my God! Why have you forsaken me? Why do you remain so distant? Why do you ignore my cries for help? Every day I call to you, my God, but you do not answer."[3] Yet later in the same psalm he states his trust in God's presence:

> Yet you brought me safely from my mother's womb and led me to trust You when I was a nursing infant. I was thrust upon You at my birth. You have been my God from the moment I was born... Praise the LORD, all you who fear Him!... For He has not ignored the suffering of the needy. He has not turned and walked away. He has listened to their cries for help.[4]

Two Dutch women during World War II experienced God's omnipresence. Corrie and Betsie ten Boom became involved in hiding Jewish people during the Nazi occupation of their country. As a consequence, the Nazis sent the two elderly women to Ravensbruck, one of the most dreaded concentration camps. There they endured incredible depravation and suffering. Yet they ministered to hundreds of other prisoners who needed to hear about their Lord and Savior. Their barracks were transformed into a Bible study and prayer center, and the cruel, harsh attitudes of many prisoners were turned to compassion and love.

THE BASIS FOR ALL PRAYER RESTS ON THE FACT THAT GOD IS OMNIPRESENT.

Eventually, Betsie became deathly ill. As she was taken to the prison hospital, Corrie tried to shield Betsie from the sleet that stung their bodies. After the orderlies set Betsie's stretcher on the hospital floor, Corrie leaned down to hear the words on her sister's weak lips, "...must tell people what we have learned here. We must tell them that there is no pit so deep that He is not deeper still. They will listen to us, Corrie, because we have been there."[5]

Betsie died the following day. Soon after, Corrie was miraculously discharged from the camp—only days before all women her age were put to death. For the rest of her life, Corrie traveled the globe telling her story of God's presence and faithfulness even in the worst of places.

Our confidence is that "there is no pit so deep that God is not there." We cannot face a situation in which He does not walk beside us.

GOD IS PRESENT WITH US DURING EVERY CRISIS

What crisis are you facing right now? Unemployment, serious health problems, the break-up of your marriage, rebellious teenage children, rejection by those who once loved you? God walks with us, gives us strength, understands our pain, and knows how to handle our problems. He will help us if we only ask Him and are willing to do things His way and in His time.

Isaiah 43:1–3 records God's precious promise to be with us in times of crisis:

> The LORD who created you says: "Do not be afraid, for I have ransomed you. I have called you by name; you are mine. When you go through deep waters and great trouble, I will be with you. When you go through rivers of difficulty, you will not drown! When you walk through the fire of oppression, you will not be burned up; the flames will not consume you. For I am the LORD, your God, the Holy One of Israel, your Savior.

One of the most basic crises each of us faces is our own death. For many people, even Christians, the terror of leaving this world is very real. One of my fellow staff members faced such a crisis just after her thirtieth birthday. Days after her doctor admitted her to the hospital, she began having problems breathing. Although she pressed the nurses' call button, no one responded.

Panicked, she realized that she was dying in a hospital bed— and no one knew. As her breathing became more labored, she began to lose consciousness. She was helpless, yet she desperately wanted to live to see her young daughter and husband again.

Within seconds of her panic, a supernatural peace flooded over her. God impressed this promise clearly on her heart: "If you awake and are in heaven, I am with you. If you awake and are in this hospital bed, I am with you. Either way, I am just as close to you."

With that promise ringing in her ears, she put her future in God's hands. Then through eyelids barely cracked, she saw the elevator doors slide open in the hall outside her room. Out walked her pastor! By the time he reached her bedside, she drifted into un-consciousness. But because of his quick response, her life was saved.

The comforting words of Psalm 23:4 ring beautifully. "Even when I walk through the dark valley of death, I will not be afraid, for You are close beside me. Your rod and Your staff protect and comfort me." I encourage you to memorize and meditate upon this beloved psalm.

GOD IS WITH US WHEN WE WITNESS FOR HIM

Jesus promises, "Be sure of this: I am with you always, even to the end of the age."[6] This was given as part of the Great Commission —the challenge to go into the entire world and preach the gospel and disciple those who come to faith in Christ. It is when we are fulfilling the Great Commission that Jesus' promise to be with us becomes most precious. He has given us the challenge to reach every person on earth with God's message of love and forgiveness. Yet He did not leave us alone to accomplish this impossible task. He has sent us His Holy Spirit who empowers us to do what is humanly impossible—but possible with God.

I take great comfort in the fact that Jesus is with every one of our ministry's 20,500 full-time staff and over 660,000 trained volunteers in 181 countries of the world.[7] His Holy Spirit is the one who works within the hearts of all believers so that His work will be accomplished.

You can take comfort in knowing that God is present and working during any ministry He gives you to do. As you share your faith in Jesus Christ with your neighbor, God is with you. When you teach your children about God's love, God is with you. When you witness to that coworker who is an atheist, God is with you. God will bring forth the fruit and help us be faithful to Him in introducing others to Christ as Savior and Lord.

Nothing We Do Is Hidden From God

Jesus promised that our heavenly Father, "who sees what is done in secret, will reward you."[8] Just think about that. When we privately do something good that no one else knows about, God still sees it and rewards us accordingly.

When a Sunday school teacher labors teaching preschoolers about God's love, she may not receive many affirmations from others, yet the Lord sees every smile and hug she gives them. When a godly pastor spends hours in his office in heartfelt prayer for people who dislike him, try to thwart his ministry, or are apathetic about the church, God sees his deep concern. For the bedridden elderly person who adopts a prayer ministry in behalf of loved ones, neighbors, and friends, God hears. For the godly parent who prays hours into the night for a prodigal child, God sees. God knows about the businessman, betrayed by his business partner, who does not take revenge but responds in forgiveness and love. To these faithful servants, our ever-present God says, "Love your enemies, do good to them, and lend to them without expecting to get anything back. Then your reward will be great."[9]

> GOD'S OMNIPRESENCE ENABLES US TO BE IN CONSTANT COMMUNION WITH HIM.

On the other hand, God also sees the wrong things we commit in secret. We only fool ourselves by thinking that no one will ever know. Scripture says, "Nothing in all creation can hide from Him. Everything is naked and exposed before His eyes. This is the God to whom we must explain all that we have done."[10]

There is no place we can hide when we do wrong. God sees and is beside us. As believers, we may break our fellowship with God when we sin, but He does not leave our presence. He is still dwelling within us, convicting us, helping us to do what is right through His loving discipline, and waiting for us to repent of our wrongdoing.

Some people see God as a "great traffic cop" in the sky watching their every move. I like to think that He loves me so much that He cannot take His eyes off me. I am the "apple of His eye." Thank You, Father, for watching over us.

CONSCIOUSLY LIVING IN HIS PRESENCE

God's omnipresence enables us to be in constant communion with Him and to depend on Him in every situation. But at times we ignore His presence because we are so preoccupied with our lives and focused on material concerns (food, clothing, shelter, finances, and jobs). Sometimes we even forget that He is with us while we are busy serving Him. Brother Lawrence discovered this truth when he began to practice the presence of God. For fifteen years, his responsibility was to wash greasy pots and pans in the monastery—a job he disliked. Practicing the presence of God transformed what he considered a chore into an exciting privilege. He writes, "My day-to-day life consists of giving God my simple, loving attention. If I'm distracted, He calls me back in tones that are supernaturally beautiful."[11] This is what he considered important in walking with God:

> The most holy and necessary practice in our spiritual life is the presence of God. That means finding constant pleasure in His divine company, speaking humbly and lovingly with Him in all seasons, at every moment, without limiting the conversation in any way.[12]

Living in God's presence means realizing that God is with you and is vitally concerned about every part of your life. As I practice this, I find that throughout the day the Lord Jesus communicates with me through impressions in my mind that spring from meditating on His Word and talking to Him in prayer. This makes both prayer and the study of God's Word an exciting adventure for me. Let me give you some promises that you can rely on as you consciously practice the presence of God in your daily activities.

When we are confused, God will guide us.

Confusion is rampant in our society—even among believers. People ask: Why are these things happening to me? Where should I go and what should I do with my life?

We can have confidence that God will reveal Himself to us when we do not know where to turn. He promises, "I will instruct you and teach you in the way you should go; I will counsel you and watch over you."[13] Through His Word, prayer, the leading of the Holy Spirit, and our open hearts, He will guide us along the pathway He has planned for us.

When we are afraid, God will protect us.

No matter where we are afraid—at home alone, driving on the freeway during rush hour traffic, facing a hostile meeting, or walking alone at night—God is right beside us. He promises, "Do not fear, for I am with you; do not be dismayed, for I am your God. I will strengthen you and help you; I will uphold you with My righteous right hand."[14] What a comfort this is for us in our daily lives!

Claim this promise and consciously remember that God is with you during your times of fear and uncertainty. He will comfort you and give you courage to confront your fears. He will also protect you so that you will never experience anything outside His will for your life.

When we are tempted, God will help us resist.

Satan's main strategy with God's people has always been to whisper, "Don't call, don't ask, don't depend on God to do great things. You'll get along fine if you rely on your own cleverness and energy." The devil is not terribly frightened of our human efforts, but he knows his kingdom will be damaged when we lift our hearts to God.[15]

Although we can be tempted by our own flesh and by worldly influences, Satan is a major player in our desire to disobey God. Radio Bible teacher David Jeremiah puts temptation in a new light:

> Suppose you and one of your friends are on the border of doing something wrong. Both of you know it is wrong. But you are about to do it anyway. But if you should say to your

friend, "Go right ahead and do it, but I think you should know that I just heard from heaven and God will be here in a few moments." Maybe your friend will respond, "Wow, if God is going to be here soon, maybe I will do this tomorrow or next week, but I don't want to do this if God is going to show up in a few minutes."[16]

Surprise! God has already shown up. He is here...now! When facing temptation, we should say to ourselves, "This is being carried out in the presence of almighty God." Meditating on this truth will give you conviction to face temptation in your life.

I encourage you to practice the presence of God by asking our Lord to help you resist temptation. The Bible promises that "God is faithful. He will keep the temptation from becoming so strong that you can't stand up against it."[17]

When we are hurting, God will comfort us.

How could Paul and Silas sing praises to God in the depths of a stinking, cold Roman prison? Their backs were raw because they had been beaten with whips and rods. Their feet were in stocks and the jailer had threatened to execute them if they tried to escape. Paul and Silas could sing because God was with them in the inner dungeon while they were hurting.

The psalmist writes, "The LORD is close to the brokenhearted; He rescues those who are crushed in spirit."[18] Whether we experience physical, emotional, or mental pain, the Holy Spirit will comfort us and give us strength and courage to triumph over our hurts.

Several of our Campus Crusade for Christ staff members have lost small children to accidental death or disease. Vonette and I are thankful that this is a trial we have never had to endure, but we feel their pain. They tell me that it is one of the most agonizing crises that a person can ever go through. Tears flow for months; muscles are sore from sobbing. Many unbelieving couples break up afterwards due to guilt and blame. But many followers of Christ testify, "That was the most difficult thing I have ever experienced, but I have to tell you that God was so very near to me that I felt His presence like I have never felt Him before."

Although Scripture is clear that God is present everywhere at once, parents who have lost children give evidence that God manifests His presence in special ways at particular times of need. In 2 Corinthians 1:3,4, Paul assures us, "[God] is the source of every mercy and the God who comforts us. He comforts us in all our troubles so that we can comfort others."

When we are discouraged, God will encourage us.

Do you struggle with insurmountable bills? Have friends betrayed you? Do you feel inadequate at your job or as a parent? Scripture instructs us, "Cast all your anxiety on Him because He cares for you."[19] We are encouraged in Joshua 1:9, "Do not be afraid or discouraged. For the LORD your God is with you wherever you go." Not only will God help you conquer every discouragement, He will help you climb every mountain in your life! And when you come through the valleys of discouragement, you will find that God was there all the time. Sometimes He was waiting patiently for you to exhaust your means and energy and turn to Him for His help. What a tremendous encouragement! We can trust that kind of God for anything!

When we are lonely, God will be our companion.

Some of our most lonely moments can be when we are in a crowd, and yet no one notices us. Our hearts ache when we think no one cares. But Jesus is our ever-present friend.[20] He promises, "Never will I leave you; never will I forsake you."[21]

He is also with us as we face lonely tasks. When David Livingstone sailed to Africa for the first time as a missionary, a group of his friends accompanied him to the pier to wish him bon voyage. They were concerned for his safety and reminded him of the dangers of that unexplored land. One of the men even tried to convince him to remain in England. But Livingstone opened his Bible and read Jesus' words from Matthew 28:20: "Lo, I am with you always." He turned to the man who was especially concerned about his safety and smiled. "That, my friend, is the word of a gentleman...So let us be going."

No person or circumstance can ever remove us from the presence of our loving God. Paul writes, "I am convinced that nothing can ever separate us from His love. Death can't, and life can't. The angels can't, and the demons can't. Our fears for today, our worries about tomorrow, and even the powers of hell can't keep God's love away. Whether we are high above the sky or in the deepest ocean, nothing in all creation will ever be able to separate us from the love of God that is revealed in Christ Jesus our Lord."[22]

He is here with us right now and forever—because He is our ever-present God. He is our guide for life and for eternity. What an incredible truth! What a powerful motivation for us to know, love, trust, obey, worship, and enjoy the presence of our wonderful God and Savior.

LIFE APPLICATION

WRITE IT ON YOUR HEART—Commit the following statement and verses to memory. Then as you encounter situations during this week where you need the comfort of knowing God is near, claim these promises by faith.

- Because God is ever-present, He is always with me.

- Joshua 1:9—"I command you—be strong and courageous! Do not be afraid or discouraged. For the LORD your God is with you wherever you go."

- Psalm 16:11—"You will show me the way of life, granting me the joy of Your presence and the pleasures of living with You forever."

COUNT ON GOD—Our ever-present God is everywhere you have been and everywhere you will go. He is in the classroom, the courtroom, the office, the home, and the hospital room. He is with you in life and in death. He is the only one who can be with you no matter what. Are you in the midst of a struggle or situation where you need His guidance? Turn to Him now and place your trust in the One who is always with you. Study His Word and let it guide you.

OBEY GOD—God is present with you each minute of every day. He knows what you do and think every moment. Is there some area in your life in which you are not obeying God? Your ever-present God knows, so commit yourself to obeying Him today.

CHAPTER 8

GOD
KNOWS
EVERYTHING

M any people consider Albert Einstein the most dazzling intellect in history. Did you know that the beginnings of his theory of relativity came from an essay he wrote when he was 16 years old? By age 26, he had published five major research papers in an important German journal. For one of those papers, he received his doctorate. The ideas he introduced in those papers were so revolutionary that they changed the way we view the scientific universe.

When the Nazis came to power, they denounced Einstein's work, confiscated his property, and burned his books. Soon after, he moved to America and became a U.S. citizen. In 1939, Einstein learned that German scientists had split the uranium atom. He wrote a letter to President Franklin D. Roosevelt warning him about the German discovery, which he predicted would lead to the invention of the atomic bomb. Because of Einstein's advice, the U.S. government established the Manhattan Project, which developed the first two atomic bombs in 1945.[1]

Einstein's ideas impacted not only the way scientists think about matter, but also the way war is waged. They even spilled over into the moral realm. To Einstein's shock, modern philosophers took his scientific theory of relativity and applied it to the moral realm as *relativism*. This philosophy destroyed society's belief in absolute truth and helped produce acceptance for situational ethics. While Einstein's discoveries about the atom have advanced the arenas of energy and medicine, they have been used to destroy physical and moral lives.

God is the only source of all knowledge, understanding, and wisdom; everything we know and understand originated with Him. As the prophet Isaiah declares:

> Who has understood the mind of the LORD, or instructed Him as His counselor? Whom did the LORD consult to enlighten Him, and who taught Him the right way? Who was it that taught Him knowledge or showed Him the path of understanding?[2]

What great news! We do not need an intellect like Einstein's. We know Someone who knows the answers to all of life's questions. "Oh, what a wonderful God we have! How great are His riches and wisdom and knowledge!"[3]

THE GREATEST KNOWLEDGE

What a person knows can lead to riches, power, and advancement. Major corporations and companies pay consultants handsomely for what they know. Consider the computer industry. Fortunes are being made because people want quicker ways to find and manage information.

In 1953, there were only 100 computers in use around the world. These machines each weighed many tons and filled huge rooms. Today, there are more than 110 million computers in homes, schools, businesses, and government offices. Some of the newest computers are so small that they can fit into a coat pocket.[4]

Our knowledge base doubles every few years. College graduates often discover that what they learned in their many years of study quickly becomes obsolete due to this information explosion. Every day new discoveries change what we previously accepted as factual. Yesterday's cutting-edge concepts are being replaced by today's insights. These in turn will give way to tomorrow's breakthroughs.

Yet the more we learn, the more we realize how much we still do not know. To compensate for our lack of knowledge, we are always trying to build a faster, smarter way to access knowledge. Some of today's sophisticated supercomputers can perform nearly 32 billion calculations per second and can store a billion characters in their memories. They can do in one hour what it would take your desktop computer forty years to perform. Scientists are also using technology called parallel processing in which they link networks of computers to be able to use each computer's idle time. The goal is to create a network that can perform a trillion calculations per second, a measure known as a teraflop.[5]

> WE KNOW SOMEONE WHO KNOWS THE ANSWERS TO ALL OF LIFE'S QUESTIONS.

At the same time, many of these scientists and experts reject the one Person who has the greatest knowledge of all. According to 1 John 3:20, "He knows everything." Our magnificent Creator God not only knows everything but also is the source of all knowledge. His knowledge is absolutely pure, totally true and accurate, and undefiled by distortions or wrong perspectives. Unlike man's knowledge, God's knowledge is never superseded or made obsolete by new discoveries.

Most scientists spend their lives trying to understand and solve the mysteries of life and the universe. But for our all-knowing God, there are no mysteries. He has a clear understanding of everything that baffles mankind. To Him, a teraflop is nothing.

OUR ALL-KNOWING GOD

Theologians call God's unlimited knowledge *omniscience* (all knowing). What does God's omniscience mean? Nearly 150 years ago, one of the last century's great theologians, Stephen Charnock, wrote:

He knows what angels know, what man knows, and infinitely more; He knows Himself, His own operations, all His creatures, the notions and thoughts of them.[6]

Because God knows absolutely everything that can ever be known, He has never had to learn anything. He does not need a computer because all knowledge is instantly accessible to Him and He remembers everything at all times. He is never bewildered or confused or perplexed. He never has to figure something out; everything is always absolutely clear to Him. Nothing ever surprises God; He is always completely aware of all events because He sees everything. Nothing ever turns out differently than He expected or planned.

In this chapter, I want to highlight four areas of God's omniscience. They will help us more fully understand how much we can trust God with everything in our lives.

ONLY GOD KNOWS EVERYTHING ABOUT HIMSELF

As humans, we do not understand much about ourselves. For example, has anyone ever pointed out a task you messed up and said, "You should have known better than that"? But you thought you did know what to do when you started—until you failed.

Now imagine what it would be like to deal with a god who has inadequate knowledge about himself and his creation. At Shinto shrines in Japan, people tie messages to tree branches to inform their gods of needs. These worshippers have never experienced a God who knows everything, so they operate on the premise that their deity needs the most elemental information.

Not so with the God of the Bible. He knows His own essence and infinite perfections. He knows what is unknowable to anyone else. First Corinthians 2:11 says, "No one can know what anyone else is really thinking except that person alone, and no one can know God's thoughts except God's own Spirit."

If God did not know Himself completely, then His knowledge of everything else would be incomplete as well. We could not trust Him with our problems. Let us take this a step further. If God did not know Himself perfectly, then He would be ignorant of His own ability; He would not know how far His power extends. That would mean He could not govern everything, for He would not know how to exercise His power. Let me give some examples of the importance of God's knowledge of Himself.

As humans, we do not know ourselves, let alone what is going on in the heart of another person. That is why many of our laws when put into practice work against what they were intended to do. For example, malpractice laws intended to help patients injured during a medical procedure can also be used by a dishonest person to cheat the system out of millions of dollars. In a similar way, if God did not fully know His own holiness, He could not discern the difference between evil and good. Consequently, He could not prescribe laws or execute justice, for He would be limited in His knowledge of a person's heart attitudes. But He does understand His holiness, so He is the perfect judge.

Second, if a king did not know his own authority or the borders and nature of his kingdom, how could he rule? His authority would suffer from serious lapses. But God does know every detail about His creatures, and His ability to rule in majesty and fairness is unequaled.

Third, in sports, we sometimes say about a rookie who makes it to the major leagues, "He doesn't know his own strength." Therefore, he plays well below his capabilities. We can never say that about God. No one but God is capable of truly understanding His divine magnificence and His many attributes.

Jesus tells us, "No one really knows the Father except the Son and those to whom the Son chooses to reveal Him."[7] What we know about God is possible only because He has revealed Himself through creation, the Bible, and Jesus Christ.

Only God Knows Everything About His Creation

Some people believe that our vast and orderly universe originated as a result of a massive explosion known as the "Big Bang." This theory proposes that billions of years ago, before there were stars or planets, all of the energy and matter of the universe were crammed together into a big ball. Somehow, this huge ball exploded, which caused the planets, stars, and galaxies to emerge. Yet even renowned scientists admit that no one really knows how stars originated. Abraham Loeb of the Harvard University Center for Astrophysics says, "The truth is that we don't understand star formation at a fundamental level."[8]

Where did the original matter and energy come from? How could life originate from the dead, inorganic matter of the Big Bang? And why do explosions today create only chaos and destruction instead of order and intricate design that is present throughout the universe?

How foolish to believe that this universe created itself. Truth and knowledge about creation can only originate with God.

ONLY GOD KNOWS EVERYTHING THAT HAS EVER HAPPENED OR WILL HAPPEN

Have you ever known someone who was a "know-it-all"? No matter what you say, he corrects you. If you tell a story, he has a better one. He parades his knowledge about the latest fads or news. Soon your ears tire of hearing him talk about what he knows.

Although God knows everything that has ever happened or will happen, He never comes across as a "know-it-all." He never uses His knowledge in a selfish way. Not a single event throughout all eternity has gone unnoticed by God. In the Book of Isaiah, God declares, "I am God, and there is no one else like Me. Only I can tell you what is going to happen even before it happens."[9] His omniscience is vitally important to us. As we get to know Him more intimately, we realize that we can trust Him because He does know everything we have done and will do, yet He loves us anyway.

Some people are intimidated by God because He knows the end from the beginning—and everything in between. Statements like Proverbs 15:3 unnerve them: "The LORD is watching everywhere, keeping His eye on both the evil and the good." They know that He sees their sin. This truth is disturbing for a husband who secretly looks at pornographic material and the employee who steals from the job. But God who sees what is done in secret will someday reveal such behavior publicly. On the other hand, God's omniscience is comforting to those who confess their sins as they recognize them. They know their sins have been forgiven.

God Knows the Past

None of us have a perfect memory, and we sometimes forget incidents in our past that would be helpful in the future. As a result, we run into all kinds of obstacles because we did not remember the past.

Our omniscient God, however, never forgets the past. One of the marvelous facets of God's knowledge is that He knows everything that has happened in the past as though it were happening right now. He has no dark recesses in his memory where some past action lies hidden. Since He knows our past perfectly, as we submit to the Holy Spirit, He illuminates what we need to know to take proper action.

The only time God promises not to remember our past is when we seek His forgiveness. God says, "I, even I, am He who blots out your transgressions, for My own sake, and remembers your sins no more."[10] Even though He is aware of our sins, He consciously does not "remember" them after we confess them.[11]

God Knows the Present

If God did not know all the present, then He could be deceived and misled. But God knows everything about all His creatures. The psalmist writes, "The LORD looks down from heaven and sees the whole human race. From His throne He observes all who live on the earth. He made their hearts, so He understands everything they do."[12]

We can compare God's knowledge to a mother who knows exactly what her child has done and is doing. Mothers often intuitively discern the real motives of their children's actions. If that is true of a mother, how much more is it true of our heavenly Father! God knows every good intention we have—as well as every temptation to rebel against His commands.

This can be very encouraging. For example, during Jesus' final meal with His disciples before the crucifixion, He predicted that Peter would deny his Lord. Jesus says to him, "Simon, Simon, Satan has asked to sift you as wheat. But I have prayed for you, Simon, that your faith may not fail. And when you have turned back, strengthen your brothers."[13] Knowing the condition of Peter's heart and that Peter would later disciple his brothers and sisters in their faith, Jesus prayed for him even before his denial. Jesus does the same for us today.

God Knows the Future

For years, highly educated and experienced economists have predicted doom for the American economy, yet we are experiencing quarter after quarter of improved profits and higher productivity.

> THERE IS NOT A THOUGHT IN YOUR MIND OR A MOTIVE IN YOUR HEART THAT GOD DOES NOT KNOW.

Stock market consultants forecasted a market decline and advised clients to switch into safer financial investments, yet the stock market continues to climb to extraordinary heights. No one really knows what the economy will do. As someone once remarked, "If you lined up all the economists in the world one after another, you wouldn't have enough to reach a conclusion."

Now consider the foreknowledge of God. At one time, nothing existed but God, yet at any point in time, He knew the past, present, and future. He knew when He would create the universe, that Adam and Eve would sin, and that He would send a Savior.

To prove His ability to predict the future, God gave us hundreds of prophecies in the Bible. One that fascinates me is the prophecy that the Jewish people would be called together as a nation.[14] The temple of Jerusalem was destroyed in A.D. 70 and the Jewish people scattered from their homeland. What were the chances that a people without a country could survive as a nation?

Every other nation since then has disappeared into oblivion. But in 1948, the Jewish people reestablished their homeland in Israel. The odds are astronomical of that happening after nearly two millennia. God's prophecies are 100 percent accurate because He not only knows the future, He also controls the future.

ONLY GOD KNOWS EVERYTHING ABOUT US

Occasionally when Vonette and I are talking together, one of us will say, "You read my mind; that was what I was about to tell you." Sometimes I will be silently praying about something, and she will ask me, "Have you thought about such and such?" To my amazement, that was the very thing I was praying about. How does that happen? I do not understand it, but I know that if human beings can be so in tune with one another, how much greater is God's ability to know our thoughts, discern our motives, and understand our weaknesses.

There is neither a thought in your mind nor a motive in your heart that God does not know. That is an awesome thought! King David explains:

> Oh LORD, You have examined my heart and know everything about me. You know when I sit down or stand up. You know my every thought when far away. You chart the path ahead of me and tell me where to stop and rest. Every moment You know where I am. You know what I am going to say even before I say it, LORD. You both precede and follow me. You place Your hand of blessing on my head. Such knowledge is too wonderful for me, too great for me to know![15]

I encourage you to take a few moments to worship God because of His knowledge and love for us. One way to worship our incomprehensible Creator is by coming before Him in silence and awe. Shut out everything else; turn off the radio, television, or music, and come into His presence. Tell Him how great are His attributes and works. Then listen in quietness as His Spirit speaks and ministers to your spirit.

LIFE APPLICATION

EXALT YOUR GOD—In silence and in awe, worship our all-knowing Lord with this Psalm:

> Oh LORD, You have examined my heart and know everything about me. You know when I sit down or stand up. You know my every thought when far away. You chart the path ahead of me and tell me where to stop and rest. Every moment You know where I am. You know what I am going to say even before I say it, LORD. You both precede and follow me. You place Your hand of blessing on my head. Such knowledge is too wonderful for me, too great for me to know! (Psalm 139:1–6).

In your own words, praise God for His knowledge of your past, present, and future. Thank Him for His forgiveness of your past, and praise Him for the peace He provides in the present, and the hope you can have because He knows your future.

REFLECT HIS IMAGE—How have you been influenced by the idea that morals are relative? Do you really believe that God knows everything and that His way is best? Spend time in the Bible and gain His knowledge. Then you can be an instrument of His wisdom, which is "far more valuable than rubies" (Proverbs 8:11). With your knowledge of God's Word, reject any relativistic ideas you may be practicing and reflect the standards of God's Word in your neighborhood and workplace.

SHARE HIS MAJESTY—Do you have friends or family members who need to know that our loving Creator knows all about them and wants to have a personal relationship with them? God's Spirit will help you find the words to say as you share the hope of Jesus with them. Today, encourage others with the Good News!

CHAPTER 9

GOD KNOWS EVERYTHING ABOUT US

Shortly after I became a Christian, a friend invited me to a celebration hosted by a man who headed one of the largest oil companies in the world at the time. As I went through the reception line, I knew I was just another nobody to this man. But afterward, the Holy Spirit began to impress upon me that I needed to talk to him about his soul. I obediently called his office, and to my surprise, he agreed to meet with me.

When I arrived for my appointment, I passed by all the various people who screen his visitors and walked into his office. He sat behind a big, mahogany desk in a high-back chair, not a sheet of paper on his desk. "What can I do for you?" he asked.

"Well, sir," I said, "I asked you for fifteen minutes of your time. I don't want to impose. I have come to talk to you about your relationship with Jesus Christ."

Suddenly, he began to cry. As he was sobbing, he told me his story. He became a Christian when he was eight years old. After attending college and getting involved in business, he turned away from God. He said, "I haven't been to church in thirty years. I have made such a mess out of my life. Some think that I am at the top of the ladder of success, but I feel like a great failure. I seem to have everything, but I have lost my family and everything dear to me."

Before I met with him, I had no way of knowing where this man was spiritually or what he was going through, but God did. As I responded to the Holy Spirit's leading, God opened the door so that this man's life could be turned around. He spontaneously volunteered, "I will be in church on Sunday."

Only God knows us perfectly and intimately. He understands our desires, motives, and thoughts. Nothing about us escapes His notice. In fact, God knows infinitely more about us than we will ever know about ourselves. God also knows what is going on in the lives of the people with whom we come into contact every day. He knows their struggles and has the answer to their problems.

God not only knows all about us, but He will never forget us. He even keeps an account of the number of hairs on our heads.[1] God promises through Isaiah:

> Can a mother forget the baby at her breast and have no compassion on the child she has borne? Though she may forget, I will not forget you! See, I have engraved you on the palms of My hands.[2]

The reference to the engraving on the palms of God's hands is a prophecy about the death of Christ on the cross when the Roman soldiers drove nails through His hands. Christ submitted to death because of His love for us; the nail holes are eternal reminders of that love. No wonder we can have assurance that God will never forget about us!

Consider a few things that demonstrate how well God knows you.

GOD KNOWS HOW YOU ARE DESIGNED

Do you ever feel that your parents do not listen to you, your boss does not respect you, or that your co-workers in the church, even the pastor, do not understand you? How devastating to realize that almost no one knows what you are like inside or the dreams you dream. Take heart. Remember that God knows how we are formed.[3]

As our Creator, He custom-designed us for a unique purpose.

David declared that the steps of a godly person are directed by the LORD.[4] That means that He will guide us as we live our lives for Him. God even "understands how weak we are; He knows we are only dust."[5]

This assurance was evident in the experience of a pastor of a small church. He became so discouraged that he was ready to give up the ministry. A friend invited him to a prayer summit of pastors. When he got there, he confessed to his group, "I've been so defeated that I don't even think God knows where I am." But God did know where he was. The next day, the other pastors stood in a circle around him and prayed for him, and he had such an overpowering sense of God's presence that he went home walking on air. God knew exactly what this pastor needed to be renewed in his heart and mind. He will help each of us in similar ways because He designed us and knows exactly what we need at every moment.

> GOD DESIGNED US AND KNOWS EXACTLY WHAT WE NEED AT EVERY MOMENT.

GOD KNOWS EVERYTHING ABOUT YOUR PAST

God is aware of everything every person has ever done—both good and bad. God told Jeremiah, "The human heart is most deceitful and desperately wicked. Who really knows how bad it is? But I know! I, the LORD, search all hearts and examine secret motives. I give all people their due rewards, according to what their actions deserve."[6]

In man's system of justice, accused murderers are brought to trial, then prosecutors use every possible tactic to get the accused convicted. On the other side, defense attorneys use every possible tactic to get the jurors to believe their client is innocent, no matter what the evidence says. Jurors are often swayed by the skill of the attorneys rather than by the facts.

However, our all-knowing God accurately judges not only the

actions of people but also the intents of their heart, no matter what excuses they give, no matter how long they seem to get away with their sins. In a later chapter we will learn more about God's justice in greater depth. But let me ask you: What is your reaction to a God who knows every sin you have ever committed? Do you fear your future is doomed because of your past? He has not left us in a hopeless condition.

God loves you unconditionally in spite of your past sin. He will forgive you when you sincerely confess it to Him. We never have to fear that He will discover something in our past that will change His mind about loving us.

GOD KNOWS EVERYTHING YOU FACE IN THE PRESENT

When we face challenges or difficulties, the fact that God knows all things is encouraging. Pastor David Jeremiah tells his congregation:

> Our God knows what we are going through. He knows every minute of our pain and suffering. He not only knows what we feel, He also knows why we feel what we feel. He knows how it happened, and how long it's going to last and how intense it is. He knows every emotion associated with it; and when you are going through such difficult times, all you can do sometimes is look and say, "Father, you know…you know."[7]

Whatever your circumstances, whatever your need, God understands and will go through it with you. He knows about your hurt, rejection, and pressures. Your feelings and struggles are not unknown to Him, but He also knows the purposes for your trials. He wants to help you accomplish those purposes and to experience His joy through them. In Him there is hope for a way out and a better tomorrow.

GOD KNOWS THE FUTURE HE WANTS FOR YOU

Amy Carmichael was one of the most beloved missionaries during the end of the 19th and beginning of the 20th centuries. She served God in India for fifty-five years. Sherwood Eddy wrote: "Amy Wilson Carmichael was the most Christlike character I ever met, and…her life was the most fragrant, the most joyfully sacrificial, that I ever knew."[8]

When she was growing up in Ireland, she desperately wanted blue eyes. With the faith of a child, she truly believed that God would change her brown eyes to blue if she asked Him. One night, she prayed fervently for blue eyes, then confidently went to bed. When she awoke the next morning, she ran to the mirror. Her same brown eyes were reflected in the glass. How disappointed she was!

Later during her years in India, she became aware of the tragic plight of many girls from poor families who were sold to Hindu temples as prostitutes. Amy began rescuing these young girls and bringing them to her home in Dohnavur to raise them and teach them how much God loves them. She would stain her white skin with coffee grounds and dress in Indian clothing so she could sneak into the temples unnoticed. One day as she dressed, she realized that her disguise worked only because she had brown eyes. Blue eyes would have been a dead giveaway! At that moment, she realized that one of the reasons God said no to her prayer as a child was because He had a plan for her future that involved the lives of hundreds of other precious little ones. God had known her future—even when she was a little girl half a world away.

In Ephesians 2:10, Paul tells us, "He has created us anew in Christ Jesus, so that we can do the good things He planned for us long ago." God knew what He had planned for our lives before we were even conceived. He understands our capabilities, opportunities, and life mission. We can trust Him with every moment of our future.

GOD KNOWS WHICH CHOICES WILL LEAD TO HIS BEST FOR YOU

As you were sitting in the classroom in high school or college, you probably thought many times, *I don't see any purpose in all the stuff I'm having to learn.* Or maybe you have a friend who is a sports trivia addict who can spew out an incredible number of statistics on players who were active in the '40s and '50s. What purpose is his knowledge, except to amaze his friends?

God uses His omniscience for more than categorizing information. Peter tells the crowd that Jesus "was handed over to you by God's set purpose and foreknowledge."[9] What was the purpose of this foreknowledge? To establish a way for us to have an intimate relationship with God through His Son, Jesus Christ, whose death and resurrection would result in victory over Satan and eternal death. His purpose was our freedom.

GOD USES OUR ADVERSITY, HEARTACHE, TESTINGS, AND PERSECUTIONS TO BLESS US.

God knew that once you chose to become His child, you would become "holy and blameless" before Him.[10]

Unfortunately, sometimes we think we know better than God does and do not listen to Him. How many times have you gotten impatient with the way your life is going and wanted to go directly from point A to point C? But it is not just getting to the destination that is important. God knows that by taking us through point B, the process of the journey will change us so we will be the kind of people we need to be when we arrive at our destination.

In Jeremiah 29:11, God promises, "I know the plans I have for you," declares the LORD, "plans to prosper you and not to harm you, plans to give you hope and a future" (NIV). Following His plan leads to the best choices for our lives—right now, in the future, and for eternity.

GOD KNOWS YOU NEED WISDOM

Because God's Spirit resides within us, we can rely on Him as our Teacher, Counselor, and Guide into all truth. He is willing to share His great knowledge with us. God promises:

> If you need wisdom—if you want to know what God wants you to do—ask Him, and He will gladly tell you. He

will not resent your asking. But when you ask Him, be sure that you really expect Him to answer, for a doubtful mind is as unsettled as a wave of the sea that is driven and tossed by the wind.[11]

God is never surprised when we have problems, and He is always with us to help us. But believers often deprive themselves of God's solutions because they do not take time to study His Word.[12] Or they may know the Word but not want to obey it or meet the conditions of God's promises. Thus they do not receive full benefit from God's omniscience.

Solomon writes, "Trust in the LORD with all your heart; do not depend on your own understanding. Seek His will in all you do, and He will direct your paths."[13] But God's help does not guarantee us a life free of trials and tribulations. In fact, James 1:2–4 and Romans 5:3,4 inform us that God uses our adversity, heartache, testings, and persecutions to bless us.

Trusting God does not eliminate temptation either. Remember how we read earlier, "No temptation has seized you except what is common to man. And God is faithful; He will not let you be tempted beyond what you can bear. But when you are tempted, He will also provide a way out so that you can stand up under it."[14] We sometimes wish we knew what that way out would be. Yet when we accept the fact that the God who knows the end from the beginning is providing the way out, we can relax. He has the power to make us victorious.

God knows all about you and loves you unconditionally. I encourage you—yes, I plead with you—to open your heart to Him and determine to walk with Him regardless of the cost. Remind yourself every day of the truth of our all-knowing God. You will never again feel the same way about your daily personal fellowship with our wonderful God.

In the next chapter, we will put all of God's attributes of ability (omnipotence, omnipresence, omniscience) together to discover another characteristic that sets Him far above anything or anyone else—His sovereignty. This attribute is one that gives us complete hope for the future.

LIFE APPLICATION

WRITE IT ON YOUR HEART—Commit the following statement and verses to memory. Then as you encounter situations during this week where you need God's wisdom, claim these promises by faith.

- Because God knows everything, I can go to Him with all my questions and concerns.

- James 1:5,6—"If you need wisdom—if you want to know what God wants you to do—ask Him, and He will gladly tell you. He will not resent your asking. But when you ask Him, be sure that you really expect Him to answer, for a doubtful mind is as unsettled as a wave of the sea that is driven and tossed by the wind."

- Psalm 147:5—"How great is our Lord! His power is absolute! His understanding is beyond comprehension!"

COUNT ON GOD—It is often difficult to trust other people. They can be wishy-washy or simply forget to do something they have promised. But God never forgets! Spend time in God's Word gathering His many promises. Choose one that applies to a situation you are facing right now and trust Him to fulfill it.

OBEY GOD—God not only knows the past, present, and future, He knows what is best for you. Is there something you have been reluctant to do? Decide today to do everything God's way and obey Him in the areas you turned over to Him.

CHAPTER 10

GOD IS SOVEREIGN

People around the world are fascinated with royalty. Pictures of the late Princess Diana, Prince Charles, and other British royalty fill the tabloids and television screens. Why does their every appearance captivate our attention? Perhaps it is the grandeur in which they live.

Since we live in a democracy in a time in which sovereigns do not rule grand empires, it is hard for us to understand the depth of feeling that people have toward their kings and queens. When King Hussein of Jordan died in February 1999, his entire country mourned. Nearly a million people lined up to see the funeral procession—almost one-sixth of Jordan's population! Hundreds of Jordanians broke through the security barrier to get near the coffin.

As the coffin reached Raghadan Palace, it was placed on a cannon carriage, accompanied by the king's favorite Arabian stallion. A pair of boots were placed backward in the stirrups in remembrance of the fallen leader. All over Jordan, black flags waved from doorposts and car antennas. The country was almost shut down for a week for official mourning.

From earliest days, kings and queens have received honor and respect. One example is in 1911 when the former Indian rulers' courts paid homage to King George V and Queen Mary of England on the Delhi plain. The royal couple sat on a dais while the princes advanced according to protocol and did their salutes. The first prince gave the king a necklace that held a ruby the size of a pigeon's egg. His Highness of Panna presented the king with a twelve-inch umbrella made from a single emerald. Dressed in gold and silver brocade, Sir Tukoji Rao of Indore came with a gold stick that had jeweled engravings and a hilt carved from a single ruby.[1]

One of the rulers' dearest treasures are their titles. This was the title of the Seventh Nizam:

> Lieutenant-General His Exalted Highness Seventh in Line Equal to the Rank of Asaf Jah, Victor of the Realm and the World, Regulator of the Realm, Regulator of the State, Viceroy Sir the Honourable Osman Ali Khan, the Brave, Victorious in Battle, Faithful Ally of the British, Grand Commander of the Star of India, Knight Grand Cross of the British Empire, Nizam of Hyderabad and Berar.[2]

English royalty held lavish ceremonies to establish their positions, often spending months on elaborate preparations. When Queen Elizabeth II was crowned in Westminster Abbey in London, she rode in a gold coach pulled by eight magnificent grays. Anne Edwards describes a portion of the 1953 coronation ceremony:

> The Queen was next garbed in the gold Robe Royal and one by one was given the symbols of authority. The Sceptre was placed in her right hand and the Rod in her left. "Be so merciful that you be not too remiss," prayed the Archbishop, "so execute justice that you forget not mercy. Punish the wicked, protect and cherish the just, and lead your people in the way wherein they should go."
>
> …A great gust of sound raised up through the Abbey, "God Save the Queen." Trumpets sounded, drums rolled, and then the great guns of the Tower and in Hyde Park were shot off.[3]

The Queen was crowned with the large solid-gold, pearl- and

ruby-studded St. Edward's Crown worn at all coronations in the 20th century. Then the peers of her realm performed the Act of Homage by kneeling before her and swearing allegiance to the crown. Even the Queen's husband, Prince Phillip, performed the Act of Homage.

THE GREATEST SOVEREIGN

Yet, there exists another Royal King whose majesty, splendor, and awesomeness are almost indescribable. Compared to Him, no other ruler or reign is even a blip on the screen of eternity. He does not need ceremony or to drape Himself in grandeur to appear more regal. Jewels and wealth mean nothing to Him. Yes, this divine Ruler is none other than the Sovereign God. His throne is far above the universe in heaven; He rules over all.

David, himself a king, asked, "Who is this King of glory?" Then he answers his own question,"The LORD, strong and mighty, the LORD, invincible in battle…The LORD Almighty—He is the King of glory."[4] In one of the final chapters in the Bible, John identifies Him as "KING OF KINGS AND LORD OF LORDS." John describes how he heard a loud voice of a great multitude in heaven shouting, "Hallelujah! Salvation and glory and power belong to our God…Hallelujah! For our Lord God Almighty reigns."[5]

As John continues to describe his vision of God's throne, he tries to convey what cannot be adequately described in words. I want to quote a portion here:

> I saw a throne in heaven and Someone sitting on it! The One sitting on the throne was as brilliant as gemstones— jasper and carnelian. And the glow of an emerald circled His throne like a rainbow. Twenty-four thrones surrounded Him, and twenty-four elders sat on them. They were all clothed in white and had gold crowns on their heads. And from the throne came flashes of lightning and the rumble of thunder …In front of the throne was a shiny sea of glass, sparkling like crystal.
>
> In the center and around the throne were four living beings…Day after day and night after night they keep on saying,

"Holy, holy, holy is the Lord God Almighty—the One who always was, who is, and who is still to come."

Whenever the living beings give glory and honor and thanks to the One sitting on the throne, the One who lives forever and ever, the twenty-four elders fall down and worship the One who lives forever and ever. And they lay their crowns before the throne and say:

"You are worthy, O Lord our God,
to receive glory and honor and power.
For You created everything,
and it is for Your pleasure that they exist
and were created."[6]

The throne of an earthly king or queen, however grand it may be, cannot compare to the glories of God. If we took away the royal trappings from any human sovereign, he would look just like one of us. His honor is derived from ceremonies and the homage paid him by other people, which can be removed in a moment. He may have the power of an army behind him, but in himself, he is a sinful, imperfect human just like you and me.

God's reign is different. God does not derive His right to rule from anyone or anything. No title was bestowed on Him by another, and there is no higher authority anywhere than His. The great I AM always does what He knows is best and answers to no one. His reign is so magnificent that we cannot even comprehend any part of it.

God's rule is supreme, paramount, and absolute. He has power to do anything that needs to be done. He is present everywhere so no one can hide from Him or escape His scrutiny. He is all-knowing, so there is nothing about which He is unaware. Amazingly, this great God loves you and me unconditionally, caring for the smallest need of the least of us.

THE GREAT PUZZLE OF LIFE

Submitting to God's sovereignty can be compared to putting together a billion-piece picture puzzle. History is like that giant picture. Only by looking at the photograph on the box cover can you see what everything will look like once all the pieces are in place.

Now imagine that you are given one piece of the puzzle. This is where you fit into God's great plan for the universe. What can you do with this piece? You have never seen the picture on the outside of the box. All you know is that your piece has a little dark color here and a few bright spots there. So you run around trying to match what you are doing with someone else's puzzle piece. The chances of finding one other person who has a piece that matches yours is almost zero. Therefore, there is no way you could ever understand what the completed picture will look like.

From a human standpoint, it is impossible to understand the many puzzles in life. But if you let God direct you, He will help you place your puzzle piece in the right place. He is not only big enough to see the whole picture, He created it.

We can see part of the picture of where God is taking history by reading the Bible. God gives us clues as to what His purposes are for us. In His sovereignty, He will fulfill all He has promised in His Word. We will look at three truths about the scope of God's sovereignty.

GOD SOVEREIGNLY RULES THE UNIVERSE

God reigns so supremely above His creation that we cannot question any of His actions. Whatever God wants to have happen will happen; His will cannot be thwarted. Daniel explains, "He determines the course of world events; He removes kings and sets others on the throne."[7]

God's creative actions set the stage for His sovereignty. He was able to create because He was in absolute control of every particle of material even before He brought it into being. Once He formed something, no matter how simple or complex, He remained in absolute authority.

Jeremiah reminded God's people of how completely God is in control. Because of their disobedience, they wanted to escape the judgment of the God they had spurned. God sent Jeremiah to the house of a potter. As the potter worked on a piece of clay, he skillfully shaped it with his hands into a beautiful vessel. But when another pot he was making was marred, he tossed it aside and began a new pot. He did what seemed best to him.

Through this illustration, God pointed out His limitless sovereignty. "O Israel, can I not do to you as this potter has done to his clay? As the clay is in the potter's hand, so are you in My hand."[8] As Creator, God could do whatever He wanted with His creation. No matter how much the clay complained or rebelled, it was shaped by the strong hand of the potter. Centuries later, Paul points out: "Shall what is formed say to Him who formed it, 'Why did You make me like this?'"[9] Norman Geisler explains God's sovereignty this way:

> If it is a power that you can manipulate, it is not God. If it is a power that created the universe that chooses to express itself one way this time, and another way at another time, for our good and His glory, then it is God.

GOD SOVEREIGNLY WORKS THROUGH HIS LAWS OF NATURE

Stephen Charnock writes, "We cannot suppose God a Creator, without supposing a sovereign dominion in Him."[10] God dominates nature to accomplish His purposes:

> He directs the snow to fall on the earth and tells the rain to pour down…God's breath sends the ice, freezing wide expanses of water. He loads the clouds with moisture, and they flash with His lightning. The clouds turn around and around under His direction. They do whatever He commands throughout the earth. He causes things to happen on earth, either as a punishment or as a sign of His unfailing love."[11]

God established the scientific laws that regulate the universe; only He can overrule their effect. For God, miracles are "routine."

I am amazed when I hear from Christians who doubt God's supernatural intervention in their lives. God did mighty miracles through Noah, Moses, and other Old Testament characters. He spoke through the prophets. He personally invaded our time and space in the form of His Son, the Lord Jesus Christ. Jesus performed miracles, died for our sins, rose from the grave, and ascended bodily into heaven. His resurrection is the greatest miracle of all. Now His Spirit lives in the hearts of millions of believers around the world. We sometimes take these miracles for granted.

God still suspends His natural laws today. I love the story told by former Campus Crusade staff members Dick and Carolyn Edic:

> In 1967,...300 staff and 300 selected students converged on the [University of California] Berkeley campus for a week of intense evangelism in every facet of the campus. We would meet as a group every morning for prayer, Bible study, and challenge before going out with our particular assignment on campus. Our plan was to culminate the week with a large rally in the Greek Outdoor Theatre with Billy Graham as the speaker. The Amphitheatre held about 8,000 people.
>
> Friday morning, we met as a group as usual. Billy Graham spoke to us. It was raining very heavily, so we feared that the heavy rain would prevent our final evangelistic outreach with Billy Graham. So we got on our knees as a group and prayed for about 45 to 60 minutes, asking God to stop the rain and prepare the way for the outreach.
>
> When we finished praying at about 11:30 a.m. and looked outside, the sun was shining! By meeting time, the seats had dried enough to attract 8,000 students, and Billy Graham's preaching went forward. After the rally, at about 2 p.m., it started raining again!
>
> This was the highlight of an exciting week of outreach to a tough crowd. During that week, 23,000 of the 27,000 students received a direct witness of the Lord Jesus Christ personally, in small groups, or in the mass meetings. We saw miraculous answers to prayer that demonstrated God's power to change lives and control the weather.[12]

Yet sometimes God chooses to let it rain and to work despite the floods or sloshing through mud as at Campus Crusade's EXPLO '72 in Dallas and EXPLO '74 in Korea. God is in the business of turning tragedy into triumph and sorrow into joy—at His choosing.

GOD SOVEREIGNLY FULFILLS
HIS ETERNAL MASTER PLAN

God actively directs His creation toward a pre-determined conclusion. Therefore, He controls all other authorities. The psalmist
Asaph wrote, "It is God who judges: He brings one down, he exalts
another."[13] Let me give you one example from Scripture.

God chose to use King Nebuchadnezzar as His instrument of
judgment upon Judah's wicked kings and rebellious people.[14]
Nebuchadnezzar's armies seemed unstoppable as they captured a
vast empire including Jerusalem and took most of Judah's resi-
dents into captivity in Babylon. When Nebuchadnezzar began to
boast about what *he* had accomplished, God removed him from
the throne until he was humbled.

Seventy years later, in keeping with God's prophecy that He
would bring His captive people back to Judah, God raised up
another king. As prophesied, Cyrus sent the captives back to Jerusalem to rebuild the city.[15] This was all a part of God's magnificent plan to eventually send His Son, the Messiah, who would be
born of a Jewish girl living near Jerusalem.

Someone has aptly said that God's master plan on earth is to:

1) Make sinners sons (spiritual children of God).[16]

2) Make sons like Jesus.[17]

3) Help the sons share the good news of eternal life through Jesus.[18]

Scriptural evidence supports the fact that God's work on earth
is primarily of a spiritual, eternal nature.[19] Such a spiritual kingdom
is in vast contrast to the material, physical, and temporal kingdom
that occupies most people's efforts today.[20]

RESPONDING TO THE REIGN
OF THE KING OF KINGS

We do not live under the jurisdiction of a dictatorial ruler who is
out to deprive us of all the fun and happiness in life. The King of
kings and Lord of lords has our best interest at heart at all times.
He orchestrates events to enable us to praise Him and glorify His

name. When times get tough, we can remind ourselves of the conditions under which He reigns. The following paragraphs describe several ways in which He reigns in our lives.

God reigns through His omniscient wisdom.

As a young businessman I made great plans for my business and my future. I had carefully considered what I wanted out of life and what I would have to do to achieve my objectives. Then I met the Son of God! As I discovered the attributes of God—His love, holiness, wisdom, sovereignty, power—I began to realize I could trust His wisdom much more than I could trust my own intelligence.

> HE ORCHES-TRATES EVENTS TO ENABLE US TO PRAISE HIM AND GLORIFY HIS NAME.

God's sovereignty operates through righteousness.

In the 20th century, many men have held tremendous power and used it for evil— Stalin, Hitler, Mao Tse Tung, and Pol Pot, the vicious head of the Khmer Rouge in Cambodia. These few men, responsible for the deaths of tens of millions of innocent people, reigned in unrighteousness. But God sits on a throne of righteousness because He is holy. We never need to fear that He will act out of evil intentions. Submitting to His sovereignty will always be best for us.

God's sovereignty reveals His goodness.

Because God is good, He is a gracious Sovereign and obliging Benefactor rather than an arbitrary tyrant. The writer to the Hebrews encourages us to "come boldly to the throne of our gracious God" because we have a High Priest who "understands our weaknesses, for He faced all the same temptations we do, yet He did not sin."[21] God has bridged the gap of understanding between us and Him. We can count on His goodness when He deals with us.

THE MOST ASTOUNDING CONTRAST

Can you imagine Queen Elizabeth II giving up her crown to live as a pauper? Putting aside her jewels and dressing in rags? That is unthinkable.

But that is exactly what God did. Reread the description of His throne at the beginning of this chapter. What majesty, perfection, honor, and glory envelops our great God and Savior! Heaven is a place of such beauty and peace, where no sin mars the atmosphere. Pain and hurt are unknown. Angels and all other beings continually praise God.

When God's Son, Jesus Christ, was voluntarily born in a humble manger in Bethlehem, the only people who worshipped Him were lowly shepherds. The stable must have been drafty and not very private. What kind of place was this for the Sovereign of the universe? Where were His crown and His scepter?

Jesus did not live like a king either. He became tired and hungry, was ridiculed, beaten, spit upon, humiliated. The soldiers ripped off His clothes, and He was taken to court before a cruel ruler named Herod. The crowd shouted that they wanted Him killed. All His friends ran away, afraid for their own lives. Then He was cruelly nailed to a cross in front of a jeering crowd. He could have shaken the world in defiance, but all He said was, "Forgive these people, because they don't know what they are doing."[22]

Jesus did this because God loves us so much. His love motivated Him to communicate His love and salvation to us. To do this effectively, He had to become one of us—to walk, talk, eat, and look like us. Just the thought of our sovereign God putting aside His magnificent glory brings me to tears. How can we ever reach the depths of that love? How could we ever fear putting our lives into His hands?

Part of our problem with accepting God's authority and honoring Him is that we have lost our concept of majesty. With little sense of the majesty of God, we have trouble submitting to His sovereignty and worshipping Him. For most Christians, true worship is not something they practice very often or well. A. W. Tozer explains our dilemma:

The modern Christian has lost a sense of worship along with the concept of majesty [of God], and of course, reverence as well. He has lost his ability to withdraw inwardly and commune in the secret place with God in the shrine of his own hidden spirit. It is this that makes Christianity, and we have all but lost it. Added numbers, yes, but lost fear. Multiplied schools, yes, but lost awareness of the invisible. Tons of literature being poured out, of course, but no consciousness of the divine Presence. Better communication, certainly, but nothing to communicate. Evangelistic organizations, yes, but the concept of majesty and worship and reverence has almost left us.[23]

Understanding God's sovereignty causes us to focus on Him, not ourselves. Our response is to fall at His feet and give Him everything we are and own. If the royalty of England kneel before Queen Elizabeth II and pledge to submit to her reign, how much more important is it for us to kneel before God's throne and surrender ourselves to Him?

I urge you to recognize God's sovereignty right now by humbling yourself before Him. Totally and irrevocably submit to His lordship of your life. Worship Him by giving Him everything you own. Think of your life as a house with many rooms. Go through each "room" and surrender both the room and the contents to Him. If you have a closet full of fears, let Him control that part of your life. Invite Him into the room where you hide your insecurities and hurts. Let Him take down that monument of pride to your own abilities and talents that you have displayed in your living room. Ask Him to control your checkbook and bank account. Everything you "lose" by serving Him He will replace with something so much better. He controls the universe; He will without doubt enrich your life with joy, peace, happiness, fulfillment, satisfaction, and rewards far beyond your wildest imagination!

LIFE APPLICATION

EXALT YOUR GOD—Worship the sovereign Ruler of the universe with David's song of praise. As you repeat his words, meditate on how secure you are in God's care.

> Praise be to you, O LORD, God of our father Israel, from everlasting to everlasting. Yours, O LORD, is the greatness and the power and the glory and the majesty and the splendor, for everything in heaven and earth is Yours. Yours, O LORD, is the kingdom; You are exalted as head over all...Now, our God, we give You thanks, and praise Your glorious name (1 Chronicles 29:10,11,13).

REFLECT HIS IMAGE—As we increasingly commit ourselves to our sovereign Creator, we reflect God's image. Even the Son of God submitted to His Father. Jesus stated in John 8:28,29, "I do nothing on my own, but I speak what the Father taught me...I always do those things that are pleasing to Him." Yield your will to God today and determine to make submission to God a consistent part of your character. As you do, you will show others that God controls your life.

SHARE HIS MAJESTY—Does someone you know need to be reminded that God is in control? Comfort them with the fact that our sovereign Lord rules over every circumstance. Challenge them with the truth that God will accomplish His plans through them.

CHAPTER 11.

GOD DIRECTS OUR LIVES

A s members of a democratic society rife with individual-
ism, Americans have difficulty understanding God as an
absolute ruler. Did we not reject living under a sovereign
ruler when the American Colonies revolted against the
king of England? Why should we be subject to anyone now? Yes,
we Americans love our independence and freedom.

We do pay homage to our superstar heroes, especially in entertainment and sports, but only as long as they produce astonishing
performances for us. Other great champions quickly replace them.

With the decline in the belief of absolute truth, we tend to
argue and debate our points of view with everyone, even our leaders, to get our beliefs and agendas accepted. Today we negotiate to
get our own way, and compromise—even on moral issues—is
considered a virtue.

But we cannot argue, debate, or negotiate with God, the King
of the universe. If He is truly the Lord of our lives, and we are
His true disciples, we say, "Yes, Lord!" Saying "No, Lord" is a
contradiction of terms for the true disciple of Jesus Christ.

Please, fellow believers, do not follow the teaching of some who say that if you have enough faith in God, or if you repeat the name of Jesus, or quote a formula of phrases or Scripture verses, then you will get all your prayers answered. We cannot force God to do things our way. Sometimes in His wisdom and sovereign plan, His answer to our prayers is "no" or "wait." Our position is to trust, believe, and obey, not to demand.

CHOICE VERSUS OBEDIENCE

Does that mean we have no say with our sovereign God? Of course not! He does not consider us His puppets or slaves. He made us as free moral agents with minds, wills, and emotions. He will not force His love and plans upon us against our wills. Within the context of His master plan, God gives us the freedom to choose. This is a hard concept to grasp. Let me explain with an illustration. A few days ago, I flew to Dallas. I had complete freedom to get up and walk around on that jetliner. I could go get a magazine or talk to my fellow passengers. I could take a nap or make a telephone call. I had complete freedom—within limits. However, I could not alter the plane's course. That plane was going to Dallas!

Our relationship with God is like that. We are not robots mechanically programmed to follow His decrees. God has a course for us that has been charted before the beginning of time. God assures us in His Word: "My purpose will stand, and I will do all that I please."[1] His master plan for history will be accomplished, whether we choose to work with Him or follow our own stubborn way. Although He allows us to choose and suffer the consequences of our choices, He never relinquishes control of the plans to accomplish His purposes. God turns the pages of history; we do not. As you read the following truths about God's sovereignty, ask God to show you how you can restore His majesty in your life and what He wants you to do to obey Him.

GOD SOVEREIGNLY DIRECTS PEOPLE, CIRCUMSTANCES, AND EVENTS

When you read the newspaper or look at events around you, do you sometimes wonder who is in control? More and more Christians see themselves as victims of a wicked society. Many feel overwhelmed by circumstances and struggle with hopelessness, defeat, and discouragement. But God has not abandoned them.

I can clearly see how God's sovereignty has been at work throughout my life. When my mother was carrying me, she almost died many times. During that time, she asked God to spare her life. "Lord, if you will just give me time, and allow me to give birth to this little child, I will dedicate him or her to you." Not only did she survive, but she lived to be 93 years old and her godly example and powerful prayers were the greatest influence on my life. She dedicated me to the Lord and faithfully prayed that God's will would be done in my life.

After completing my college degree, I spent one year on the faculty at Oklahoma State University Extension. Then I left Oklahoma to seek my fortune in California. Although my mother was still praying for me, I had no interest in the things of God. I wanted to be a successful businessman, a man of influence and significance. I was a self-made, happy pagan.

The first day I arrived in California, I picked up a hitchhiker who invited me to dinner at his friend's house. I agreed and, as it turned out, his friend was Dawson Trotman, founder of the Navigators Ministry. After dinner, they said, "We're going to a birthday party. Would you like to come?" That celebration was in the home of America's top radio evangelist, Charles E. Fuller.

I am still awed by the fact that through God's sovereignty, I spent my first night in California in the homes of two of the most famous Christian leaders of the 20th century. That did not just happen by chance. God was orchestrating events in my life—even though I was not a believer—in gracious answer to my saintly mother's prayers.

God is sovereignly involved in directing each of our lives. Proverbs states, "Many are the plans in a man's heart, but it is the LORD's purpose that prevails."[2] God carefully supervises all that happens. No event escapes His notice. No person is beyond His influence. No circumstance exists outside His control.

There Is No Room for Luck in God's Sovereign Plans

"Good luck," I heard a man recently say. What about luck? Anyone who understands the Bible and God's revelation of Himself knows that there is no such thing as luck or chance, which implies a capriciousness of nature and the universe. When we use the word "luck," we express our unbelief or a lack of knowledge of God's attributes. With God in control, luck does not exist.

As believers, we live by faith in God and His Word and in the power of the Holy Spirit, not by luck or superstition. He also wants us to consciously acknowledge His sovereign control in the affairs of our lives. This means making our life's plans—from our simplest decisions to our career choices or our retirement plans—follow God's will. James explains the attitudes that please or displease God:

> Now listen, you who say, "Today or tomorrow we will go to this or that city, spend a year there, carry on business and make money." Why, you do not even know what will happen tomorrow. What is your life? You are a mist that appears for a little while and then vanishes. Instead, you ought to say, "If it is the Lord's will, we will live and do this or that." As it is, you boast and brag. All such boasting is evil.[3]

God has a much greater agenda than ours. As we make plans through the power of His Holy Spirit, we must allow God to change those plans at a moment's notice. We must seriously seek the will of God rather than our own will—and trust all our circumstances to His control.

God Uses Bad Things for Good Purposes

You may have wondered, *If God is in complete control of everything, why does He allow (or cause) birth defects, famines, and war? Why does He permit sin, evil, and suffering?* God's very nature opposes these things. It was not His plan for Adam and Eve, the first humans, to sin and bring sickness, disease, and death upon mankind.[4] God created a perfect world, but man chose to sin, and the penalty for sin was death—physical and spiritual. This curse of death has affected all of creation, not just humans, and all the bad things that exist are due to living in a world under judgment, a fallen world. Part of Adam and Eve's punishment was pain and suffering in childbirth, fighting against nature for food, and struggling to make a living before finally dying.[5]

God does not initiate, cause, or authorize sin, or tempt anyone to sin. Yet He tolerates evil for a season to fulfill His righteous plans for people to respond by their own free will to His love.

Pastor Charles Stanley explains that God allows troubles, accidents, adversity, and similar problems to come into our lives for a purpose. Some of these purposes are:

- To get our attention
- To draw us to himself
- To help us get to know Him
- To see Him as He is
- To taste of His goodness
- To have an intimate, close relationship with Him
- To prevent distance from and avoidance of God[6]

> GOD IS MORE CONCERNED ABOUT OUR ETERNAL FUTURE THAN OUR PRESENT COMFORT.

Our disappointments are often God's appointments. He is far more concerned about the quality of our eternal future than He is about our present comfort. In fact, difficulties and suffering are tools with which He shapes us into the image of Jesus Christ. It is never fun to be enrolled in the academy of adversity, but unless God takes us through the curriculum of trials, we will never become the quality person He wants us to be. Adversity is the touchstone of character.

Romans 8 promises, "God causes everything to work together for the good of those who love God and are called according to His purpose for them."[7] God uses even the most disastrous situations for our good.

In the summer of 1976, thirty-five female Campus Crusade staff leaders—including my wife, Vonette—gathered in Colorado for a retreat. That night, they were trapped in the Big Thompson Canyon flood.

At about 1:30 in the morning, I was awakened and informed of the flood and of the rescue of one of the women, who was now in the hospital. About an hour later, another staff member was brought to the hospital by helicopter. By this time, we had good reason to believe that several of the women had drowned.

I did not know if Vonette was safe, struggling for her life in the floodwaters, or dead. But I had incredible peace because I knew that God is sovereign and ever-present. So even though I had no idea where Vonette was and could not help her, I knew God was with her and the other women. Because He is all-powerful, God could save all the women whose lives were in danger. But God is also all-knowing. If it was best for Vonette to be taken home to heaven, I could completely trust my loving Father to do the right thing.

Soon I sadly learned that seven of our staff women perished during the flood. I knew that each of these women was rejoicing in the presence of her Savior. I also learned that Vonette and twenty-seven other staff women had escaped the raging water.

In the weeks that followed, we mourned for those dear friends we had lost. But we also felt led by God to make their last moments on earth a tribute to our sovereign God. With full approval of the grieving families, friends of Campus Crusade ministry placed full-page ads in most newspapers across the country featuring pictures of the seven women who died. The headline read, "These seven women lost their lives in the Colorado flood, but they are alive and they have a message for you." The advertisement gave readers an opportunity to read the gospel and receive Jesus Christ as their Savior.

Approximately 150 million people read those ads. The response was phenomenal. Only God knows the full extent of what happened, but many thousands wrote to say that they had received Christ that week as a result of the tragic deaths of those seven women. A foreign ambassador told us that his life was changed by the ad, and later helped open the door for ministry in his country, which had previously been closed to the gospel.

We can give all our worries and cares to God, knowing that He cares about what happens to us.[8] When tragedy strikes, take comfort in the fact that no difficulty will ever come into your life without God's permission. Knowing this truth does not make adversity pleasant, but it gives us hope that the result will be worth whatever pain we endure.

GOD OVERRULES THE EVIL INTENTIONS OF PEOPLE

What about the intentions of evil people? Is God's hand present when they devise evil against us? Throughout the Bible we see incidents of God intervening to thwart the evil intents of humans.

Sometimes it seems as if following God's will makes us more vulnerable to the evil intentions of others. That simply is not true. Yes, since Lucifer rebelled against God, and Adam and Eve sinned in the Garden of Eden, wars have existed between God and Satan, good and evil, light and darkness. God still has His plan, and He will execute it. We just do not always see His working at the beginning, in the middle of the warfare, or even at the end.

As a 19-year-old, Bruce Olsson went into the jungles on the border of Colombia and Venezuela to bring the gospel to the Bari people. God protected him from these aboriginal people who had never let a white man into their territory, and as they came to love him and his Lord, they affectionately called him *bruchko*. Then in 1988 Bruce was captured by Colombian guerrillas and held secretly in the jungle. It looked as if his ministry had been disrupted and maybe even ended.

Once the Colombian armed forces realized that the guerrillas had kidnapped Bruce, they tried to enlist the Baris, once a fierce, warlike tribe, to help rescue their beloved *bruchko*. The Baris refused, saying, "Violence only engenders violence."

Meanwhile, things were happening in the jungle. After five months in captivity, Bruce had so gained the confidence of the guerrillas that they gave him a Bible. Eventually he was able to hold Bible studies with his captors. During nine months of captivity, including one firing squad escape, Bruce led about half the guerrillas assigned to him to faith in Christ. He was so successful that the guerrilla leaders finally released him.

As the years passed after the kidnapping, these Christian guerrillas won others to faith in Christ. Finally, the entire Christian group broke away from the larger guerrilla group and surrendered themselves to the Colombian government. On April 6, 1994, Bruce Olsson wrote in a letter to his prayer and financial supporters:

> Resurrection Sunday also meant "conversion" to a great many members of the former guerrilla forces. In their camps [during my captivity] I witnessed more than a hundred break before the Lord in repentant tears, attentive to His Word and surrender their lives to the lordship of Jesus Christ. This action is prelude to the celebration of the 9th of April [when] ...descendants from the "Armed Forces for National Liberation" (ELN) and "Armed Forces for Colombian Revolution" (FARC), representing about half of the violent revolutionary forces in Colombia, will reincorporate themselves into national life at the surrendering of their arms and signature of the negotiated "Peace Plan."

DURING NINE MONTHS OF CAPTIVITY, BRUCE LED HALF HIS CAPTORS TO FAITH IN CHRIST.

God in His sovereignty protected Bruce despite the evil intentions of guerrilla leaders—and turned the whole incident into a great victory for Jesus Christ. Bruce writes, "The Bari had no doubt in God's sovereignty and trusted in His intervention in the lives and affairs of His creation. The relinquishing of arms [by the guerrillas] in the presence of Bari leaders was significant. It was vindication of the Bari's endurance and persuasion." God was sovereign through the actions of Bruce, the Bari, *and* the guerrillas! Does that give you hope in a situation you may face right now? God will sovereignly use you, too, as you follow His will.

Our Redemption and God's Sovereignty

The entire gospel is a declaration of God's sovereign pleasure concerning Christ. Writing to the Ephesians, Paul explained:

> God's secret plan has now been revealed to us; it is a plan centered on Christ, designed long ago according to His good pleasure. And this is His plan: At the right time He will bring everything together under the authority of Christ—everything in heaven and on earth.[9]

Satan plotted to defeat God's purpose by arranging circumstances so that the Son of God would be crucified. His plots were successful—at first sight. Consider all the evil intentions of men that God used to bring about our redemption:

- The religious leaders plotted to kill Jesus. They succeeded in their malicious intent.

- The court crowd asked Pilate to release Barabbas rather than Jesus. Pilate agreed to their hate-filled request.

- The soldiers beat Jesus and crowned Him with a crown of thorns. They were following the evil orders of their superiors.

- The rabble in front of the cross ridiculed Jesus as He was dying. Their purpose was to make Him look weak and insignificant. And they surely did.

- The government assigned soldiers to guard Jesus' tomb to thwart any claims that He had risen from the dead. They were successful for two days.

Today we know that all these evil intents were integral parts of God's plan. Jesus was just one man standing against the evil intentions of His physical world, and the spiritual world too, but His power was greater than anything anyone could throw at Him. We have available to us that same power, because as believers, the Holy Spirit lives within us. He will comfort us during times of trial, give us wisdom to accomplish God's will, and help us glorify God through every situation.

Do you feel as privileged as I do to be part of God's eternal plan, knowing that God has revealed to us His sovereign will for the grand scale of history? In fact, our sovereign God will ensure that grand finale! Jesus Christ, the Lamb of God, who seemed to be the "victim" of evil intentions, will reign supreme forever and ever. One more passage from John's Revelation gives us the panorama of the grand finale that will take place in the City of God:

> All the nations will bring their glory and honor into the city. Nothing evil will be allowed to enter—no one who practices shameful idolatry and dishonesty—but only those whose names are written in the Lamb's Book of Life.
>
> And the angel showed me a pure river with the water of life, clear as crystal, flowing down from the throne of God and of the Lamb, coursing down the center of the main street. On each side of the river grew a tree of life, bearing twelve crops of fruit, with a fresh crop each month. The leaves were used for medicine to heal the nations.
>
> No longer will anything be cursed. For the throne of God and of the Lamb will be there, and His servants will worship Him. And they will see His face, and His name will be written on their foreheads. And there will be no night there—no need for lamps or sun—for the Lord God will shine on them. And they will reign forever and ever.[10]

When we choose to submit to God's majesty and sovereignty, we are on the winning side. We will reign with the only One who is worthy of worship and who will be our comfort, guide, and friend throughout eternity! What a Savior! I can hardly wait for that moment!

I urge you to allow God to direct your life by surrendering your decisions, trials, hurts, and pain to Him. Give Him your joys, your accomplishments, your treasures. After all, if Indian princes chose to honor the king of England with their most precious and costly possessions, how much more should we honor God with every part of our lives! Unlike an earthly king, God will take what we give to Him and multiply blessings in our lives. We do not give up anything but pride, sin, and temporal possessions; He gives us back eternal life, joy, spiritual riches, and an eternal reign with Him! What a good God!

Now that we have some insight into the limitless abilities of God, we can turn our attention to His moral attributes. They are the basis of our laws, our justice system, and our ideas of fair treatment. In Part II, we will be examining God's high moral character: His ability to judge fairly, truthfully, righteously, and with perfect justice. We will discover why He acts as He does and how that affects our relationship with Him. We will answer questions like: Can I trust God to be fair? How will He judge events when it seems like everything is stacked against me? What does He do when His people commit wrong acts? Is He swayed by those who are more "spiritual" or who hold power in the church?

For a person who has a wrong view of God or who does not know Him intimately, the answers to these questions are unsettling. But as we learn more about God's moral attributes, we will be increasingly confident that we can put complete faith in our Perfect Judge and let Him preside over the courtroom of our lives!

LIFE APPLICATION

WRITE IT ON YOUR HEART—Commit the following statement and verses to memory. Then as you encounter situations during this week where you need to remember that God is in control, claim these promises by faith.

- Because God is sovereign, I will submit to His will.

- Jeremiah 10:23—"I know, LORD, that a person's life is not his own. No one is able to plan his own course."

- Romans 8:28—"God causes everything to work together for the good of those who love God and are called according to His purpose for them."

COUNT ON GOD—Does the fact that God is sovereign scare you? When God is in control, that means you and I are not. That may invoke fear, but it should bring comfort. How much better that our all-powerful, all-knowing God controls every circumstance rather than we who are imperfect and limited. Trust God today by placing your current situation into the hands of your capable and loving heavenly Father.

OBEY GOD—Our sovereign God controls every breath and heartbeat in your life. How foolish it is for us not to obey Him. Ephesians 2:10 states, "We are God's masterpiece. He has created us anew in Christ Jesus, so that we can do the good things He planned for us long ago." You will realize your own full potential by obeying Him. Pursue the "good things" He has for you to do—today.

PART II.

OUR PERFECT JUDGE

(Attributes of Integrity)

*They will sing before the L*ORD*,*
for He comes, He comes to judge the earth.
He will judge the world in righteousness
and the peoples in His truth.

PSALM 96:13, NIV

CHAPTER 12

GOD
IS
HOLY

C olumnist Ray Cohn writes in the *New York Times*, "I don't want to know what the law is, I want to know who the judge is."[1] How important is a judge? All over the world, we hear of court cases that are mock trials. Defendants are paraded as guilty after being forced to sign confessions—many times to crimes they did not commit. The judges in these cases are part of a system that results in injustice for the people. On the other hand, if the judge is honest and fair, he will fulfill his role so that justice is served and complaints are addressed.

Since God is the most powerful judge in the universe, we must know what He is like to understand His role as judge. What kind of court does He hold? What kind of laws does He uphold? Is His justice fair and impartial?

Today most people ignore God's role as judge of mankind. They go on with their sin as if no one will ever call them to account. Yet in both the Old and New Testaments, God's justice is repeatedly presented. Look at a few of the times God acted as judge:

- He sent Adam and Eve out of the Garden of Eden because of their sin.

127

- He destroyed the wicked cities of Sodom and Gomorrah.

- He sent plagues on Egypt for the Pharaoh's mistreatment of God's people.

- He struck down Ananias and Sapphira when they lied to the Holy Spirit.

- He inflicted King Herod with deadly worms after he accepted worship as a god.

- He sent disease into the Corinthian church for not honoring the Lord's Supper.

As we study God's role as the Perfect Judge, we will tackle some of the difficult areas and see the purity of God's moral attributes of integrity. We will learn about His holiness, righteousness, and faithfulness, and how they affect our lives. And of course, we will also discover the truth about God's justice, the basic characteristic for a good judge. Once we see how God's attributes of integrity work together, we can have confidence that every action He takes as judge is perfect. As we grow in our intimacy with God, we will also learn how we can be free of the fear of His judgment against sin. Allow me to begin by showing you the awesome magnificence of God's holiness.

THE POWER OF FIRE

They were called the Great Fires of 1988. That year, wildfires swept through 1.4 million acres of Yellowstone National Park. The park was like a huge lumberyard filled with millions of wooden poles stuck at intervals far enough apart to allow good air circulation but close enough for each old lodgepole pine to torch its neighbor. Pine needles and dead twigs littered the ground, providing tinder-dry fodder for the unquenchable appetite of the fires.

On September 6, spot fires were seen around Old Faithful Inn. Built in 1904, it is the world's largest log structure. It sits near Old Faithful Geyser surrounded by the majestic old forests of Yellowstone. Twenty-five miles north, a fire storm raged across 50 acres of forest. Winds as powerful as a tornado whipped the flames through the forest with the sound of a freight train, reducing trees to piles of white ashes and small charred spears on the blackened earth.

On September 7, wind gusts in the wildfire area enabled the fires to spread even faster. By afternoon, a large wall of intensifying black and brown smoke hovered close to the Inn, but firefighters felt confident that they could contain any outbreaks. Suddenly, fingers of fires around the Inn curled together to make a powerful fist that pounded the area. Then 50-mile-an-hour, fire-generated winds thundered in, sounding like the continuous roar of a jet taking off. Spot fires jumped up in numerous places close to the vulnerable buildings. A wall of flame higher than the tops of the trees advanced with incredible speed.

Firefighters worked furiously, soaking the Inn with water to protect it from the flames. Then as quickly as the fire had come, it turned to the northeast. The danger was past. Twenty-four buildings had burned, but Old Faithful Inn had been saved.[2]

Months later, the forest grew with new vigor. The heat from the fires split open the hulls of the pine cones, releasing their seeds and yielding a forest of little saplings sprouting everywhere. The dead underbrush had been burned away. New spears of grass turned the hillsides to spring green, and a bumper crop of wildflowers carpeted the meadows.

THE POWER OF GOD'S HOLINESS

Anyone who has been near a fire of that magnitude understands its tremendous power. When it roars through an area, everything is changed. Ancient trees turn into cinders. Buildings are reduced to ashes. Nothing can withstand its fury. In their wake, wildfires also bring new growth and regeneration.

In the Bible, God's holiness is sometimes pictured as a fire. A. W. Tozer writes:

> Only fire can give even a remote conception of it. In fire He appeared at the burning bush; in the pillar of fire He dwelt through all the long wilderness journey. The fire that glowed between the wings of the cherubim in the holy place

was called the Shekinah, the Presence, through the years of Israel's glory, and when the Old had given place to the New, He came at Pentecost as a fiery flame and rested upon each disciple.[3]

What does a fire do? It destroys the dead, purifies, transforms the landscape. It is powerful, beautiful, and awesome. No one can stand up to the heat and fury of a firestorm. Nothing can bring regeneration like a forest fire.

God's holiness has even greater power. Moses, who saw God's holiness in the burning bush, asked, "Who else among the gods is like you, O LORD? Who is glorious in holiness like you—so awesome in splendor, performing such wonders?"[4]

Of all God's attributes, nothing compares to the splendor and beauty of His holiness. It is chief among His attributes. That means His character is perfect in every way. He is totally pure. His moral excellence is the absolute standard of integrity and ethical purity for all within His universe. God's supreme holiness infinitely sets Him apart from His creation. Everything God does bears the imprint of His holiness. His holiness never diminishes.

OUR GOD IS EXALTED IN HOLY MAJESTY

Unfortunately, to a large degree, God's holiness has been ignored by modern Christianity because we are filled with the dead brush of sin and pride. Our unwillingness to acknowledge a holy God reflects our failure to recognize who God really is. The Hebrew root word for "to be holy" means to cut or to separate. The Old Testament reveals that God is above and separate from all that He created. He is exalted above everything in holy majesty.

We may also define *holy* as completely set apart from sin. It is a term describing conduct or behavior usually implying sacredness, being consecrated to God, or being worthy of God.[5] Holiness reflects a flawless, unblemished purity. God does not just match a standard of purity—He is the standard.

I feel totally inadequate to describe this attribute of God. How can I, or any sinful human being, find the right words to explain how pure and high God is in His holiness? How can I describe something that is so far removed from my experience and nature?

When I think of God's holiness, I am convicted by the sinful nature of my own being. We are all like a man wearing a beautiful white suit who was invited to go down into the depths of a coal mine. In the darkness of the mine, he was not aware that his suit was becoming soiled. But when he resurfaced into the dazzling light of the noonday sun, he was fully aware that his suit had become sooty and dirty. The light of God's holiness reveals the darkness of our sin.

> THE LIGHT OF GOD'S HOLINESS REVEALS THE DARKNESS OF OUR SIN.

Isaiah was a prominent citizen of Judah during the eighth century B.C., a prophet who followed God's commands and served his Lord. Today, we would consider him one of the "spiritual elite," a man of integrity and honor. At one point, Isaiah had a vision of heaven and the holiness of the Creator:

> I saw the Lord. He was sitting on a lofty throne, and the train of His robe filled the Temple. Hovering around Him were mighty seraphim, each with six wings. With two wings they covered their faces, with two they covered their feet, and with the remaining two they flew. In a great chorus they sang, "Holy, holy, holy is the LORD Almighty! The whole earth is filled with His glory!" The glorious singing shook the Temple to its foundations, and the entire sanctuary was filled with smoke.[6]

Prior to his vision, Isaiah was focused on the sins of others, calling them to repentance. Now that he found himself in the very presence of our holy God, he became dramatically aware of his own sin and unrighteousness. Terrified, he exclaimed, "My destruction is sealed, for I am a sinful man and a member of a sinful race. Yet I have seen the King, the LORD Almighty!"[7]

When the angels surround the glorious throne of God, they sing, "Holy, holy, holy is the LORD Almighty." Stephen Charnock comments, "Do you hear, in any angelical song, any other perfection of the Divine Nature thrice repeated? Where do we read of them crying out, 'eternal, eternal, eternal' or 'faithful, faithful, faithful' Lord God of hosts?"[8]

This repetition, "holy, holy, holy," tells us that God's holiness is the supreme attribute of His being, the foundation of His eternal existence. His sovereignty and His role as judge are rooted in and flow out of His holiness. In fact, theologians speak of God's holiness as His "central and supreme perfection."[9]

GOD'S HOLINESS REQUIRES SEPARATION

Permit me to take you back to the Old Testament times when the Israelites worshipped God in a tabernacle they carried through the wilderness and into the Promised Land. The tabernacle pictured God's holiness and His separation from sinful mankind.

The tabernacle had three sections: the large area of service, the Holy Place, and the Holy of Holies. Each area was hidden from the other two by curtains.

Any priest who entered God's tabernacle first had to sacrifice an animal on the Brazen Altar to atone for sin. These burnt sacrifices were offered twice a day, once in the morning and once in the evening. Next was the Laver in which the priest washed his hands and feet before he appeared before the Lord—once again a symbol of our need for cleansing from sin. Then he was ready to enter the Holy Place.

Inside the Holy Place were three articles: the Table of Shewbread, the Candlestick, and the Altar of Incense. The Table of Shewbread held the special Bread of the Presence; the Candlestick continually burned pure oil; and the Altar of Incense held fragrant incense which was offered every morning.

But the Holy of Holies was the place where God's presence resided. It was hidden from view by a curtain so heavy that it took four men to move it. Only the High Priest was allowed to enter this place—and only once a year. If anyone else tried, God would strike him dead. Inside the Holy of Holies was the Ark of the Covenant, the dwelling place of God Himself, where once a year the High Priest offered sacrifices for his own sins and the sins of the people.

Why was the place of God's presence in the tabernacle hidden from view? Because God is so holy that no one can look upon His glory and live. No one can approach our holy God without a covering of blood to atone for the forgiveness of his sin.

Why was a lamb offered as a sacrifice for sin? It was a picture of Jesus Christ, the Lamb of God, and His sacrifice on the cross to provide a covering against the wrath of God on unconfessed sin. The only thing that can satisfy the judgment of sin demanded by God's holiness is the shedding of pure, innocent blood. Only Jesus' blood met this high standard.

GOD'S WRATH IS PART OF HIS HOLINESS

God is the absolutely pure and righteous being who abhors evil. He cannot tolerate any unrighteousness. Habakkuk 1:13 tells us, "Your eyes are too pure to look on evil; You cannot tolerate wrong" (NIV). God cannot secretly inspire any evil in us, for in His very nature He cannot accept any evil in any form.

God's holiness demands consequences for sin. We have broken His standard of holiness, and His holiness demands that He judge sin, not ignore or excuse it.

Throughout the Bible, God's wrath is pictured as a destroying fire. Think back to the story of Sodom and Gomorrah. The cities were filled with sin; the only righteous person was Lot. God allowed Lot and his family to flee from Sodom before He brought judgment. What was that punishment? The Lord rained down fire and burning sulfur upon those cities. All who lived there perished. Yet God's wrath is not uncontrolled anger, like we may sometimes think. Instead, it is a planned and just act that has its roots in God's holiness.

In the secular world, many people believe that actions do not have consequences. If you want to have extramarital "safe" sex, just use a condom. If you commit a crime, hire a good lawyer who can get you off on a technicality. Stealing items from your employer is okay because everyone else is doing it. The lack of teaching on morality in our public schools and in society in general has lowered the bar of standards for holy and righteous living.

This is how we sometimes approach God too. "Our sins are not so wrong," we say. "What others do is much worse." The person who believes this has not confronted the holiness of God. One small sin, one white lie, one hurtful word is enough to separate us from God's holiness.

GOD'S HOLINESS IS DEMONSTRATED IN HIS LAWGIVING

In recent years, numerous laws passed by state and federal legislatures have been struck down by the Supreme Court. In some cases, the judges ruled that a law could not be fairly applied. Other laws the Supreme Court decided had a fatal flaw that would prevent justice from being evenly distributed.

As the supreme, absolutely holy lawgiver, God has never announced a law that was not perfect in all respects. He has no need of a Supreme Court to determine whether His laws are fair or can be evenly applied. All His laws are an expression of the purity of His holiness.[10]

> TRUE KNOWLEDGE OF GOD'S HOLINESS ALWAYS ELICITS A WORSHIPFUL RESPONSE.

Jude's epistle provides numerous examples of people who rejected God's laws —and suffered the judgment of a holy God. Jude mentions "godless men, who change the grace of our God into a license for immorality."[11] They thought they could get away with their sin. Not so, Jude writes, for we are dealing with a holy God who, after delivering the people of Israel out of Egypt, "later destroyed those who did not believe."[12] Even the angels who rebelled against God "He has kept in darkness, bound with everlasting chains for judgment on the great Day."[13]

Over and over again, we set up our own standards of what ought to please God: "I deal fairly with people." "I do not abuse my wife or my children." "I give to the needs of others in the homeless ministry I support." "I'm a good neighbor."

We slight the holiness of God when we think we can manage

on our own. We fool ourselves when we assume that keeping the Golden Rule[14] will cover our sins. How ridiculous our standards are when compared to His standards of righteousness. When Joshua gave his farewell address to the people of Israel after they had settled into the Promised Land, he knew that the people still worshipped foreign gods. He told them, "You are not able to serve the LORD, for He is a holy and jealous God. He will not forgive your rebellion and sins."[15]

None of our manmade standards of behavior meet the requirements of a holy God. God's holiness mandates that we keep all His laws perfectly at all times. The only way we can come into His presence is by having our sins covered by the blood of the Lamb, Jesus Christ. Only through Christ's payment can our holy Judge extend His mercy to us.

RESPONDING TO GOD'S HOLINESS

If we could just grasp even a part of the magnificent holiness of God and the miracle of His mercy to His sinful creatures, then our homes, offices, schools, and in fact, the whole earth would shake with people falling prostrate on the ground in worship and adoration of Him. Such a view would precipitate a healthy fear of God, which is a necessary starting point.[16]

True knowledge of God's holiness always elicits a worshipful response from us. Moses fell to his face before the burning bush. Isaiah said, "Woe is me!" We cannot stand in the presence of God without acknowledging His holiness and seeing our own sin. Author Beth Moore writes in *A Woman's Heart: God's Dwelling Place:*

> The light of God's glory shines two ways: it sheds light on the knowledge of God so we can see Him more clearly, but it also sheds light on us so that we can see our own sin more clearly. Remember, the closer you approach the light, the brighter it shines on you. This is the marvelous two-edged sword of intimacy. We see Him more clearly and we see ourselves more clearly. It is the perfect safeguard against pride. You can mark His word on this: true intimacy breeds true humility![17]

When we concentrate on God's holiness—His moral perfections and absolute purity—the only appropriate response is humble adoration. Adoration is the basis for all worship.

Whenever I meditate on the holiness of God, I am impressed with how worthy He is of our worship. I think of the verse, "Worship the LORD in the splendor of His holiness; tremble before Him, all the earth."[18] I want to become absorbed with His holiness, rather than with His might, His wisdom, or His other magnificent attributes.

As we meditate on God's supreme holiness, we cannot help but be overcome with a sense of awe. Music can help us express our awe for our Lord. Many of the old Christian hymns capture the spirit of worship. I encourage you to select one of them, such as *Holy, Holy, Holy,* and begin to worship God in song and praises right now.

After Isaiah humbled himself before the Lord during his vision, one of the seraphim flew over to the altar in the temple and picked up a burning coal with a pair of tongs. Isaiah says, "He touched my lips with it and said, 'See, this coal has touched your lips. Now your guilt is removed, and your sins are forgiven.'"[19] Worship God also for the Lamb of God who bridged the separation between God and the repentant sinner. *The Old Rugged Cross* is a hymn which tells that story in song. Read through the words of this classic hymn; then exalt God's holy name as one of His children who has caught a glimpse of His holiness and His merciful salvation.

LIFE APPLICATION

EXALT YOUR GOD—Exodus 15:11 records that, after Moses and the Israelites safely crossed through the Red Sea, they sang a song of praise to the Lord.

> "Who else among the gods is like you, O LORD?
> Who is glorious in holiness like You—
> So awesome in splendor,
> Performing such wonders?"

Make a list of the wonders our holy God has displayed in your life this past year. Be specific. Now, thank God for them and praise Him by singing the beautiful hymn *Holy, Holy, Holy.*

> Holy, holy, holy! Lord God Almighty!
> Early in the morning our song shall rise to Thee;
> Holy, holy, holy, merciful and mighty!
> God in three Persons, blessed Trinity!

> Holy, holy, holy! Tho' the darkness hide Thee,
> Tho' the eye of sinful man Thy glory may not see;
> Only Thou art holy; there is none beside Thee,
> Perfect in pow'r, in love, and purity.

REFLECT HIS IMAGE—We are called to be holy, which means "set apart," "dedicated to the Lord." First Peter 1:16 says, "God Himself has said, 'You must be holy because I am holy.'" Are there areas of your life you are ashamed of, aspects of your character or lifestyle that are not pure? Submit them to the Lord and ask for His cleansing and forgiveness.

SHARE HIS MAJESTY—Moral integrity is not very common today. Does a friend or family member need to hear that there is someone who acts with complete integrity and can always be trusted? Share the truth of God's holiness with them today.

CHAPTER 13

GOD GIVES US THE POWER TO BECOME HOLY

Have you ever known anyone who was extremely talented but morally flawed? It does not take long to realize that great ability without the moral guidance of good character can cause immense tragedy and grief. An individual's character, rather than his abilities, determines the lasting value of his accomplishments.

For example, the president of a famous university was discovered using his computer to transfer pornographic material to minors. The head of a prestigious charitable organization was convicted of embezzling from the charity. Several top political leaders have been accused of committing adultery with interns and staff. Obviously, not all people in these professions are guilty of such crimes, but these problems are so rampant that although we are a nation of achievements, we are morally bankrupt.

Christians also struggle with moral purity. Some time ago a man who held an influential position in a Christian ministry confided in me that he had never surrendered his life to Christ, although for years he pretended that he had done so. He said and did all the right things so that his friends and all who met him would think he was a committed follower of Christ. But he admitted to deliberately saying "no" to the Holy Spirit's leading and choosing to live a lie.

I was shocked that anyone who was exposed to the inspired Word of God, Christian fellowship, and ministry would dare to deliberately disobey God. But as we talked, I learned that he was simply afraid to live a holy life. The thought of complete surrender to the Lord was unappealing to him, and as a result, he had run from God for many years.

Holy Living, the Secret to Life

Like this man, a false view of holiness causes many Christians to stop short of complete surrender to God. They have a distorted view of holiness because they define it from a secular viewpoint. They imagine a holy person as some kind of religious fanatic, a "kook," or an isolated monk devoted to prayer and fasting. Others think that holiness has only to do with the way a person dresses or socializes. These misinformed believers decide they do not want to give up their lifestyle, pleasures, and pride and allow God to renew their minds. They do not let Him mold them into people with tastes and desires that bring true happiness and joy in fellowship with Him.

Tragically, some believers continue to wrestle with their childhood experiences with strict, legalistic parents or churches. I have heard some confess, "I tried to live up to the high expectations of my parents or pastor, but I have failed many times. I just can't live the Christian life!" They conclude that the Christian life is difficult to live. I agree—and go one step further: It is impossible to live a holy life on your own. Even with determination and our best efforts, we will always fail. We can never become holy in our own strength and abilities.

But the story does not end with our feeble efforts. Paul proclaims:

> There is no condemnation [guilt] for those who belong to Christ Jesus. For the power of the life-giving Spirit has freed you through Christ Jesus from the power of sin that leads to death. The law of Moses could not save us, because

of our sinful nature. But God put into effect a different plan to save us. He sent His own Son in a human body like ours, except that ours are sinful. God destroyed sin's control over us by giving His Son as a sacrifice for our sins. He did this so that the requirement of the law would be fully accomplished for us who no longer follow our sinful nature but instead follow the Spirit.[1]

This is the secret: We can live a holy life if we yield to the Holy Spirit who came to glorify Jesus Christ. Jesus is the only person to ever live a holy life, and now He resides within every believer through His Holy Spirit. His presence and power give us the strength to live a holy life moment by moment.

Holy, righteous living is the secret to a life of joy, power, victory, and fruitfulness. When we are holy, we are set apart and separated from sin for God's special use. God gives us the power to experience a whole new life based on His holiness and purity. But we must obey His direction and laws. In this chapter, we will learn about several ways God wants us to respond to His holiness.

Because God is holy, we must give Him reverential respect.

In 1996, I was privileged to receive the prestigious international Templeton Prize for Progress in Religion. As part of the honor, Vonette and I went to Buckingham Palace to meet with Prince Philip and Sir John Templeton. Because we were meeting royalty, we were very conscious of our appearance and our behavior.

Do we have less concern when we come before our Sovereign God, the ruler of the universe? He deserves much more reverence and respect than any human being who ever lived! He is not the "man upstairs." He is the great, holy, righteous, all-powerful, loving, creator God.

Many Scripture passages tell us to fear God. King David writes, "Serve the LORD with reverent fear, and rejoice with trembling."[2] Solomon explains, "The fear of the LORD is the beginning of wisdom. Knowledge of the Holy One results in understanding."[3] Fearing God does not mean to be afraid of God, but rather to express reverential awe and deep respect before Him.

Vonette and I get on our knees every morning to praise and worship God out of reverential awe for Him. I encourage you to examine how you come before God, how you honor His name before others, and how you respect His Word. In your daily quiet time with Him, give Him the honor He deserves. Spend more time worshipping Him than asking for your own needs.

Because our holy God abhors sin and evil, we must turn away from every evil.

God created the universe to function according to His standard of holiness. God's holiness is so complete that He cannot look on even one sin. Not one.

Picture God's holiness in this way. Envision a beautiful bride on her wedding day, dressed in white and looking radiant. The white dress symbolizes purity. It does not have a spot or wrinkle anywhere. If one ink spot stained the dress, people would focus on the ugliness of the stain rather than the loveliness of the dress. That is a picture of God's purity. God, who has never sinned in any way, is so pure and holy that He "cannot tolerate the slightest sin."[4] His heaven is pure and holy, absolutely free of all sin and evil.

> WE CANNOT EXPECT GOD TO ALLOW US INTO HEAVEN WHEN WE HAVE SIN-STAINS IN OUR LIVES.

No matter how religious, self-disciplined, or good we may try to be, we cannot expect God to allow us into His heaven when we have sin-stains in our lives. If God allowed one sin to mar His pure dwelling place, it would cease to be a holy city. Since God cannot even look on sin, our sinful, human situation is hopeless.

This is where a miraculous paradox comes in. Jesus Christ came to take away the sins of the world. He became sin for us. The perfect, holy Son of God took on the stain of our sin. He endured and satisfied the judgment of a pure God for our misdeeds —not just one or two sins, but every sin you and I have ever committed or will commit in our lifetimes!

Remember how the Holy of Holies in the tabernacle illustrated God's holiness and His separation from humans? The heavy curtain separated sinful people from God's presence. The sacrifices of lambs and goats symbolized a holy God who would take upon Himself the sins of the world. This ultimate sacrifice also included death—Christ's death on the cross.

The physical agony of the cross was nothing compared to the spiritual agony of God becoming sin for us! All the sins and evil ever committed, or that ever will be committed, were laid on Jesus Christ just before He died. Although Jesus abhorred sin and evil, He willingly took on the sins of all people. The Book of Hebrews explains this so much better than I ever could:

> What God wants is for us to be made holy by the sacrifice of the body of Jesus Christ once for all time…For by that one offering He perfected forever all those whom He is making holy…Now when sins have been forgiven, there is no need to offer any more sacrifices. And so, dear brothers and sisters, we can boldly enter heaven's Most Holy Place because of the blood of Jesus. This is the new, life-giving way that Christ has opened up for us through the sacred curtain, by means of His death for us.[5]

That is why during Christ's crucifixion God miraculously tore in two the heavy curtain that kept men and women from the Holy of Holies. Christ had paid the ultimate price. Those who accept God's forgiveness become spotless and pure so they now have access to God. In fact, all believers become God's holy temple as the Holy Spirit comes to live within them at the moment of their spiritual birth.

As His temples—His Most Holy Place—our lives are no longer temples of evil, immorality, stealing, or lying. Because God lives within us, we should abhor evil the way He does. When we understand how holy God is and what His Son endured to make us the temple of the living God, our motivation should be to live pure and sin-free lives.

Of course, living a pure life is possible only through the enabling of the Holy Spirit. We are given power over sin and temptation as we are indwelt, filled, and anointed by Him.

According to God's Word, we do not have to sin. But if we do sin, there is Someone to plead for us before the Father. This is explained in 1 John 2:1,2: "My dear children, I am writing this to you so that you will not sin. But if you do sin, there is someone to plead for you before the Father. He is Jesus Christ, the one who pleases God completely. He is the sacrifice for our sins. He takes away not only our sins but the sins of all the world."

Becoming holy is more than obedience; it is a liberating, cleansing freedom from all unwholesomeness. Sin in our lives creates a barrier to fellowship with God. It blocks the communication lines between us and God so He does not hear our prayers.[6] Restored fellowship with God comes by confessing our sin and turning from it. As the holiness of God is absorbed into every fiber of our being, we become even more sensitive to sin and learn to abhor it all the more as we walk in an intimate, joyful relationship with Him.

Because God's holiness dispels darkness, we must walk in His light.

In the early '60s, I went to Rangoon, Burma, to speak to a gathering of students. When I arrived, I was told that a group of radical Communist students planned to kill me by stoning me at the meeting.

When I began my speech, there was so much heckling that I could not be heard. Since I knew that God inhabits the praises of His people, I asked the few Christians in the audience to join me in singing the praise chorus, *Hallelujah*. Satan cannot stand it when believers praise God. As we praised God, the hecklers leaped from their chairs and ran out of the meeting. We continued with the meeting and several students received Christ.

Sin and evil always seek refuge in darkness. But God's holy radiance exposes and destroys the darkness of sin and evil. Paul writes, "God lives in light so brilliant that no human can approach Him."[7] The more we meditate on the holiness of God, the more we become aware of our sinfulness. In comparison to His purity, everything else appears dull and dirty.

First John 1 says that "God is light and there is no darkness in Him at all…If we are living in the light of God's presence,… then we have fellowship with each other, and the blood of Jesus, His Son, cleanses us from every sin."[8] Jesus said, "I am the light of the world. If you follow Me, you won't be stumbling through the darkness, because you will have the light that leads to life."[9] As we follow Jesus, His light illumines our way and unbelievers see the holiness of God through our attitudes and actions.

Because our God is holy, we must serve Him with life-changing devotion.

Scripture gives us God's directive: "Now you must be holy in everything you do, just as God—who chose you to be His children—is holy."[10] Christians have been set apart by God for this divine purpose. If you want to see the holiness of God, examine the life and teachings of Jesus Christ. He is the visible expression of God's holiness. God wants us to place our lives under His lordship and conform to the moral character of His Son and reflect the beauty of His holiness and character.

Out of respect for God, I want to be holy as He is holy and never disappoint Him in any way. I would rather die than bring dishonor to His holy name. I have often prayed that if there is any possibility that I might be unfaithful to my beloved wife or in any other way bring dishonor to our Lord, that He would take my life before it happened.

George Muller, well-known for his great faith and ministry to orphans, was asked the secret of his fruitful service for the Lord. He said, "There was a day when I died…utterly died." As he spoke, he bent lower and lower until he almost touched the floor. "I died to George Muller—his opinions, his preferences, tastes, and will—died to the world, its approval or censure—died to the approval or blame even of my brethren and friends—and since then I have studied only to show myself approved unto God."

Everyone I know who has been greatly used by God for the cause of Christ has gone through an experience of "dying to self" as described in Galatians 2:20. It is not until we know the reality of "death to self" that we can live for Christ and God can truly use and bless us. My Galatians 2:20 experience happened in the spring of 1951 when Vonette and I signed a contract to become slaves of Christ. I daily reaffirm this contract.

Holy living involves a daily decision to surrender to the lordship of Christ. It involves yielding our will to God and adopting His perspective for life.[11] God wants our minds and hearts to be filled with His holy qualities. As our lives are transformed, we will project the light of His holiness into the darkness of our evil world. Real life—abundant life—begins with dying to self.

Because God expects holiness from His people, we must turn away from any idols in our lives.

God is very possessive of our affections. He warned the Israelites, "Do not worship any other gods besides Me. Do not make idols of any kind…You must never worship or bow down to them, for I, the LORD your God, am a jealous God who will not share your affection with any other god!"[12] He alone has the right to occupy the throne of our heart. He is to be exalted to the highest place in our lives. Everything else must be of lower importance.

THE FALSE GODS OF OUR SOCIETY CLAMOR FOR OUR ATTENTION.

Yet we are all guilty at one time or another of idolatry. The false gods and idols of our society may not be as obvious as those of ancient Israel or other cultures, but their presence is just as real. They clamor for our attention. They bargain for our allegiance. Here are some of the most common:

- The god of affluence. Many are convinced that wealth is the key to happiness. They place their trust in bank accounts and hoarded assets. The spirit of greed has gradually transformed their values so that money is now their master.

- The god of pleasure. Multitudes are convinced that fun is the chief goal in life. Couch potatoes vegetate in front of the TV screen. Sports fanatics cannot watch enough games. Some seek entertainment, thrills, and adventure in hopes of conquering boredom in their futile search for happiness.

- The god of achievement. The ambitious sacrifice themselves to this god. Pride is their relentless taskmaster. For these workaholics, accomplishments are the building blocks of self-esteem. No challenge is too great in their quest for significance.

- The god of infatuation. Some people idolize a celebrity, a hero, a friend, or even a relative. Their entire world revolves around that individual. The spirit of obsession amplifies healthy feelings of love and admiration into unholy worship.

- The god of self-worship. Many are convinced by the spirit of vanity that appearance is everything. Their life is preoccupied with beauty, fashion, and body-building.

- The god of sensuality. The spirit of lust has ensnared many with immorality. For them God's gift of sex has been distorted into perversion and tragically often ends in addiction, abortion, disease, and death.

Substitute gods usurp the worship and devotion that rightfully belong to our holy God. In reality, these idols can never fill the God-shaped vacuum within the heart of man. God's Word calls us to a higher focus: "You must be holy because I am holy."[13]

As believers who belong to the universal Church, we are the bride of Christ. God promises that the Church will one day shine faultless before Him. At the end of this age, Christ will present us to God clothed in Christ's purity and holiness.[14]

I can hardly wait for that day. That will be the moment when all of us, the Church of Christ universal with millions upon millions of believers, will give glory to God as the spotless bride of Christ. It will be one of the most moving moments in all eternity. We can prepare ourselves for that momentous occasion today by living our lives in the light of God's holiness and purity by faith through the enabling power of the Holy Spirit.

LIFE APPLICATION

WRITE IT ON YOUR HEART—Commit the following statement and verses to memory. Then as you encounter situations during this week where you need to be reminded of God's purity, claim these promises by faith.

- Because God is holy, I will devote myself to Him in worship and service.
- 1 Peter 1:16—"[God] Himself has said, 'You must be holy because I am holy.'"
- Psalm 96:9—"Worship the LORD in the splendor of His holiness; tremble before Him, all the earth."

COUNT ON GOD—Our holy God is perfect. Give your imperfections and limitations to Him. Trust Him to bring good out of your current circumstances and bring glory to His holy name.

OBEY GOD—God's very nature is holy, and His holiness abhors sin and evil. In order to have a healthy relationship with your loving Father, you must not have sin in your life. Search your heart for any hidden sin and confess it to your holy God. Commit yourself to turn away from temptation that you struggle with today.

CHAPTER 14

GOD
IS ABSOLUTE
TRUTH

A story is told about a banquet speaker who was introduced as a very smart businessman. His business growing and selling potatoes in Maine netted him $25,000 the previous year. After a long introduction, he arose to speak. "Before I begin," he said, "I must set the record straight. What was said about my business is only partially true. First, it was not Maine, but Texas. It was not potatoes, but oil. It was not $25,000, but $250,000. And it was not a profit, but a loss. And one more thing about this introduction—it was not me who lost the money, it was my brother."

As the story illustrates, truth matters. And in some situations, it *really* matters. We all laugh at jokes about the doctor coming out of surgery to tell the waiting family, "I've got good news and bad news. Which do you want first?" But when one of our own loved ones faces a life-threatening illness or accident, we do not want jokes, we want medical experts to tell us the truth.

Josh McDowell, one of Campus Crusade's most well-known ministry directors, speaks to college students all over the world. One of his most frequent topics is "safe sex." Josh was invited to give the concluding talk during "Safe Sex Week" at the University of North Dakota to 3,000 students in a jammed auditorium. When he began by saying, "You've been brainwashed," a rumble spread through the crowd. Josh describes what happened next:

> When the students settled down, I continued, "You've had an entire week of 'safer sex' indoctrination: speakers, experts, videos, films, classes, and symposiums. You've been challenged, motivated, encouraged, indoctrinated, and pressured about using condoms to ensure safe sex. To top it all off, you were given a 'safer sex packet.' But you've been lied to."
>
> At this point, the crowd was becoming a little indignant with me. Then I lowered the boom with one more question: "After all the information on 'safer sex' you have received this week, how many of you know the statistical failure rate of the condom?" *Not one hand went up!* Suddenly, the auditorium was as quiet as a cemetery. They looked at each other with expressions of astonishment. They realized they hadn't been told the whole truth about safer sex.[1]

TRUTH HAS BEEN A MAJOR CASUALTY IN OUR MODERN CULTURE.

Josh finds a similar reaction in every university crowd he addresses. Invariably, the students have been thoroughly coached about how to have "safer sex," but are never told how unsafe "safer sex" really is. In essence, what they heard was a lie.

Read these statistics that fly in the face of "safe sex." Research conducted by Planned Parenthood (a group advocating the practice of safer sex) states that within one year of using a condom to prevent pregnancy, the pregnancy rate is more than 10 percent for all ages, and the rate is almost double for teens.[2] Statistics also show that a girl who becomes sexually active at 14 years old and practices birth control has an 87 percent chance of becoming pregnant before she graduates from high school.[3] If she is your daughter, niece, or a friend's child, does she not deserve to know the *whole truth* before she engages in risky behavior? Does shading the truth *really* matter to her—and consequently to her unborn baby? Of course!

But the consequences go even further. Physician Robert C. Noble writes in *Newsweek*:

> I can't say I'm comforted reading a government pamphlet called "Condoms and Sexually Transmitted Diseases Especially AIDS." "Condoms are not 100 percent safe," it says, "but if used properly will reduce the risk of sexually transmitted diseases, including AIDS." *Reduce* the risk of a disease that is 100 percent fatal? That's all that's available between us and death? How much do condoms reduce the risk? They don't say. So much for Safe Sex.[4]

In fact, all latex condoms have microscopic holes that are *fifty times larger* than the HIV virus. The oil-based lubricants used with condoms can also damage them. If a condom is too old, or has been exposed to heat or cold, it may be less effective.[5]

What comfort is the lie of "safe sex" to the young man who contracts gonorrhea or to the young woman who develops herpes or to the newborn who is born with AIDS? Telling incomplete "truths" can change a life—or cause death. It is vital that we know and tell the absolute truth.

THE WHOLE PROBLEM WITH ABSOLUTE TRUTH

Most Americans believe in absolute truth, right? Wrong! Truth has been a major casualty in our modern culture. In a study by George Barna of Americans between ages 26 and 44, only 20 percent of those surveyed strongly disagreed with the statement: "There is no such thing as absolute truth; different people can define truth in different ways and still be correct."[6] Shockingly, only 27 percent of those who described themselves as born-again Christians strongly disagreed! Fifty-two percent actually agreed at least somewhat with the statement![7]

If we look at the phrase "there is no absolute truth," it is logically inconsistent. It states an absolute truth about absolute truth while claiming there is no absolute truth!

The whole idea that truth is relative contradicts God's Word.

Second Timothy 3:16 says, "All Scripture is inspired by God and is useful to teach us what is true and to make us realize what is wrong in our lives. It straightens us out and teaches us to do what is right." For example, the Bible teaches that homosexuality is wrong.[8] Yet I recently read that a school board in Massachusetts voted unanimously to teach pre-schoolers (ages 3–5) about homosexual lifestyles. Pre-schoolers! This is a symptom of a culture that has rejected absolute truth.

Many people argue that even religious people cannot agree on what is absolute truth. As Christians we say that the Bible is true. The Hindus reject that, preferring the writings, or Vedas, of their holy men. The Muslims put their faith in the Koran, claiming Mohammed received it as a prophet of God. The Mormons are convinced that Joseph Smith got his messages straight from God.

To make the situation more confusing, other people claim to have received absolute truth. Today, more than a million people have purchased the bestseller *Conversations with God, Books 1 and 2*, which the author, Neale Donald Walsch, insists were dictated to him by God. Listen to the "absolute truth" that Walsch's god advocates: "I do not love 'good' more than I love 'bad.' Hitler went to heaven. When you understand this, you will understand God."

In his column in *The Wall Street Journal,* Charles Colson writes, "Mr. Walsch's God liberates us from traditional authorities—rabbis, ministers, parents, the Bible…He confidently attempts—in dialogue form, with his own questions and comments and God's replies and explanations—to repeal or modify every known religious truth and propound his own version of God's message as authoritative."[9]

A famous New Age believer made a statement in a television interview with Kathie Lee Gifford that everyone goes to Paradise after they die. Then with a question uncharacteristic of the media, Kathie Lee, a strong Bible believer, asked, "Are you saying you believe that the same thing happens to Hitler as to Mother Teresa?" The New Ager stuttered and stumbled and had no reply. Kathie Lee's poignant question demonstrated the ludicrous nature of those who reject truth.

WHAT IS ABSOLUTE TRUTH?

If you were asked to describe absolute truth, what would you say? By what standard can we measure truth to determine if it is truth? If you do not believe there is such a thing as absolute truth, how do you find anything to be true and trustworthy? Following are three qualities of absolute truth.

Absolute truth is internally consistent. No matter which way you approach a true statement, it remains unassailably true. When we say that our God is absolutely truthful, we mean above everything else that He is internally consistent in His character and being. Proverbs 30:5 says, "Every word of God proves true." In fact, the Hebrew word for *truth* means conformance to a standard—God's standards.

Internal consistency of character is vital to all of God's attributes. If you can prove that God is not truthful in any aspect of who He is and how He acts, then His other qualities have no validity. If He were not absolutely consistent, then God's unlimited power, for example, could be compromised by His love. He would be like a powerful president of a country who fails to take action against evil because he lets his emotions, his wrong understanding of love, negate his power.

Absolute truth is true for all people in all places at all times. Not everything qualifies as absolute truth. For example, if you said, "Today, the interest rate for home mortgages is at 6.5 percent," that could be true for you living in America. But for someone living in Brazil, the interest rate might be 50-plus percent. And a month from now, the interest rate for you could change to 8 percent. Because interest rates fluctuate, the percentage rate is not true for all people in all places at all times. The rate is not an absolute truth.

On the other hand, if you say, "Adultery is always wrong," you would be stating an absolute truth.[10] Whether you live in Bangladesh, Japan, or the United States, adultery is still wrong. Adultery was just as wrong a thousand years ago as it is today. Adultery is wrong for the wife living with the alcoholic husband, or the business or military person separated from a spouse by extended travel.

Absolute truth has its source in our holy God. No human can think up or discover a new truth. Truth has always existed in God's nature; He is the author of truth.

We must always measure our beliefs by the truth in God's Word. Since He is the author of truth and since absolute truth resides in Him, He is the only One who can guide us to absolute truth. With Him, we see truth face to face. Any other guide will only lead us into confusion and deception.

Moses said, "God is not a man, that He should lie. He is not a human, that He should change His mind. Has He ever spoken and failed to act? Has He ever promised and not carried it through?"[11]

> WE CAN BREAK GOD'S COMMANDMENTS, BUT WE CANNOT CHANGE THEM.

Whatever God says is absolutely right. Whatever He promises will always be fulfilled.

NOTHING CAN CHANGE GOD'S ABSOLUTE TRUTH

Have you ever heard the phrase, "written in stone"? This usually refers to some statement that cannot be changed. The phrase comes from the Old Testament account of when God gave the Ten Commandments. About two months after the Israelites had left their slavery in Egypt, they reached Mount Sinai where God revealed Himself to the people. God's holiness and power were very evident:

> All Mount Sinai was covered with smoke because the LORD had descended on it in the form of fire. The smoke billowed into the sky like smoke from a furnace, and the whole mountain shook with a violent earthquake.[12]

Moses went up the mountaintop into a cloud that looked like a devouring fire and stayed forty days and nights. During that time God wrote the Ten Commandments with His own finger on tablets of stone. God required His people to obey these timeless gems of absolute truth.

Meanwhile, the people, under the leadership of Moses' brother, Aaron, began to think that Moses would never return. So Aaron built them a golden calf to take God's place.

Aware of the peoples' disobedience, God told Moses to go back down the mountain. As Moses strode downward clutching the stone tablets, he heard noises like the sounds of celebration. When he got near, he saw God's people worshipping a golden calf. The people who had promised to obey all of God's law had already broken one of the Ten Commandments. In anguish and anger over the sight, Moses hurled the tablets to the ground, shattering them.

Then God said to Moses: "Prepare two stone tablets like the first ones. I will write on them the same words that were on the tablets you smashed."[13] Once more Moses climbed that cloud-covered mountain; once more God etched the Ten Commandments into stone with His finger.

Do you see the picture of absolute truth in this account? God wrote the commandments in stone. No one can erase or alter them; they are absolute truth. Moses, in his anger, shattered the stone tablets. As humans we can break God's commandments, but we cannot change them. The broken laws are not any less true. Once shattered, God just wrote them on stone once more. Nothing we can do will ever change God's absolute truth.

GOD'S ABSOLUTE TRUTH LASTS FOREVER

A woman received directions to a home for a baby shower, complete with the street name and the house number. But she never found the correct house and went home embarrassed. The next day she discovered some pranksters had switched several street signs in the area. She failed to reach her destination *even though she had true directions.*

If you have ever had an experience like that, you may be skeptical whenever you receive directions to an unfamiliar setting. That is how many people approach what God has said. They are not at all sure that His truth is absolutely accurate or applies to modern life. *Maybe He has forgotten about a turn, a detour, or a switched street sign,* they think. *Times change, so how can we rely on truth given centuries ago?*

Because God knows the end from the beginning, not one of His statements ever turns out to be a misdirection. He does not shade the truth or leave out an essential part. His absolute truth applies to every situation in history.

I encourage you to read Psalm 119, the greatest chapter in the Bible, about the endurance and truth of God's Word. Verse 160 says, "All Your words are true; all Your just laws will stand forever." Not only is God's truth absolute, but it lasts forever! We can count on it for eternity.

How God Reveals His Absolute Truth to Us

God wants us to know the absolute truth, so He has taken the initiative to show us truth in several ways: in His Word, the Bible; by the life, death, and resurrection of His Son; and through His Holy Spirit.

God recorded truth for us in the Bible.

The Bible is God's absolute truth in written form. Jesus tells us, "Your word is truth."[14] We can read it, memorize it, and meditate on it. God uses the Bible to reveal truth about Himself, ourselves, and about life.[15] There is no way anyone can live a holy, satisfying, fulfilled life without spending regular time in the Word of God.

It has been my practice for years to read through the Bible each year. My most important priority every morning is to read God's Word, even before I eat breakfast. Somehow the time I spend with God in the morning is more than compensated in the way the rest of the day unfolds.

God manifested truth to us through the life, death, and resurrection of Jesus Christ.

Truth is not just a concept, it is embodied in a person—Jesus Christ. While many people claim to *know* the truth, only Jesus could honestly claim to *be* the truth. Jesus explains, "I am the way, the truth, and the life. No one can come to the Father except through Me."[16]

John Wesley writes: "The word of His truth and wisdom is more ardent and more light-giving than the rays of the sun, and sinks down into the depths of heart and mind." The words of God put into human form by Jesus purify us when we let them sink into our hearts.

God guides us into truth through the working of the Holy Spirit.

As Christians, we have the Holy Spirit living within us. One of His primary responsibilities is to reveal truth to us. Jesus calls Him "the Spirit of truth."[17] The Holy Spirit is Christ's representative who communicates directly with us, illuminating God's truth, and giving us the power to obey that truth. In fact, when we worship God, we are to worship Him in spirit and in truth.[18]

I often use the illustration that the Holy Spirit represents one wing of an airplane and the Word of God represents the other. Our Lord Jesus Christ is the pilot. No airplane will fly with just one wing. If we do not rely on the Holy Spirit to guide us and also saturate ourselves with God's truth—His holy, inspired, inerrant truth—then our holy life will not fly. We must also allow Jesus to be the navigator of our plans, desires, wills, and emotions, for He is the truth.

We do not need to be confused about what is right or wrong —we can look to God's Word. We cannot complain that we do not have an example of how to put God's truth into practice—we have the truth in the flesh, Jesus Christ. And we cannot excuse ourselves from knowing and following God's truth—we have the power of the Holy Spirit who leads us into all truth.

Spirit-filled worship leads us to a reverence for God's truth, which in turn leads us to daily obedience. We put our worship into action when we say "yes" to God's truth in each and every decision of our lives. If you find yourself misrepresenting the truth to an employer, ask God to help you be completely honest out of respect for Him. The following Life Application gives more suggestions to help you worship God in Spirit and in truth.

LIFE APPLICATION

EXALT YOUR GOD—The Bible states in Hebrews 6:18, "It is impossible for God to lie." Praise your heavenly Father that He is truth. Thank Him that in this world of "half-truths" and "double speak," His Word can always be trusted.

REFLECT HIS IMAGE—Jesus stated, "I am the truth." Are you known as a truthful person, someone whose word can be trusted? In God's book, there are no such things as "fibs" or "white lies." Our God of truth wants His children to be reflections of His character. Ask Him to help you tell the truth in situations you face where it would be easier to compromise.

SHARE HIS MAJESTY—Prayerfully ask God to show you an area in your church or ministry where you can stand up for God's absolute truth. Perhaps you can help high school students to understand the importance of God's command to be sexually pure. Or maybe you can explain the importance of being truthful to your spouse during a couples' Bible study. Be sure to back up your teaching with God's Word.

CHAPTER 15

GOD'S TRUTH SETS US FREE

On February 3, 1998, Karla Faye Tucker died. She had known the date of her death since December because she was scheduled to be executed in a Texas prison for the double murders she had committed.

Karla Faye Tucker was the first woman since the Civil War to be executed in the Texas prison system. In 1983 after three days of non-stop drug taking, she and Daniel Garrett broke into a Houston apartment and killed Dean and Deborah Thornton. Karla Faye was the one who swung the pickax. If anyone deserved a sentence of death, she did.

But something miraculous happened to Karla Faye during her fourteen years on death row. Soon after her arrest, she learned the truth that God loves even the vilest sinner and that He pardons completely the person who asks Him for forgiveness. Karla Faye said in an interview a month before her execution, "I asked [God] to forgive me and I knew I needed forgiveness. And I knew I had done something really horrible. But I think right at that moment what mostly hit me was His love. His love. It just surrounded me."[1] In that moment, the murderer became a child of God.

Although she would never again set foot outside a prison, God's truth had made her free. George Sechrist, who represented Karla Faye in her appeal process, saw her change as she grew in her faith. He says, "I've represented a number of folks on death row. All of them certainly are deserving of their day in court, regardless of what they've done, but I've never seen anyone who has genuinely transformed in any way as she has. And, quite frankly, I doubt I'll ever see it again!"[2]

Karla testified to the power of the Holy Spirit to change a life that had been ruined by sin. Her testimony was broadcast over radio and television to millions.

No one can commit a sin so rotten that God cannot transform that life into one which brings glory to Him. Although Karla reaped the consequences for her crime with the death penalty, she also influenced thousands of others for Christ with her testimony before she died.

Every day, we make decisions based on beliefs and values that we assume are true. Too often, we later discover our beliefs were an illusion of truth projected by our corrupt society. As John the apostle explains, "They are from the world and therefore speak from the viewpoint of the world, and the world listens to them."[3] The world's viewpoint is based on wrong values and misguided purposes, not absolute truth, and its ideas fluctuate with the time, the person, and the culture. Eventually, the world's viewpoint enslaves us to sin. But as we read in John 8:32, God's truth sets us free.

God's liberating truth is our anchor point for life. Solomon writes, "Truth stands the test of time; lies are soon exposed."[4] God's truth has endured for thousands of years. Man's "truth" has not. And since God's truth lasts for eternity, its power to free us from sin will never diminish.

WE CAN TRUST GOD'S WORD

Most of us have at least one friend we consider very honest. When we ask that person for his opinion, we find out what he really thinks. If we ask him to take care of something important for us, he will be open about whether or not he can complete the job.

We would not consider him a faithful friend if there were areas of his life where he acted dishonestly.

That is even more true of our holy God. We can trust His Word —completely and implicitly. The psalmist writes, "All Your commands are true. Long ago I learned from Your statutes that You established them to last forever."[5] It would violate God's truthfulness if His Word could not be trusted.

During the first centuries of the Church, false teachers tried to argue that the Bible was not completely truthful. Paul quickly defended the Bible.[6] He proclaimed that all Scripture is God's truth! That assurance is what gave Paul such incredible confidence as he traveled about the Roman Empire proclaiming the Good News of Jesus' death and resurrection. His life of service through incredible pressures and persecutions is proof that God's Word has power to sustain us.

> THE WORLD'S VIEWPOINT ENSLAVES US TO SIN, BUT GOD'S TRUTH SETS US FREE.

We can absolutely trust God's Word —to the last period on the last page. After more than fifty years of studying the Bible, I am convinced beyond any shadow of doubt that it is the holy, inspired, and inerrant Word of God. During these years, I have anchored my life of service to Jesus Christ on a God who is faithful and stands behind His holy Word. God has never failed me, and never will.

GOD'S PROMISES ARE TRUE

If God's Word can be trusted, we can be sure that the promises in His Word are also true. The writer to the Hebrews encourages us: "Let us hold unswervingly to the hope we profess, for He who promised is faithful."[7] God's truthful nature backs up His promises; therefore, we can immerse ourselves in His promises, applying them to our life situations. For example, consider Jesus' promises:

- "When everything is ready, I will come and get you, so that you will always be with Me where I am."[8]

- "The truth is, anyone who believes in Me will do the same works I have done, and even greater works, because I am going to be with the Father."[9]
- "I am leaving you with a gift—peace of mind and heart. And the peace I give isn't like the peace the world gives. So don't be troubled or afraid."[10]

The Bible is full of thousands of other wonderful promises from God, for every imaginable occasion. They mean so much to me that years ago I wrote a devotional book called *Promises: A Daily Guide to Supernatural Living*. The promises highlighted on each of the pages are still blessing the lives of those who read them. I encourage you to read through the Old and New Testaments, highlighting the amazing promises of God. You will be greatly blessed with what you find! Memorizing them will bring an invaluable source of encouragement.

GOD'S TRUTH EXPOSES
DECEPTION AND IGNORANCE

Because our secular society has rejected God's holy inspired Word as the absolute standard for truth, we have lost our reference point for reality. Now our society often defines truth based on public opinion polls. We live in a media culture of sizzle and hype which influences public thinking. Advertising hucksters and spin-doctors are constantly at work to influence our thinking about events and issues. Educational institutions promote diversified views at the expense of truth. Even many journalists are no longer satisfied with reporting the facts. Instead, they slant the news to fit their own, often anti-God, interpretation.

This is the nature of the world system controlled by Satan, who is the father of lies.[11] These masters of deception, distortion, and manipulation take truth out of context or give only half-truths. Anyone who accepts this world system becomes bound up in deception, manipulation, lies, and ignorance. Many Christians have bought into these lies.

But God's truth is a light that shows us the difference between falsehood and truth. Jesus taught, "I am the light of the world. If you follow Me, you won't be stumbling through the darkness, because you will have the light that leads to life."[12] Without His truth, we are left to grope about in spiritual darkness. But His light frees us to see and do what is right and good.

Consider some of the deceptions promoted by our culture and the contrast of God's truth, as shown in the following table. Of the six options, which of the two columns are you tempted to base your life on? Every day, each of us makes choices about what we want to do or perceive to be true. Only God can free us from the deceptions and distortions of the world system. He has given us the Bible as a handbook for identifying truth and His Spirit,

SOCIETY'S LIE	GOD'S TRUTH
Money is the key to happiness. Wealth provides comfort and security, prestige and respectability. If you have a nice house in the suburbs and own the things you always wanted, you will find fulfillment in life.	"Stay away from the love of money; *be satisfied with what you have.*"[13] "Seek first His kingdom and His righteousness, and all these things will be given to you as well."[14] "My God will meet all your needs."[15]
Think of yourself first. Otherwise, your needs will go unmet. You deserve more out of life. Go ahead, reward yourself. You owe it to yourself.	"If you try to keep your life for yourself, you will lose it. But *if you give up your life for Me, you will find true life.* And how do you benefit if you gain the whole world but lose your own soul in the process?"[16]
You have a right to satisfy your sexual appetites and passions in whatever way you want. It's nobody's business what you do as long as you are not hurting anyone. Besides, biblical standards for sexual purity are prudish and old-fashioned.	*"Run away from sexual sin!"*[17] "Remain faithful to one another in marriage. God will surely judge people who are immoral and those who commit adultery."[18] "Do not commit adultery."[19]
It's okay to sin a little. Nobody's perfect. Loosen up and have some fun. No one will ever find out what you do. Lighten up. Get a life.	"The time is coming when everything will be revealed; all that is secret will be made public."[20] "Do not be deceived: God cannot be mocked. *A man reaps what he sows.*"[21]

Society's Lie	God's Truth
You have a right to get even. You're a wimp if you let people get away with anything. If someone hurts you, hurt them back. It's an eye for an eye and a tooth for a tooth.	*"Get rid of all bitterness, rage and anger."*[22] "Do not repay anyone evil for evil…Do not take revenge."[23] "Love your enemies. Do good to those who hate you."[24]
Character doesn't matter. If you want to get ahead in life, tell people what they want to hear. Bend the rules to achieve your purposes because the end justifies the means. Ability is more important than conduct.	*"I the LORD search the heart and examine the mind,* to reward a man according to his conduct, according to what his deeds deserve."[25]

the Counselor of Truth, within us as our Guide.

Do your decisions and lifestyle demonstrate that you are listening to God through His Word and His servants? Or are you living in the darkness of the lies of society and popular culture? Like a powerful floodlight, God's truth will expose for us the foolishness and destructiveness of every myth promoted by the world.

How God's Truth Sets Us Free

God's truth frees us to live as God has intended. On the other hand, the Deceiver wants us to base our lives on false assumptions. Jesus said to His followers, "You are truly My disciples if you keep obeying My teachings. And you will know the truth, and the truth will set you free."[26] Here are several ways God's truth sets us free.

We are free from death and eternal damnation.

Jesus said, "I give them eternal life, and they will never perish. No one will snatch them away from me."[27]

Paul wrote to Titus about the certainty of eternal life: "a faith and knowledge resting on the hope of eternal life, which God, who does not lie, promised before the beginning of time."[28] Paul knew that way back in eternity past God had promised salvation for those who believe in Him. That promise became reality in Paul's life, as it will for all of us who accept the message of Jesus' death on the cross for sin. The Book of Hebrews assures us:

> God also bound Himself with an oath, so that those who received the promise could be perfectly sure that He would never change His mind. So God has given us both His promise and His oath. These two things are unchangeable because it is impossible for God to lie.[29]

That is why the hope of eternal life based on God's promises is so firmly anchored for us.

We are set free from bondage to sin and guilt.

Our society has tried to cleanse itself from guilt by removing the Ten Commandments from our public schools, buildings, and courts so that no one will be reminded of breaking them. Those who sin try to rationalize all kinds of wicked behavior by blaming it on their background, circumstances, a parent or spouse. With society saying, "Don't worry, it's not your fault," why are so many guilt-ridden people filling up psychiatrists' couches? Because we are all born in bondage to sin and guilt, and only God can break those bonds. Only He can break the chains of blame shifting, bad habits, and addictions.

Nick Smith, a 17-year-old who participated in Josh McDowell's "Right From Wrong" campaign, understood this principle. By attending the meetings, he prepared himself to make godly decisions. While he was at an out-of-town track meet, he discovered several teammates glued to a less-than-wholesome movie on the HBO channel. He had two choices: to follow the biblical guidelines he had learned about keeping himself pure or to go along with his friends. Nick said, "Y'all shouldn't be watching that. It messes up your mind."[30]

One of the boys agreed with Nick and left the group. Not only did Nick resist the temptation to do something wrong, he also influenced another young man to do the same! If you turn your temptations over to God and trust in His power, He will help you step out of that pile of chains as a free man or woman.

Paul writes in Romans 6:22, "Now that you have been set free from sin and have become slaves to God, the benefit you reap leads to holiness, and the result is eternal life" (NIV). In Jesus we can live freely and joyfully.

We are set free from self-centeredness.

If you want to take a test to see how self-centered you are, note your instinctive reaction the next time you see a photograph showing a group of people including yourself. Whose face do you look at first? Your best friend's or your own? How about when you hear good news about someone close to you? Do you immediately think about how your friend is feeling or wonder why you do not get the "lucky breaks" in life?

You are not alone. We all have a self-centered nature. It's part of the human condition.

Jesus told His disciples, "If any of you wants to be My follower, you must put aside your selfish ambition, shoulder your cross, and follow Me. If you try to keep your life for yourself, you will lose it. But if you give up your life for Me, you will find true life."[31] Only Christ can free us to be more other-centered as we walk in the power of His Spirit. He fills us with His powerful love, which "does not demand its own way. Love is not irritable, and it keeps no record of when it has been wronged."[32]

We are set free from bondage to fear.

Paul informs us, "You did not receive a spirit that makes you a slave again to fear, but you received the Spirit of sonship."[33] Yet many Christians still live in fear. It robs us of joy and limits what we can do for our Lord. But God enables us to live in freedom through the power of His Holy Spirit—if only we will trust and obey Him!

We are set free from a life of mediocrity and insignificance.

God, the creator of over 100 billion galaxies, also created us in His image and has a wonderful plan for our lives.[34] Nothing the world offers can even come close to what God has planned. We will only be significant to whatever degree we are willing to fulfill the plan for which God has created us.

You Can Begin to Live
Freely in God's Truth

Many years ago, a young missionary from Africa came to see me for counsel. He told me that he had little knowledge or experience of the Holy Spirit. He had spent several years on the mission field with no tangible results and felt like a miserable failure.

As we sat together, I explained that his ministry had been fruitless because he did not draw on the power of the Holy Spirit to help him. I further explained how important it is that we confess all known sin to God, turn from our sin, and walk in obedience to Him. Then as we surrender to the Lordship of Christ, we can by faith ask God to fill us with His Holy Spirit.[35] We can claim His promise to fill us knowing that if we ask anything according to His will, He hears us.[36]

In response, the man exploded in anger. He said, "I have spent my life serving God at great sacrifice. I have faced death and all kinds of persecution on the mission field. And now you offer me this simplistic solution to my problem?" He was irate and stormed out of my office.

A few days later he called me for another appointment. He said, "I don't agree with you. I believe that your explanation of the Spirit-filled life is too superficial and simple, but you obviously have a quality in your life that I don't have and I want very badly. I will ask God to show me if what you say is true."

I will never forget a letter I received from him a few weeks later. He wrote out of a joyful heart overflowing with praise and thanksgiving to God. He said, "I now understand what you have been trying to tell me. I did what you told me to do and now I want to return to the mission field and teach other defeated believers what you taught me. I've been liberated. I'm free!"

The choice is ours. Every day we must choose whom we will believe, God or Satan. Those who diligently seek truth in the right places will find only God's truth. Base your life on it because His absolute truth will set you free.

LIFE APPLICATION

WRITE IT ON YOUR HEART—Memorize the following statement and verses, and as you encounter the temptation to lie this week, claim them as promises from our God of truth.

- Because God is absolute truth, I can believe what He says and live accordingly.
- John 18:37—"I came to bring truth to the world. All who love the truth recognize that what I say is true."
- John 8:31,32—"You are truly My disciples if you keep obeying My teachings. And you will know the truth, and the truth will set you free."

COUNT ON GOD—God's Word can always be trusted because He never lies. Is there something that you have difficulty trusting God with in your current situation? Claim a promise from one of the following Scriptures and commit your concerns to God today.

- Romans 8:28—"God causes everything to work together for the good of those who love God and are called according to His purpose for them."
- Philippians 1:6—"I am sure that God, who began the good work within you, will continue His work until it is finally finished on that day when Christ Jesus comes back again."
- 1 John 1:9—"If we confess our sins to him, He is faithful and just to forgive us and to cleanse us from every wrong."

OBEY GOD—Is there something in the last few weeks that you have been untruthful about? First John 1:6 says, "If we claim to have fellowship with Him yet walk in the darkness, we lie and do not live by the truth" (NIV). Confess it to the LORD and tell the truth to the one you misled. Then determine to always speak the truth.

CHAPTER 16

GOD Is RIGHTEOUS

How can there be so many different views about what is right and what is wrong? Why are moral issues no longer seen as black or white but rather as varying shades of gray? Why do the standards of morality constantly change within society?

Today the distinction between right and wrong is becoming increasingly blurred. People passionately defend their sinful actions. What is right has become a matter of interpretation by the individual, the community, or the courts. However, this view is absolutely wrong because it assumes that public opinion and government legislation provide the ultimate criterion for determining what is right. But our sovereign God sets the standards for His creation. His standards do not change; they are timeless. And our American society, like many western nations, was built on the biblical principles of right and wrong.

Our culture understands how important it is to be "right" about certain things. Permit me to give you several examples:

An architect building a hundred-story skyscraper takes immense precautions to have the building's foundation perfectly level.

If the footings are off even a fraction of an inch, there are tremendous consequences. The farther up he builds on an unleveled foundation, the more unstable the skyscraper becomes.

Scientists at Mission Control in Houston also know the importance of being "right" when bringing a spaceship back to Earth. If the angle of re-entry into the Earth's atmosphere is off just a little, the spaceship will encounter too much friction and burn up before it reaches the ground.

Last, consider the speed skater in a race. Two lanes circle the track. The skaters not only race each other, but each skater is also required to stay in his own lane. If one skater crosses the line into the other lane, he is disqualified and loses the race.

Although most people understand the importance of laying the "right" foundation, having the "right" re-entry angle, or staying in the "right" lane, they have problems understanding the "rightness" of moral laws. When it comes to stealing, for example, most people divide stealing into categories like "borrowing," petty theft, robbery, and embezzlement. They feel that some categories are okay, such as taking a few supplies from their employer or school, or keeping the excess when a cashier gives them too much change. But to them it would be wrong to break into someone's home or rob a bank. Moral laws, they believe, are not as rigid as other laws. Therefore, we can bend them a little without incurring any penalty. But that is contrary to how God sees His righteous laws.

God Is Always Right

It is easy to understand God's righteous role as Creator. Everything He created functions according to the laws applying to its creation. All His natural laws perform the way He intends for the good of His creation. Look at the way a coastal marsh works. Each day, tides bring fresh nutrients for the millions of tiny plants that grow in the soil and water. At high tide, all kinds of shellfish dine on these tiny plants. Fish such as spotted sea trout spawn in the calm water and the tiny hatchlings feed in their own little marshy nursery. Ducks and other birds build nests to raise their young. A stew of vegetation provides a smorgasbord for the ducklings and gos-lings. Natural laws and processes work together as a system to benefit all of God's creation.

It is easy to recognize how God created nature in its right order. But it is far less common to understand that God has created the moral realm to function in its right order, too.

In fact, as humans we often purposefully overlook one wrong to right another. In recent years, juries have declared a defendant "not guilty" of a crime despite evidence that clearly convicts him. Through their actions, jury members hope to make a statement about some other moral wrong connected with the crime. Many experts believe the jury in the O. J. Simpson murder trial did this to right the wrong of minorities often not getting equal justice in the court system. But ignoring one wrong to address another wrong will not make things right. We just end up with two wrongs —and no right.

As humans, we sometimes fail to do what is right in our daily lives. Have you ever said to yourself, "I know the right thing to do, but if I do what is right, I will mess up my situation"? Perhaps you are in a college class when someone advocates an immoral viewpoint. You do not challenge the speaker's opinion because you do not want to be viewed as a moral extremist. Standing up for what is morally right might cause you to be ridiculed, lose friends, receive a lower grade from the professor, or lose your job. As fall-en human beings, we have a hard time even understanding per-fect righteousness much less living righteous lives.

Only God is righteous because He is holy. He has never acted unrighteously; never had an evil thought; never rationalized a questionable act to make something else right.

What Is Righteousness?

We learned previously that God is holy. But His holiness and His righteousness are not the same. Holiness is "a condition of purity or freedom from sin."[1] God's righteousness is "the quality or at-tribute of God by virtue of which He does that which is right or in accordance with His own nature, will, and law."[2]

In other words, holiness describes God's nature; righteousness describes how God acts according to His holiness. God's laws are holy because they come from His nature. God's standards for enforcing His laws are always righteous.

Let me give an example of one law. God says, "Do not commit adultery." That simple statement arises out of God's holiness. He can never be disloyal when He has made a commitment; it is against His nature. In the Old Testament, God made covenants or promises to His people. He made a covenant with Noah that He would never again destroy the earth with a flood. The rainbow in the sky is the evidence of His covenant. Over the many centuries since the flood, God has acted rightly regarding this covenant. That follow-through with His holy covenant shows His righteousness.

> HOLINESS DESCRIBES GOD'S NATURE; RIGHTEOUSNESS DESCRIBES HOW GOD ACTS.

In the same way, when we stand before a minister and promise to love our spouse and be faithful to him or her the rest of our lives, we are making a covenant that reflects God's holiness. We act righteously when we keep that commitment or covenant.

But do not imagine that righteousness is reaching a standard like climbing a ladder to a higher level. That is what most people think when they consider righteous acts. "If I tell the truth more times than I tell lies, I'll be more righteous." "If I make up for the money I stole from my employer, then I'll be okay." No one can work up to righteousness because it begins as purity. It comes out of holiness; it does not reach up to holiness.

Holiness sets the standard. Righteousness is the result of a relationship that fulfills that standard.

GOD IS THE SOURCE OF ALL RIGHTEOUSNESS

How righteous is God? Everything God does is perfectly right in every way. David tells us, "The LORD is righteous in all His ways and loving toward all He has made."[3] For God, righteousness is not an external standard that He must adhere to; righteousness is part of His very nature. It emanates from His inner being. As a result, whatever God wills is perfectly right. It is impossible for God to do anything wrong.

All righteousness within the entire universe has its origin in Him. The psalmist exclaims, "Your righteousness reaches to the skies, O God, You who have done great things. Who, O God, is like You?"[4] Every action God has ever taken or will take is righteous. As a judge, He has never made a wrong determination. He has never had to reverse a decision when He learned more facts. No one can question His judgment in all His actions.

Heaven is filled with God's righteousness. "Righteousness and justice are the foundation of His throne."[5] Because God is righteous, He wants righteousness to fill His universe.

GOD AS RIGHTEOUS JUDGE

When you walk into a courtroom and face the judge, you may wonder, "Who gave this judge the power to decide between right and wrong? Who gave the judge the moral and legal authority to pronounce what is righteous behavior and what is grievous misbehavior deserving punishment?"

Whether judges are elected directly by the people or appointed by the politicians we elect, they ultimately owe their authority and legal power to us, the people. These judges are subject to human passions, can misuse their authority, and be removed. A New England judge was recently removed after a grand jury indicted him for forcing young men to have sex with him in his private chambers—in return for dismissing their cases. An Illinois judge was removed for "fixing" speeding tickets in return for illegal bribes.

But when we discuss the righteousness of God, we are not talking about an appointed judge, prone to weaknesses. An infinite and powerful God does not need anyone to elect or appoint Him, to give Him righteousness. He was righteous before the beginning of time and always will be.

God told Jeremiah, "I am the LORD, who exercises kindness,

justice and righteousness on earth, for in these I delight."[6] He is the standard by which every evaluation of righteousness must be compared. If God were not inherently holy and just, He could not act righteously.

GOD'S LAWS DEFINE RIGHTEOUS BEHAVIOR

The *Dred Scott v. Sanford* Supreme Court case in 1856 shows how little righteousness we really have as humans. The case began when Henry Blow filed a suit trying to free a slave, Dred Scott, who worked for him. The problem, however, was that Henry did not own Mr. Scott. A Mrs. Emerson did. Although she lived in New York and Dred Scott lived in Missouri, she would not give him his freedom.

The case wound its way from the lower courts to the Supreme Court. By the time the Supreme Court Justices heard the case, the abolition movement in the U.S. had grown strong. Abolitionists wanted slavery outlawed in new territories and states like Missouri. Southern slave owners were desperate to keep their right to own slaves because of their labor-intensive farms. To complicate the case, Dred Scott had lived for a time in free Wisconsin territory. Because of that fact, Blow argued, Scott should be a free man.

The Supreme Court could not make up its mind. It heard oral arguments twice, then the Justices recessed for two months. They were so divided on the issue that they did not even meet during that time. Finally, each Justice wrote his own opinion. Seven of them ruled that Dred Scott was still a slave, while two ruled that he was free. Since the Supreme Court ruled that slavery could not be prohibited in new territories, only a constitutional amendment could outlaw the expansion of slavery. This decision was one of the principal causes of the Civil War.[7] Years later, The Supreme Court reversed its decision on slavery.

Throughout history, human judges have had a hard time determining right from wrong. Just like us, they are caught up in the culture, swayed by their own personalities, and limited to the evidence presented in court, which may not accurately portray the truth.

A more recent miscarriage of justice was the *Roe v. Wade* case in which the Supreme Court ruled that abortion is legal. Lawful killing of preborn babies is certainly not righteous. Yet the Court approved of this travesty. I am praying that, like its reversal on the slavery issue, the Supreme Count will reverse its decision in *Roe v. Wade* that legalized abortion on demand.

God does not struggle with right and wrong. The psalmist declares, "Righteous are You, O LORD, and Your laws are right."[8] His laws reflect His own righteous nature and the moral perfection of His character. Cultural bias, a lack of knowledge, or any other factor does not alter His rulings.

God's spiritual laws are every bit as absolute as His physical laws. If we break God's natural laws, we pay the consequences. For example, if you jump off of the Empire State Building in New York City, the law of gravity will guarantee your death. Likewise, if you lock yourself in a garage and breathe carbon monoxide instead of the oxygen that your body needs, you will die.

> GOD'S SPIRITUAL LAWS ARE THE PILLARS FOR JUSTICE AND MORALITY IN ANY NATION.

God's spiritual laws are no less binding. As the perfect Judge and Lawgiver, God is also the law enforcer. His laws lay out the responsibilities for which God holds us accountable. They are a yardstick by which God measures our righteousness. When His laws are broken, He must punish anyone who defies His righteous laws.

You may wonder why God is so exacting about His spiritual laws. He did not make rules just for the "fun of it." His righteous laws focus on standards for acting rightly toward one another.

Consequently, God's spiritual laws are the pillars for justice and morality within any nation. To restate this fact, the laws of a nation are just only to the degree that they conform to the laws of God. When national leaders reject and disobey God, they cut their nation loose from the anchor of morality, and set it adrift in an ocean of moral relativity. Without God they lose their moral compass and doom their society to injustice, dishonesty, and depravity. In our next chapter, we will see how important righteous laws are to our nation.

WE CANNOT MEET GOD'S RIGHTEOUS STANDARD

Ever since Adam and Eve first disobeyed God, every person has been born with a sinful nature that insists on exerting self-will, even against the Creator. Isaiah describes our dilemma, "How can people like us be saved? We are all infected and impure with sin. When we proudly display our righteous deeds, we find they are but filthy rags. Like autumn leaves, we wither and fall. And our sins, like the wind, sweep us away."[9]

Imagine a contest between an Olympic gold medal winner and me to see who can jump across the Grand Canyon, which is miles wide and deep. Who do you think would win that match? While I am sure the Olympian would jump far beyond me, he would still fall short of the other side. We would both plummet to our deaths.

That is similar to our attempts to be righteous. Even when we try our very hardest, we still fall far short of God's perfect standard. Because of our sinful nature, it is impossible for us to live the righteous life God demands. As we read earlier, if we are ever to be acceptable to God, He has to intervene on our behalf.

FAITH IS THE KEY TO RIGHTEOUSNESS

We can be righteous only when God's righteousness is imputed, or freely given to us as we place our faith in God's only Son, Jesus Christ. Abraham was an Old Testament illustration of this truth, which was not fully revealed until Jesus came some 2,000 years later. Genesis 15:6 explains, "[Abraham] believed the LORD, and He credited it to him as righteousness" (NIV). This "righteousness" is sometimes referred to as "right standing" with God; in other words, God considers us right with Him. Abraham came into right standing with God because Abraham believed Him!

Since God's standards for morality and virtue are 100 percent perfect and we are imperfect and inadequate, we can only be righteous as a gift from God. Through our faith in His Son, He "credits" His own righteousness to our account.

In the New Testament, Paul referred to this passage about Abraham and then gave us the wonderful news that "the words 'it was credited to him' were written not for him alone, but also for us, to whom God will credit righteousness—for us who believe in Him who raised Jesus our Lord from the dead."[10] This is one of the most wonderful truths in the universe: God declares us righteous by faith, and sees us as having the righteousness of His own Son! This is grace, or unmerited favor—a free gift purchased for us by our Lord Jesus Christ through His death on the cross.

What is our worshipful response to the knowledge that God gives us righteousness because of His Son? The Bible contains many examples of prayers that we can offer up to God. One such prayer was written by Paul and is found in 1 Thessalonians: "Now may the God of peace make you holy in every way, and may your whole spirit and soul and body be kept blameless until that day when our Lord Jesus Christ comes again. God, who calls you, is faithful; He will do this."[11]

Make this prayer the cry of your heart. God will respond by touching your heart, spirit, soul, and body. We can be assured that He will answer this prayer and make us righteous in His sight.

LIFE APPLICATION

EXALT YOUR GOD—Worship our righteous God with the words of Psalm 119:137–144:

> O Lord, You are righteous, and Your decisions are fair. Your decrees are perfect; they are entirely worthy of our trust.
>
> I am overwhelmed with rage, for my enemies have disregarded your words. Your promises have been thoroughly tested; that is why I love them so much.
>
> I am insignificant and despised, but I don't forget Your commandments. Your justice is eternal, and Your law is perfectly true. As pressure and stress bear down on me, I find joy in Your commands.
>
> Your decrees are always fair; help me to understand them, that I may live.

REFLECT HIS IMAGE—We are called to be righteous, but we cannot do this in our own strength. Ask your heavenly Father to reveal areas of unrighteousness in your heart and life. Then repent and confess them to Him. Ask the Holy Spirit to empower you to live righteously in those areas you are most tempted to disobey God.

SHARE HIS MAJESTY—One of the ways we can testify of God's righteousness is by displaying our faith in Him. When you are with your friends, relatives, or neighbors who do not know Christ as Savior, relate your experiences with faith-building answers to prayer and share the gospel message of love and forgiveness. As people see your faith in a God who is trustworthy, many will want to live a righteous life as a child of God.

GOD HELPS US LIVE RIGHTEOUSLY

We live in a world where many believe that the end justifies the means. They say it is acceptable to compromise God's standards to get ahead. But the fact is we always lose when we violate God's standards of righteousness. On the other hand, it is not always easy to do what is right.

I think of a situation in which we found ourselves as a ministry when we moved our headquarters from San Bernardino, California, to Orlando, Florida. We had been unable to lease or sell some of our property in San Bernardino. The buildings remained empty, yet every month we still had to make our mortgage payments.

I was counseled by some successful Christian businessmen to default the payments and allow the bank to repossess the property. After all, many businesses had done this during the economic downturn. Financially, we would be far better off, but that would be wrong since we had signed a contract with the bank. We purposed to trust God to help us pay the bills and sell the property in a way that would bring honor and glory to Him. Some would say, "Boy that's stupid." But we had given our word. Five years passed before we finally sold the property.

Although making those payments was a financial hardship, God has greatly blessed the ministry of Campus Crusade. Contributions have dramatically increased year after year. I believe God has blessed us because we run Campus Crusade for Christ in His way. We depend on Him to help us pay our bills.

As Dr. Bob Jones, Sr., once said, "It is never right to do wrong in order to get a chance to do right." In other words, if we had defaulted on our agreement, we could have saved a lot of money every year. Think of all that the ministry could have done with that money—but we would have violated our word and our contract. That would not have honored God. Living righteously means making sacrifices and saying no to desires. We cannot live this way in our own strength.

Let us look at a few action points that will help us do what is right no matter what.

DEPEND ON GOD'S RIGHTEOUSNESS RATHER THAN OUR EFFORTS

We are so fortunate that "the LORD is gracious and righteous; our God is full of compassion."[1] Otherwise we would be doomed by our lack of righteousness. Our righteousness does not depend on what we do, but on whom we place our faith. Paul explains:

> We are made right in God's sight when we trust in Jesus Christ to take away our sins. And we all can be saved in this same way, no matter who we are or what we have done. For all have sinned; all fall short of God's glorious standard. Yet now God in His gracious kindness declares us not guilty. He has done this through Christ Jesus, who has freed us by taking away our sins. For God sent Jesus to take the punishment for our sins and to satisfy God's anger against us. We are made right with God when we believe that Jesus shed His blood, sacrificing His life for us."[2]

There was not anything we could do to earn this gift of grace. We accepted it by faith. Now God no longer sees our sinfulness, but only the righteousness of Christ which covers us.

When we put our faith in Christ, we received a new nature—one of holiness and righteousness. Christ wants us to display His righteousness in our new life. We are commanded: "Throw off your old evil nature and your former way of life, which is rotten through and through, full of lust and deception. Instead, there must be a spiritual renewal of your thoughts and attitudes. You must display a new nature because you are a new person, created in God's likeness—righteous, holy, and true."[3]

Yet we are all tempted to achieve righteousness under our own power. That never works. We cannot live righteously without the enabling of the Holy Spirit, and His power is released through our faith. For example, if a person has a problem with swearing, he could try his hardest to quit using foul language. For the most part, he would be able to control his tongue, but when someone cuts him off on the freeway or breaks in front of him in a line, his mouth curses before he even realizes what he is saying. All his efforts to control this reaction come to nothing.

> WE CANNOT LIVE RIGHTEOUSLY WITHOUT THE ENABLING OF THE HOLY SPIRIT.

The secret to changing bad habits like cursing is to turn the problem over to God. By faith, admit that you are helpless to change your bad habit. By faith ask His Spirit to give you righteous language to replace the filthy language. As you walk in the Spirit moment by moment, your heart is prepared to act righteously the next time someone angers you. When this happens, take a deep breath and start praising God for something good in the situation. Trust God to take over and work out the problem. This will make the difference in your reaction and the results of the problem.

SEEK GOD FIRST AND TURN AWAY FROM WORLDLY ATTACHMENTS

The only way we can live a life of faith is by submitting our will to the Holy Spirit moment by moment and depending on Him to empower us. When doing this, Jesus instructs us to "seek first His kingdom and His righteousness."[4] As a result, we will enjoy the rewards of righteous living and agree with David, "Surely, O LORD, You bless the righteous; You surround them with Your favor as with a shield."[5]

A friend of mine lived in a palatial home in El Paso, Texas. He was a very successful manufacturer who had accumulated considerable wealth. Following his retirement he ministered weekly to the poor people across the border in Juarez, Mexico.

However, one woman greatly ministered to him. She lived in a little hut with a dirt floor. Her earthly possessions were a small stove, a pot, a pan, a plate, a knife, fork and spoon, and one change of clothes. Every time she saw him she would tell him, "God is so good to me, He is so wonderful and faithful to me." This successful businessman loved God, but this godly woman was far happier than he was. Through her, he discovered that joy and fulfillment are not found in material possessions, but in a relationship with God and in obedience to His commands.

Seeking God first will lead to a new perspective on life. Old, worldly attachments will seem insignificant and God's blessings will be apparent in righteous living. I challenge you to rearrange your priorities, schedule, and finances to put God first and follow His "right" plan for your life.

ADJUST YOUR LIFE TO GOD'S STANDARDS

Some years ago, a Christian man from a Middle Eastern nation attended a Campus Crusade conference in another country. While there, he felt God calling him to join our staff. That decision meant much more sacrifice to him than it does to someone who joins our staff in the United States. Because of Muslim persecution in his country, his decision to follow the Lord in ministry could result in harm to him and even death—and the same consequences for his family. But he felt sure that God wanted him to tell his countrymen about the love of God as revealed through Jesus Christ our Lord.

After the conference ended, he went home and told his wife what God was leading him to do. Her reaction was amazing. She said, "If God wants you to join Campus Crusade for Christ, then I agree with your decision. I am willing to follow your decision."

She realized the ramifications that this change meant for her and her family. In fact, today she and her husband are exiles from their homeland because of their witness for Christ. But she adjusted her plans to fit into God's plans for their lives—and she and her husband saw tremendous fruit in their country before their exile. God continues to use them mightily in their new assignment.

We have discussed confessing sin when our lives take a turn from God's perfect standard, but God wants us to do more than that. Henry Blackaby and Claude King explain in their book *Experiencing God*, "God wants you to have no hindrances to a love relationship with Him in your life. Once God has spoken to you through His Word, how you respond is crucial. You must adjust your life to the truth."[6]

This means adjusting your life in areas in which you have been disobeying Him. If you are not sharing your faith, you begin witnessing to others. If you read questionable—even pornographic —books or magazines, or watch such videos, get rid of the objectionable materials at once. Start spending more time reading God's Word or other materials that edify your spirit, instead. If you are not spending enough time with your family, readjust your schedule.

Adjusting your standards also may mean making changes in your life that fit God's leading. If God directs you to change careers, you take the necessary steps to do what He asks. If you feel the Holy Spirit guiding you to help with the preschoolers in Sunday school, you willingly give up that Sunday morning class that you enjoy. If a need arises for someone to work with boys at church one night a week, you must stop working late that night. If He leads you to share His good news in other countries and cultures, you must step out in faith and respond. Knowing God's truth and holiness always leads to righteous action. But the rewards, friends, for you and those you serve are exciting and fulfilling.

BE AN ADVOCATE FOR RIGHTEOUSNESS
WHERE YOU LIVE

As disciples of Jesus Christ we are to live righteous lives. But how does righteousness impact the course of a nation? The Bible declares, "Righteousness exalts a nation, but sin is a disgrace to any people."[7]

In the Book of Deuteronomy, God promised to bless the nation of Israel for obedience, but He also warned of judgment upon His people if His laws were disregarded. Second Chronicles 7:14 gives this wonderful promise: "If My people who are called by My name will humble themselves and pray and seek My face and turn from their wicked ways, I will hear from heaven and will forgive their sins and heal their land."

America has a unique heritage—one rooted in a dependence on God and His biblical principles. The scriptural principles for a godly nation were well understood by the Pilgrims. Their purpose, as stated in the Mayflower Compact, was to plant colonies "for the glory of God, and advancement of the Christian faith."[8] Ninety-nine percent of the colonial population professed to be Christians and most of our founding fathers were true followers of our Lord Jesus Christ. Early in the 19th century, the French philosopher and historian Alexis de Tocqueville did a study of democracy in our country and came to this conclusion:

> I sought for the greatness and genius of America in her commodious harbors and her ample rivers, and it was not there. I sought for the greatness and genius of America in her fertile fields and boundless forests, and it was not there. I sought for the greatness and genius of America in her rich mines and her vast world commerce, and it was not there. I sought for the greatness and genius of America in her public school system and her institutions of learning, and it was not there. Not until I went to the churches of America and heard her pulpits aflame with righteousness did I understand the secret of her genius and power. America is great because America is good, and if America ever ceases to be good, America will cease to be great.[9]

For many decades after our country's founding, American leaders advocated God's righteousness in government.

- George Washington said, "It is impossible to rightly govern the world without God and the Bible."[10]

- John Adams, the second president and co-drafter of the Declaration of Independence said, "Our Constitution was made only for a moral and religious people, it is wholly inadequate to the government of any other."[11]

- Noah Webster believed, "The Christian religion is the most important and one of the first things in which all children, under a free government, ought to be instructed."[12]

- Nearly all of the first 119 colleges and universities of our nation, including Harvard, Yale, Princeton, Dartmouth, William and Mary, and Columbia, were founded primarily to train young scholars in the knowledge of God and the Bible.

- Abraham Lincoln said, "But for the Bible we would not know right from wrong."[13]

- The first U.S. Supreme Court Chief Justice John Jay said, "Providence has given to our people the choice of their rulers, and it is the duty, as well as the privilege and interest of our Christian nation to select and prefer Christians for their rulers."[14]

- In 1892, the U.S. Supreme Court made the following ruling, "No purpose of action against religion can be imputed to any legislation, state or national, because this is a religious people …This is a Christian nation."[15] That court ruling cited 87 different historical precedents.

Then at the turn of the 20th century, a bloodless revolution began to change our nation. Unrighteous philosophies such as relativism and evolution spread throughout mainstream America. Without a single previous precedent, the Supreme Count in 1947 declared the separation of Church and State. This action was widely interpreted as separation of godly principles from public life. In 1962 and 1963, the Supreme Court declared school prayer to be unconstitutional and the Bible was outlawed from our schools.

Within a decade, the Supreme Court made it lawful to kill our unborn children yet unlawful to display the Ten Commandments in public schools. As a result, God's righteous foundation in America is systematically being destroyed. As the foundation crumbles, so does the nation. It is obvious from every social indicator that the secular and humanistic system has failed.

As believers, we dare not continue to be silent. For many years, I have had a deep burden for our country's moral condition. I firmly believe that if Christians will stand firm on the righteous standards of God's law, we can turn our country back to its godly heritage. We must hold fast to the righteous standards set forth by the sovereign Creator and Ruler of the universe in our own lives and be advocates for His standards in our culture.

GOD'S RIGHTEOUS FOUNDATION IN AMERICA IS SYSTEMATICALLY BEING DESTROYED.

I have seen exciting gains in advocating God's righteousness through the fasting and prayer movement sweeping our country. In Houston, Texas, people joined together from November 22, 1996, to January 1, 1997, every day and evening for intercession, evangelistic messages, corporate repentance, racial reconciliation, and praise and worship. They renamed the large outdoor amphitheater in which they met "Prayer Mountain." Throughout the forty days, worship was held in Spanish, Korean, Chinese, Japanese, Indonesian, English, and other languages. Messianic Jewish pastors publicly embraced Arab ministers; Chinese and Japanese leaders prayed for one another; walls between people fell as they worshipped the Lord in unity. People streamed to the altar every night, eager to get right with God.

The fasting and prayer effort resulted in righteous action. Five thousand needy families received groceries, clothes, blankets, food, and toys. Lives were changed in miraculous ways. "I was involved in gangs," a 19-year-old man explained, "and two months ago was released from prison. A friend of mine invited me to come to Prayer Mountain tonight. Jesus saved me."

On January 1, Houston symbolically passed the baton to Dallas. On January 3, Dallas believers began forty days of fasting and prayer for their city. In February, believers in both Kansas City, Missouri, and Pasadena, California, started their forty days of city-wide fasting and prayer. Katy, Texas, located just outside Houston, also got involved in the fasting and prayer movement. The "domino effect" of one city's example produced amazing results![16]

Regardless of the beliefs and behavior of a nation, ultimately God will hold every person accountable. Whose standards of "right" will you follow? God's or man's? What we do in our personal lives and how we serve as an advocate of God's righteousness to our neighborhoods, cities, states, and country will help change the world for Christ.

Every day I review and meditate on the Ten Commandments. I urge you to keep the Ten Commandments clearly in mind by writing them on a card and displaying them in your car, on your refrigerator, or at your desk.

In the following Life Application, you will find ways you can be an advocate for righteousness. I urge you to begin right now through prayer and witnessing to help others know and apply the righteous standards of our loving God.

LIFE APPLICATION

WRITE IT ON YOUR HEART—Commit the following statement and verses to memory. Then when you are tempted to compromise God's righteous standards this week, claim them as promises from our God of righteousness.

- Because God is righteous, I can live by His standards.
- Psalm 145:17 (NIV)—"The LORD is righteous in all His ways and loving toward all He has made."
- 1 Peter 3:12 (NIV)—"The eyes of the Lord are on the righteous and His ears are attentive to their prayer."
- 1 John 3:7 (NIV)—"Dear children, do not let anyone lead you astray. He who does what is right is righteous, just as He is righteous."

COUNT ON GOD—Because God is righteous, He will never do wrong. How simple and wise to place your trust in Someone who cannot wrong you. So far, we have studied a number of God's attributes. Which one is the most difficult for you to understand or accept? This week, ask God to give you assurance that He uses all His attributes righteously for our good.

OBEY GOD—Our world today often calls right wrong and wrong right. We honor the immoral and ridicule the upright. Even the most "moral" programs on mass media today advocate immoral solutions to problems: living together before marriage to see if you are compatible partners; using violence to resolve disputes; using foul language to look "cool." As you watch television, listen to the radio, or read secular books and magazines, compare the ideas you encounter with standards in God's Word. Ask God to help you separate the unrighteous morals of our culture and exchange them for God's righteous rules.

CHAPTER 18

GOD
Is
JUST

D o you ever wonder what happened to justice? Why is it becoming increasingly elusive? What has gone wrong with the manmade judicial system?

In one of the worst travesties in American justice, four young men from Chicago with no history of violence were convicted of kidnapping, rape, and double murder. The bullet-riddled bodies of a young couple were found on May 12, 1978. Acting on an anonymous telephone tip, the police arrested Dennis Williams, Verneal Jimerson, Kenny Adams, and Willie Rainge. News reports declared that the crime had been solved. The men were soon convicted, and two were sentenced to death row. Appeals failed; all looked hopeless.

In September 1981, a tattered envelope with a return address of the "Condemned Unit," Menard, Illinois, arrived at the offices of the *Chicago Lawyer* magazine. That letter led Rob Warden, editor and publisher of the *Chicago Lawyer*, and Dennis Protess, professor at Northwestern Medill School of Journalism, to investigate the case. They uncovered substantial evidence that exonerated the four convicts, including the first use of DNA to prove that multiple defendants were excluded as suspects in a rape case.

On July 2, 1996, more than eighteen years after the murders took place, Judge Thomas Fitzgerald ended the defendants' fight against an unjust sentence by reading, "All the convictions are vacated."[1] The four prisoners were free! The next day, the state attorney's office charged the real killers, Ira Johnson, Arthur Robinson, and Juan Rodriguez.

Justice is a pillar of any society. It vindicates the innocent and punishes the guilty. All too often though, this standard is compromised for personal gain. Corrupt judges sometimes tilt the scales of justice; unscrupulous lawyers manipulate laws and juries; witnesses lie. Truth is often distorted to benefit the rich, famous, and powerful.

Today, people are becoming less concerned about doing what is right. Instead they look for ways to cover their tracks, believing they will never get caught. If their transgression is discovered, they assume they will never be convicted. If they are found guilty, they can always appeal. If the appeal is denied, they will likely serve only a fraction of their sentence anyway.

Since our justice system can often be manipulated, many people mistakenly believe they can manipulate God's system of justice. They think that their excuses and alibis fool God. But oh how wrong they are! God told Jeremiah, "I the LORD search the heart and examine the mind, to reward a man according to his conduct, according to what his deeds deserve."[2] You can always count on God being just. He will always act according to what is morally upright or good.

GOD IS A PERFECT JUDGE

The Supreme Court is the highest court in our country. If we could expect justice anywhere, it should be when a case comes before these esteemed justices. Yet they are just human. Their caseload is so overwhelming that the solicitor general of the Justice Department chooses from thousands of potential cases to be brought before the court. The Supreme Court Justices are ten times more likely to hear a case if the solicitor general files it.

The staff of the solicitor general has mushroomed in recent years. They file briefs and make appearances in about 150 to 175 cases a year. But think of how many petitions are denied! There is so much paperwork in the Supreme Court system that detailed rules are applied to the way documents are filed, from the precise wording that must appear on the cover to the length of the brief.[3]

With all these constraints, most cases do not make it to the bench. Perfect justice is therefore not being rendered. It is humanly impossible.

But God does not need a brief to examine a case. He does not run out of time to consider the evidence. No research or investigation is needed in His court—He already knows it all. He knows the motives, thoughts, actions, and purpose for everything done. Our only option is to confess before a holy, omniscient, omnipresent, omnipotent, just God.

Justice is not an external system to which God tries to adhere. He did not have to go to law school to learn how to apply the law. His justice comes out of His inner being and is based on His holiness, truthfulness, and righteousness. Moses observed, "Everything He does is just and fair. He is a faithful God who does no wrong; how just and upright He is!"[4] God cannot be bribed or corrupted because His judgments are grounded in integrity. Because He has all the facts at His disposal, He cannot be fooled. His decisions are always based upon absolute truth. And when God pronounces judgment, He has the power to carry out the punishment.

God's standard is the benchmark by which all human behavior is measured. God "always acts in a way consistent with the requirements of His character as revealed in His law. He rules His creation with honesty. He keeps His word. He renders to all His creatures their due."[5]

God's attributes assure us of justice. If He were not all-knowing, how could He know whether we sinned wittingly or manipulated the facts to serve our purposes? If He were not present everywhere at once, how could He know all the circumstances surrounding the issue before Him? If He were not all-wise, how could He carry out the judgment in a totally just way?

When Abraham learned that God planned to destroy Sodom and Gomorrah, Abraham argued that God could not destroy the righteous with the unrighteous. He pleads his case by saying: "Far be it from You to do such a thing—to kill the righteous with the wicked, treating the righteous and the wicked alike. Far be it from You! Will not the Judge of all the earth do right?"[6] In the New Testament, James writes, "There is only one Lawgiver and Judge, the one who is able to save and destroy."[7] To get a clearer picture of God's role as Perfect Judge, let us look at a few characteristics of an effective judge.

A judge must have authority.

Our government endows judges with authority through the oath they take to execute justice. The law enforcement and prison systems back up the judge's authority. The robe that he wears and having everyone in the courtroom stand as he enters help to emphasize that authority. His gavel and his elevated seat in the courtroom show that he commands the proceedings.

> "WILL NOT THE JUDGE OF ALL THE EARTH DO RIGHT?"
>
> GENESIS 18:25

We learned that God, as Creator, has the authority to do whatever He deems best with His creation. He is the potter; we are the clay. His throne is high above us in the heavens. His pronouncements are final. There is no higher authority than God.

God will judge every wrong act ever committed, every sinful motive, every evil word. The sentence for these crimes is eternal separation from God and His holiness.

But there are those who will live in safety with God. These are the ones who have accepted Christ's payment for our sin when He died on the cross. Our loving Savior, Jesus Christ, paid the sentence pronounced by the Perfect Judge. God sees these "sinners saved by grace" as righteous in His courtroom. Therefore, they will live eternally in the love, peace, and joy of God's presence.

A judge must have the power to execute his authority.

Can you imagine what would happen if judges had no authority to carry out sentences? Our prisons would be empty. No criminals would be deterred for fear of what the courts would do. Murderers, rapists, robbers, and child molesters could walk the streets terrorizing law-abiding citizens.

Since God is omnipotent, whatever He decides to do, He can carry out. He does not have to ask anyone's permission; He does not need a police force to back Him up. In His courtroom, His authority is the last word. No one can appeal His decisions. That is why He is pictured in heaven on a throne. As Sovereign of the universe, His authority is total and complete.

A judge must understand and know the law.

Many times, a higher court will throw out the ruling of a judge in a lower court. Why does this happen? Sometimes it is because the judge in the lower court, such as a municipal court, did not have the authority to apply the overarching laws of the state. The defendant can appeal his case to the State Supreme Court, which has greater power and can overturn the verdict.

God also follows laws—which He established. We find them in His Word as commands and rules. There is no higher law than God's laws. Not only is He the judge, He is also the lawmaker. Since God's laws are perfect, His justice is also without flaw.

A judge needs high moral qualities to judge fairly.

Without high morals, a judge will fail miserably. Our court system would fall apart, for our trials are only as good as the judges who preside over them. Judge Robert Bork tells the story of Judge Martin Manton, a Court of Appeals judge who was almost nominated to the U.S. Supreme Court:

> When it became known that Manton took bribes from parties appearing before him, he claimed innocence on the interesting ground that he took bribes from both sides, decided the case on its merits, and then returned the money to the losing party. That defense caused Judge Learned Hand,

perhaps the most distinguished court of appeals judge in our history, to call Manton a moral moron.[8]

Would you like to bring your case before a judge like Manton? Corrupt judges lead to injustice and unfairness. Victims do not receive proper consideration. The wronged are helpless; the wicked hold the power. If the judge is not truthful, honest, and wise in presiding over the courtroom, justice cannot be served.

A JUST GOD HATES SIN

As the holy and righteous sovereign of the universe, God cannot ignore or overlook any act of sin. David writes, "God is a judge who is perfectly fair. He is angry with the wicked every day."[9]

God's anger over sin should never be underestimated: "You spread out our sins before You—our secret sins—and You see them all. We live our lives beneath Your wrath…Who can comprehend the power of Your anger? Your wrath is as awesome as the fear You deserve."[10]

I urge you to live in reverential fear of God, continually searching God's Word and examining your heart for sins that you need to confess to Him. One of the greatest truths I have discovered in over 50 years of walking with the Lord is a concept called *Spiritual Breathing*. This process is similar to physical breathing. As we become aware of our sins, we exhale by confessing our sin.[11] Then we inhale to appropriate the power of the Holy Spirit, based on God's command to be filled with the Spirit.[12] We can know that God will fill, enable, and equip us because He promised to hear and answer our prayers in accordance with His perfect will.[13] This spiritual principle has allowed me to walk in fellowship with God and help others come to know and serve Him. This is the privilege of every believer.

GOD WILL EVENTUALLY PUNISH ALL SIN

The Bible tells us, "God will bring every deed into judgment, including every hidden thing, whether it is good or evil."[14] Yet, I am sure there have been times when you have asked, "Why are the wicked so prosperous? Why are evil people so happy?"[15] There may be several reasons why someone appears to be getting away with wrongdoing without being punished.

- God delays His judgment because He patiently provides an opportunity for repentance. But while God is waiting for repentance, the severity of future punishment is mounting.
- Sometimes we do not recognize God's judgment because it occurs in a way that we did not expect. Paul explains, "Do not be deceived: God cannot be mocked. A man reaps what he sows."[16] The more seeds of sin a person sows, the more harm will be caused. Sin is like an addictive poison. If you drink a little poison you may only get sick. But if you keep on drinking poison, it will eventually kill you.

The final judgment will occur at the end of time. Are you spiritually ready for that day of judgment? We will look at what is going to happen during that awesome time later in this chapter.

GOD BUILT NATURAL CONSEQUENCES INTO SIN

God does not wait until judgment day to settle sin accounts. He also built natural consequences into sin as a deterrent for our disobedient behavior.

I am reminded of a friend who was one of the most remarkable preachers and pulpit personalities I know. He was a pastor of a thriving church. Then one day, a prostitute came to his office seeking his counsel. He felt sorry for her and asked his wife if this prostitute could live in their home so they could rehabilitate her.

After living with them for three weeks, the prostitute told his wife that she wanted her husband. The wife just laughed in disbelief. They had a happy home and several children. He was one of the pillars in the Christian community. Yet to everyone's shock, he eventually left his family to live with this prostitute.

Many people from the Christian community pleaded with him to repent from his sinful lifestyle, but he persisted. This former pastor had several illegitimate children, and in time the prostitute deserted him for another man.

Finally, this former pastor did come back to the Lord, but he had been brought so low that despite his giftedness he could not hold a job. The last time I saw him, he was a haggard man weeping over his illegitimate children, wishing they would come to know the Lord. Finally, he went to his grave prematurely—a broken man, his life in shambles, and his family devastated.

We cannot thumb our noses at God's righteous principles and not expect to experience the just consequences of our actions. A reverential fear of God will help us avoid doing anything to hinder our relationship with Him. I live daily in reverential fear of God because when we disobey Him, we open the door to greater temptations. Sin grows until it totally engulfs us in destruction.

> WHEN WE DISOBEY GOD, WE OPEN THE DOOR TO GREATER TEMPTATIONS.

GOD WILL EXERCISE THE FINAL JUDGMENT

We need mention only two of God's judgments in the Old Testament—the flood in Noah's time and the destruction of Sodom and Gomorrah during Abraham's time—to recognize that many sinners receive God's judgments here on earth. For example, have you ever stopped to consider how many vicious dictators like Hitler, Mussolini, Stalin, and Ceausescu have met terrible ends?

God predicts judgment for the ungodly: "It is mine to avenge; I will repay. In due time their foot will slip; their day of disaster is near and their doom rushes upon them."[17] Yet many live as though they will never be judged. They scoff at the idea of an eternal hell.

The final judgment has, however, been part of the biblical message for thousands of years. The Holy Spirit inspired Paul to write this ominous warning:

> Because of your stubbornness and your unrepentant heart, you are storing up wrath against yourself for the day of God's

wrath, when His righteous judgment will be revealed. God "will give to each person according to what he has done." To those who by persistence in doing good seek glory, honor and immortality, He will give eternal life. But for those who are self-seeking and who reject the truth and follow evil, there will be wrath and anger.[18]

Those are hard words from a holy, just God. In Revelation, we have a visual description of that final Judgment Day of wrath:

> Then I saw a great white throne and Him who was seated on it. Earth and sky fled from His presence, and there was no place for them. And I saw the dead, great and small, standing before the throne, and books were opened. Another book was opened, which is the book of life. The dead were judged according to what they had done as recorded in the books. The sea gave up the dead that were in it, and death and Hades gave up the dead that were in them, and each person was judged according to what he had done. Then death and Hades were thrown into the lake of fire. The lake of fire is the second death. If anyone's name was not found written in the book of life, he was thrown into the lake of fire.[19]

I never want to face that judgment seat! Thankfully, those of us who have trusted Christ will not appear before the Great White Throne judgment of sinners. But all believers will appear before Christ's judgment seat. This is a not a judgment of sin, but of how faithfully we have served our Savior with the opportunities and talents He gave us. Then, we will receive rewards for what we have done for Christ. In our next chapter, we will learn more about how God's justice works on the behalf of believers.

LIFE APPLICATION

EXALT YOUR GOD—Praise our just God with the words of Moses:

> "Listen, O heavens, and I will speak! Hear, O earth, the words that I say! My teaching will fall on you like rain; my speech will settle like dew. My words will fall like rain on tender grass, like gentle showers on young plants.
>
> I will proclaim the name of the LORD; how glorious is our God! He is the Rock; His work is perfect. Everything He does is just and fair. He is a faithful God who does no wrong; how just and upright He is!" (Deuteronomy 32:1–4)

REFLECT HIS IMAGE—The Lord spoke through Isaiah, saying, "I, the LORD, love justice" (Isaiah 61:8). God wants His children to mirror His nature through the power of His Holy Spirit. Search your heart by answering the following questions:

- Do you love justice?
- Does seeing injustice make you angry and/or sad?
- Do your actions line up with what you believe? What proof from your life experiences can you give to show that you truly love justice?
- Could those around you say that everything you do is just and fair? What recent actions can you recall that show how you will sacrifice convenience or something else to do what God deems just and fair?

SHARE HIS MAJESTY—Does a friend or family member need to be told that God is a God of justice? Think of someone who has been wronged and give them the comforting news that God is the perfect Judge. Lovingly warn someone who has not acted justly that God judges those who do wrong.

CHAPTER 19

GOD'S JUSTICE WORKS FOR OUR GOOD

D o you remember your years in junior high and high school? Every class seemed to have a student who was a prankster who deliberately violated school policy. When the teacher became aware of students' possessions disappearing, no one would confess or expose the guilty party. Then the teacher would announce, "No one is leaving this room until I find out who did this." Although you were an honest student, you sat with the rest of the class, twiddling your thumbs, and wondering, *Why can't I be excused? I've done nothing wrong and the teacher knows it. The teacher is not being fair!*

At every age, we recognize that many situations in life are not fair or just. If you have watched preschoolers play, you will soon hear, "That's not fair. I had it first." A high school student is killed in an accident caused by a drunk driver and the parents question, "Where's the justice? The drunk driver has barely a scratch, and our child is dead!" A pastor faithfully serving the Lord watches his wife, the mother of their three children, die of cancer. In his despair he wonders aloud about the justice of it all.

Yet the Bible is very clear in announcing that God is just. After leading the people of Israel for forty years in the wilderness, Moses publicly sang this song: "The Rock! His work is perfect, for all His ways are just; a God of faithfulness and without injustice."[1]

There is, however, not always a clear relationship between what we have done and what happens to us. Because questions about the justice of God plague us, let us consider practical implications of the statement, "Our God is just."

GOD'S PATIENCE TOWARD SINNERS

Justice delayed is often justice denied. If a defense lawyer can keep postponing a murder case, for example, evidence that is available in a speedy trial becomes useless. Witnesses may die or move away. The defense can challenge the validity of a witness's memory. Police departments misplace evidence.

What about justice for Christians? Sometimes they are unjustly targeted because of their faith. Nina Shea writes in *In the Lion's Den*, "Christians are the chief victims of this religious persecution around the world today."[2] Today 480 Christians will die or suffer brutality because of what they believe.

In Morocco, Rachid Cohen, a Jewish man who had received Christ as his Savior, was arrested and tortured for ten hours a day. He was burned with cigarettes, shocked in a low-voltage chair, and forced to sit in his own excrement. In China, persecutors beat, starve, and shock believers with electric probes. Thousands of stories of injustice toward believers have been documented.

Consider how God felt about the evil people living during the time of Noah. They all deserved the maximum punishment. If you had been God, how quickly would you have followed through on your threat to destroy the wicked? Would you have waited a week? A month? A year? More than five years?

Although the violation of God's justice had been described in detail, God did not act immediately. He invited Noah to build an ark to save himself, his family, and representatives of every animal group. Without modern tools, it took Noah 120 years to build that ark. Did the sin of the people decrease at all during that period of divine patience? No. Even after 120 years, only Noah and his family qualified to be rescued from the destructive flood.

So why did God not act immediately after declaring that He would destroy all humans except Noah and his family? Second Peter 3:9 says, "The Lord is not slow in keeping His promise, as some understand slowness. He is patient with you, not wanting anyone to perish, but everyone to come to repentance" (NIV).

All believers are saved because God delays His justice. At what age did you discover God's love and forgiveness? At 15 or 30 or 70? Whatever age you and I received God's promise of eternal life was more than enough time for God to have caused His wrath to fall on us. How many evil deeds had we committed before that day? How many people had we hurt? How many sins had we excused? None of us deserve even one day of life because of our sinful, depraved nature, so we must be grateful for a just God who delays punishment.

I am sure you have your own story of a friend or relative who received Christ late in life after years of self-centered living. One example is the famous skeptic Dr. Cyril E. M. Joad, who for years was head of the Philosophy Department at the University of London. Dr. Joad and his colleagues, Julian Huxley, Bertrand Russell, H. G. Wells, and Bernard Shaw, have probably done more to undermine the faith of the collegiate world of recent generations than any other group. Dr. Joad believed and taught that God was an impersonal part of the cosmos and that there is no such thing as sin.

> GOD'S DELAYED JUSTICE IS AN OPPORTUNITY FOR HIS MERCY TO BE SHOWN TO MANY.

Did God strike him dead? Did He send a crippling disease? No, but before he died, Dr. Joad became convinced that the only explanation for sin was found in the Word of God—and the only solution for sin was the cross of Jesus Christ. He became a zealous follower of the Lord Jesus. No doubt many of his followers turned to faith in God through his testimony and writings. God's long-suffering and incredible patience brought this skeptic to his knees at the cross. Truly, God's delayed justice is an opportunity for His mercy to be shown to many.

GOD IS AWARE OF INJUSTICE

In 1960, Raleigh Washington joined the army. He was quickly promoted from captain to major and then lieutenant colonel. He was well on his way to becoming a general when a group of white officers falsely accused Raleigh, who is black, of conduct unbecoming an officer.

Although none of the accusations were proven, he was given the choice of retirement in lieu of being discharged. But to get his retirement benefits, he had to admit that he was guilty. He refused. He was discharged one day short of twenty years of service, and therefore was disqualified from all of his retirement benefits. At the time, his wife was pregnant with their fifth child.

How would you have reacted? Since he had become a Christian two years earlier, Raleigh decided not to be bitter against the whites who had mistreated him. Instead, he applied to Trinity Divinity School to study to become a pastor. As a student, his income dropped by 90 percent. How he could have used that retirement income! But the Lord provided for the family's finances in exciting ways. When he graduated, the Evangelical Free Church recruited him to plant churches. Although he was their only black pastor, the white church members enthusiastically supported his church-planting efforts.

While he was planting his church, he met a Jewish lawyer named Jeff Strange, who learned about his military case. For the next nine years, Jeff worked to reverse the decision the army had made. Raleigh says, "Finally, I was reinstated for one day, so that I might retire. My retirement was made retroactive to 1980, and I received the accrued retirement benefits. In addition, they cleared my record and every document against me was destroyed. My military record was made immaculate.

"God uniquely sustained me and my wife and protected me from becoming bitter when falsely accused. Because I did not get bitter, God used whites to embrace my ministry, to support me, to befriend me. God used that time after my dismissal from the Army to teach my wife and me to walk by faith."[3]

We may encounter injustice in any place at any time. But God has His own way of righting wrongs. Even if someone deals with us unfairly, God is still in control. If you are the only Christian on a police force, in a fire station, or on a school faculty, you may be experiencing ribbing, even harassment for your faith. In fact, you may even be passed over for promotion because of your unwillingness to become part of the sinful activities of your culture. At one point the coach of the Toronto Maple Leaf hockey team made it very clear that he wanted no Christians on his team. He called them sissies. He traded the one Christian he had on the team, even though he was an excellent player. Where was the justice for this Christian player? Why did God not act?

That is a question only God can answer, but we do know that He is aware of every injustice. Within the scope of eternity, He makes everything right.

Through the prophets the Lord demonstrated His concern for those who were being mistreated, receiving abuse, and being denied opportunities to participate fully in the life of the community. For example, foreign armies oppressed the people of Israel and Judah. Instead of seeing rich and fertile fields, choice vineyards and pleasant gardens, God saw crops of injustice, bloodshed and oppression. He saw how the greedy landowners oppressed the poor. He saw the injustice in the courts, where the bribes of the affluent deprived the poor of justice. He knew of the murder of innocent people.[4]

Jesus told a story about a judge who was approached by a widow pleading, "Grant me justice against my adversary."[5] For some time this judge refused to respond to the widow. Finally she became so persistent that he said, "I will see that she gets justice, so that she won't eventually wear me out with her coming!"[6] Jesus relates this story to the suffering of the ones He loves: "Will not God bring about justice for His chosen ones, who cry out to Him day and night? Will He keep putting them off? I tell you, He will see that they get justice, and quickly."[7]

Sometimes we will see almost instant justice. On other occasions, we must wait. And at times we will not receive justice until after we join our heavenly Father in His home in heaven. But we can be assured that God sees it all—and that He cares about the mistreated even more than we do.

BLESSINGS AND JUDGMENT

When the Supreme Court was formed in the late 1700s, the first order of business was to fill in the details of the judiciary. After the lower federal courts were established and the new justices appointed, it was time to hear cases. The initial Court session began on February 1, 1790, in the Royal Exchange Building in the heart of what is now New York City's financial district. Robert Wagman writes, "When it became apparent that the five justices would have absolutely nothing to do, the session was adjourned after ten days."[8] On August 2, they met again, but once more they had nothing to do, so they adjourned for the year. It was not until February 1793 that the Court heard its first case.

> "WE HAVE BECOME...TOO PROUD TO PRAY TO THE GOD THAT MADE US."
>
> ABRAHAM LINCOLN

Although the Supreme Court's jurisdiction was more narrow back then, can you imagine if today's Supreme Court adjourned early for a lack of cases to hear? Because of the tremendous number of cases presented to the Supreme Court today, it must limit itself to four cases per day. Each side gets one hour to present its arguments. The Justices hear cases two weeks, then recess for two weeks to allow them to write their opinions on these cases. The docket is always packed. Obviously, much has changed in two hundred years!

America has been greatly blessed because our ancestors acknowledged God's supreme sovereignty and their complete dependence on Him. They believed Psalm 33:12, "Blessed is the nation whose God is the LORD" (NIV). Christian values were cherished and laws were established that reflected biblical morality.

As we prospered we began to feel self-sufficient and to see our greatness as the product of our own abilities rather than the result of God's blessing. Abraham Lincoln said in 1863:

> We have been the recipients of the choicest bounties of Heaven; we have been preserved these many years in peace and prosperity; we have grown in numbers, wealth, and power as no other nation has ever grown. But we have forgotten God. We have vainly imagined in the deceitfulness of our hearts that all these blessings were produced by some superior wisdom and virtue of our own. Intoxicated with unbroken success, we have become too self-sufficient to feel the necessity of redeeming and preserving grace, too proud to pray to the God that made us.[9]

For the past several decades, our nation has taken drastic steps to divorce itself from God's standards of righteousness. What has been the result? Scholastic Aptitude Test (SAT) scores have dropped dramatically. Pregnancies, rapes, aggravated assaults, and murders have increased at an alarmingly epidemic rate among our teenagers. Suicide has become the second leading cause of death among adolescents. Gangs have turned many urban schools into war zones. The U.S. now leads the world in illegal drug use, exporting of pornography, divorce rates, abortion, and violent crime, and we lead the Western world in teenage pregnancies and illiteracy.

Thomas Jefferson wrote about the foolishness of abandoning God:

> God who gave us life gave us liberty. And can the liberties of a nation be thought secure when we have removed their only firm basis—a conviction in the minds of the people that these liberties are the gift of God? That they are not to be violated but with His wrath? Indeed, I tremble for my country when I reflect that God is just; that His justice cannot sleep forever.[10]

We are in danger of reaping God's judgment. If our country is lost, it is only because we as Christians have not obeyed our Lord's command to be salt and light to the people around us. You may be asking, "What can I do to help turn the tide of godlessness and immorality?" In 2 Chronicles 7:14, God's conditional promise begins with your willingness to humbly come before Him to admit your disobedience and indifference and seek His forgiveness. Then ask God to cleanse your heart from all wrongdoing. Pray that He will rekindle your first love for Him and once again send revival to your heart, your church and community, our nation, and our world.

CHRIST WILL JUDGE BELIEVERS

Our just God is not primarily concerned with punishing disobedience, but with rewarding right behavior. Yet God will reward only those who accept Christ's penalty for sin because His payment for our sins opened the way for God to reward us for what we do for Him.

Christ will evaluate each believer's life to determine rewards for faithful obedience and service or loss for disobedience. Paul explains, "We must all stand before Christ to be judged. We will each receive whatever we deserve for the good or evil we have done in our bodies."[11] Jesus will consider several factors when we appear before His judgment seat.

- He will judge the words we have spoken.[12]
- He will judge the deeds we have done.
- He will judge our motives.[13]
- He will judge our faithfulness.[14]

God will also reward those who bring others to faith in Christ. God told Daniel:

Those who are wise will shine like the brightness of the heavens, and those who lead many to righteousness, like the stars for ever and ever.[15]

Every believer should desire to hear Jesus say these words: "Well done, good and faithful servant." Hebrews assures us, "God is not unjust; He will not forget your work and the love you have shown

Him as you have helped His people and continue to help them."[16]

Are you living for the glory of God or for self-satisfaction? There is an incredible reward awaiting the person who seeks to glorify God. Paul is so sure of this reward that he writes:

> Whatever you do, work at it with all your heart, as work-ing for the Lord, not for men, since you know that you will receive an inheritance from the Lord as a reward. It is the Lord Christ you are serving.[17]

Do you trust God's perfect justice? It is undergirded by His holiness, truth, and righteousness and perfectly administered through His omniscience, omnipotence, and omnipresence. He is the Perfect Judge.

So far we have seen God's work as Creator and His position as Perfect Judge. But God also has another side to His character—gracious Savior. Think of holiness, truth, and righteousness as one side of a coin. What is on the other side? Love, mercy, and faith-fulness. That does not mean that these qualities are the opposite of the former ones, but that one side of the coin needs the other to be complete. As we go on to the next section, "Our Gracious Savior," we will find more reasons to enjoy a lifelong, intimate relationship with our Creator and Perfect Judge.

LIFE APPLICATION

WRITE IT ON YOUR HEART—Memorize the following statement and verses. Then as you encounter situations during this week where you need to be reminded of God's justice, claim these promises by faith.

- Because God is just, I can be sure He will always treat me fairly.

- Jeremiah 17:10 (NIV)—"I the LORD search the heart and examine the mind, to reward a man according to his conduct, according to what his deeds deserve."

- Ecclesiastes 12:14 (NIV)—"God will bring every deed into judgment, including every hidden thing, whether it is good or evil."

COUNT ON GOD—Have you been wronged? Jeremiah 51:56 states, "The LORD is a God of retribution; He will repay in full" (NIV). Trust our perfect God of justice to judge your situations. Confide in Him about your anger and frustration regarding unfair treatment you've received. Then wait for Him to deal with the one who wronged you. No matter what happens, be fair and just to those around you.

OBEY GOD—The Word of God states in Galatians 6:7, "Do not be deceived: God cannot be mocked. A man reaps what he sows" (NIV). Are you sowing seeds of destruction, or seeds of mercy, justice, and goodness? Examine your motivations in the way you deal with difficult people. Which category do they fall into: destruction or mercy? Whatever you are sowing, you will reap. If you want to reap God's favor and blessings, obey His command to extend mercy.

PART III

OUR GRACIOUS SAVIOR

(Attributes of Relationship)

*There is only one God and one Mediator
who can reconcile God and people.
He is the man Christ Jesus.
He gave His life to purchase freedom for
everyone.*

1 TIMOTHY 2:5,6

CHAPTER 20

GOD
IS
LOVE

T he plan seemed so wonderful at the time. More than 100,000 people would camp out in a pristine glade in upstate New York where everyone would get along and love each other. This meeting was part of a movement—one that its followers believed would change the world. The movement really began in 1967, which some called the "Summer of Love." Its members were called hippies. The slogan expressed noble ideals: love, not hate; peace, not war. One of its cornerstones was "free love." Hippies thought they could ignore God's standards, as well as thousands of years of social rules, and gratify themselves with free sex.

The Woodstock Festival in the summer of 1969 culminated this national "Love-In." Instead of the expected 100,000 hippies descending on a quiet countryside, 1.5 million long-haired young people wearing beads and feathers flooded the area for three days of music.

Was Woodstock really a place of peace and love? No. Peter Townsend, a member of the band "The Who" which played during Woodstock, said, "What was going on off the stage was just beyond comprehension—stretchers and dead bodies, and people throwing up, and people having [drug] trips…I thought the whole of America had gone mad."[1]

Tempers flared; people were assaulted; a concession stand was almost ripped apart; roads were clogged for a twenty-mile radius. Nudity, sex, and drug dealing were going on everywhere. One young man was crushed in his sleeping bag by a backhoe. And when the uncontrollable crowd went on their way, they left behind acres of trash.

What was supposed to be a monument to free love and brotherhood was actually a hedonistic mess resulting in total chaos. Selfishness and a disregard for others reigned. The "Summer of Love" had turned into a time of disaster and disappointment.

> GOD'S LOVE IS THE *WHY* OF CREATION, WHEREAS HIS POWER IS THE *HOW*.

Love is a universal need of all humanity. Everyone wants to be loved. But what is love? Tragically, our world understands very little about true love. We must turn to our Mighty Creator and Perfect Judge to understand what love is all about.

In Part I, we glimpsed God's abilities through His power and majesty as Creator. In Part II, God's integrity as Perfect Judge shines brightly. But these facets of God's character do not mean much if we do not understand His love, mercy, and faithfulness—revealed to us in His role as gracious Savior. God's love is not just words on a page, but was demonstrated in the deepest kind of sacrifice—Christ's death on the cross. In this section, we will conclude our discussion of God's attributes by seeing God as the gracious Savior who died for us.

GOD IS THE SOURCE OF ALL LOVE

In New Testament times, there were three primary words for love: *eros* (sensual love); *phileo* (brotherly love); and *agape* (unconditional, supernatural love). Our world speaks mainly of *eros* or *phileo* love, but God's love is *agape,* the purest, deepest kind of love.

Love is the supreme expression of God's personhood and flows out of His goodness. It affects all His other attributes. The Bible does not say, "God is holiness" or "God is power," but "God is love."[2] God's heart overflows with His supernatural and unconditional love for us. The psalmist proclaims, "The LORD is good. His unfailing love continues forever."[3]

People are sometimes willing to violate standards of honesty, righteousness, and morality to please others, but God never compromises His standards. His love is pure and holy; it does not suppress or negate any of His other attributes.

Many years ago I spoke on God's unconditional love at a missions conference for the famous Park Street Church in Boston. A missionary with whom I had attended seminary twenty years earlier approached me afterward. "I would never preach a sermon like that," he scolded. "I leave talking about God's love to the theological liberals. My message emphasizes faith."

This man had lost sight of one of God's greatest qualities. Paul writes: "We know how dearly God loves us, because He has given us the Holy Spirit to fill our hearts with His love."[4]

God's love is the only reason we exist. It is the *why* of creation, whereas His power is the *how.* Love demands an object; therefore we are created as the object of God's love. Love flows from Him as a pure river of grace and mercy without detracting in any way from His holiness and righteousness. Everywhere we look we see evidence of God's loving concern for our well-being. Love is our doorway to knowing God intimately.

God's love is expressed to all people, not just those who love Him. He loved us first before we loved Him—even when we were unlovable. That is hard for us to accept at times. Yet all people benefit from His loving care: "He has shown kindness by giving you rain from heaven and crops in their seasons; He provides you with plenty of food and fills your hearts with joy."[5] When the sun rises, its warm rays are an expression of God's love; when the rains come, they demonstrate God's love to all.

God's Love Is Beyond Explanation

Dwight L. Moody, a famous pastor and evangelist at the turn of the 20th century, tells of an experience shortly after building Moody Church. The congregation wanted to emphasize the love of God so they put "God is love" over the pulpit in lights. Every night they lit the sign so passersby could see them through the windows. Moody reports:

> A man walking past there one night glanced in through the door and saw the text. He was a poor prodigal, and he kept going. And as he walked away, he said to himself, "God is love? No. God is not love. God does not love me. He does not love me, for I am a poor, miserable sinner. If God were love, He would love me. God is not love." Yet there the text was, burning down into his soul. He went on a little further, turned around and came back, and went into the meeting. He didn't hear what the sermon was, but the text got into his heart, and that is what we want.
>
> It is of very little account what men say if only God's Word gets into the heart. And he stayed after the meeting was over, and I found him there weeping like a child. But as I unfolded the Scripture and told him how God had loved him from his earliest childhood all along, the light of the gospel broke into his mind, and he went away rejoicing.[6]

Why would God stoop to love such unworthy people as we are? Our mortal minds cannot comprehend its vastness or its consistency. We will never be able to answer why, but we can believe it is true, causing us to love, appreciate, worship, and praise Him all the more in return.

God's Love Is Free

One night, I was speaking to several hundred men gathered in a skid row mission. To illustrate to these men the love and grace of God, I pulled a $10 bill from my pocket and said, "The first person who comes to take this from my hand can have it as a free gift." Out of the hundreds of people seated before me, not a single person moved.

Finally, a middle-aged man, shabbily dressed like the rest, stood timidly to his feet and asked, "Do you really mean it?"

I said, "Sure, come and get it; it is yours."

He almost ran to grasp it, then he thanked me. The rest of the crowd began mumbling, as if to say, "Why didn't I have the faith to go and accept the gift?"

This gave me a marvelous opportunity to emphasize that we do not earn God's love. God's love is a gift to all who will receive it by faith; He offers it to us freely. Nothing we do will make God love us any more; nothing we do will make Him love us any less. He loves us because He is gracious, not because of who we are, but because of who He is.

Usually, in our world, the rich, beautiful, talented, and intelligent receive the most attention and "love." But our social situation has no bearing on God's love for us. When Jesus entered Jericho, He had to pass by that greedy tax collector, Zacchaeus, who was shunned by everyone in town. Zacchaeus's spiritual hunger was so great that he climbed into a tree to see Jesus. When Jesus passed under the tree, He looked up and said, "Zacchaeus, come down immediately. I must stay at your house today."[7]

Zacchaeus did not need a second invitation. Scrambling out of the tree, he quickly welcomed Jesus into his home.

God's love reaches out to the most socially despised and brings them within the circle of His love. As in the case of Zacchaeus and the prodigal described by D. L. Moody, God's love frees a person from sin and despair—no matter who that person is.

GOD'S LOVE IS UNCHANGING AND EVERLASTING

Some of the most devastating words a child can hear from his parents are: "I won't love you if you do that." The hurt of conditional love is also contained in the words of the teenage boy who says to a girl, "If you won't have sex with me, you don't love me." She yields to his embraces in a desperate attempt to hold someone who loves her, but when he gets what he wants, he leaves her. That same hurt reverberates like the echo in a canyon when after many years of marriage one partner says, "I don't love you anymore because…"

God's sacrifice in planning for our salvation was set in motion in eternity past: "He chose us in Him before the creation of the world to be holy and blameless in His sight. In love He predestined us to be adopted as His sons through Jesus Christ."[8] There was never a moment when God did not purpose in His love to make the ultimate sacrifice for us. He planned to leave heaven's glory, beauty, and peace and take on the body of a man. You and I, who are not even worthy to call His name, are so loved that we were always on His mind!

Just before His betrayal, Jesus enjoyed the Passover meal with His disciples. They were about to experience incredible trauma when they saw their Master led away by soldiers, put on trial, and crucified. The Book of John explains Jesus' intentions during that Last Supper: "Jesus knew that the time had come for Him to leave this world and go to the Father. Having loved His own who were in the world, He now showed them the full extent of His love."[9]

> YOU AND I…
> ARE SO LOVED
> THAT WE WERE
> ALWAYS ON
> HIS MIND!

First Jesus had a meal of fellowship, then He washed the disciples' feet. As the Lord washed Peter's feet, Peter proclaimed, "I will lay down my life for you."

Jesus responded, "Will you really lay down your life for Me? I tell you the truth, before the rooster crows, you will disown Me three times!"[10]

That is exactly what Peter did. During Christ's darkest hours, Peter turned his back on his Lord.[11] Did Jesus reject Peter because of his betrayal? As the soldiers bound and dragged Jesus through the crowd, Jesus caught Peter's eye. His look seemed to say, "Peter, I know you feel badly for what you have done. Please know that I still love you."

When we receive Jesus as our Savior and Lord, God envelops and infuses us with His everlasting love.[12] We enter into a special eternal relationship with Him. John recognized this and exclaimed:

"How great is the love the Father has lavished on us, that we should be called children of God!"[13] This love will be with us for eternity.

GOD BLESSES US BECAUSE HE LOVES US

Recently in Milwaukee, Wisconsin, a homeowner was approached by a man who wanted to borrow his barbecue grill. Being good-hearted, he let the man take it. When the borrower returned it several days later, he offered the grill owner four tickets to a Milwaukee Brewers baseball game. The owner was delighted, and even though the Brewers lost the game that day, he and his family had a good time. When they returned home, they discovered that thieves had cleaned out their house of all furniture and appliances while they were gone. What had appeared like a magnanimous gift of tickets turned out to be a trick to get the family to leave so their house could be burglarized.

Sometimes, we find ourselves wondering when God's goodness to us will end and we will find the "bottom line." But we do not need to be suspicious about the good things God offers us. He will never misuse our love for Him.

Nothing we do will take away His love for us. Paul writes, "I am convinced that nothing can ever separate us from His love. Death can't, and life can't. The angels can't, and the demons can't. Our fears for today, our worries about tomorrow, and even the powers of hell can't keep God's love away. Whether we are high above the sky or in the deepest ocean, nothing in all creation will ever be able to separate us from the love of God that is revealed in Christ Jesus our Lord."[14] We need never fear that His blessings are a disguise for other intentions. All God's actions toward us flow out of His pure love for us.

GOD'S LOVE INVOLVES HIS BEST FOR US

When iron ore is dug out of a mountain, it is worth only a few dollars per ton. But when that same ore is placed in a Bessemer furnace and put under tremendous heat and pressure, it is changed into a high grade of surgical steel.

God uses adversity in our lives, not to destroy us, but to build our faith and to refine us into the kind of people He wants us to be. He cannot use self-centered weaklings. During those difficult times, God assures us that He will work for our good.[15] Only He knows the future and how things will turn out. Most of the time we selfishly ask for things that we want, but they are not necessarily the things that are good for us. I am so glad that God has not always answered my prayers and given me what I wanted. I am sure I would have made situations worse. I am going to trust God, His wisdom, and His plan for my life through my adversity.

Because He loves us, God has prepared an incredible future for us. First He gives us an abundant life on earth. This is not a temporary provision, nor is it available only when we feel holy enough to accept it.[16] In addition, God gives us a heavenly future with Christ.[17] That is the hope of the one loved by God!

The words of this grand old hymn express God's love so clearly:

> O the deep, deep love of Jesus,
> Vast, unmeasured, boundless, free!
> Rolling as a mighty ocean
> In its fullness over me;
> Underneath me, all around me,
> Is the current of Thy love;
> Leading onward, leading homeward,
> To my glorious rest above.[18]

We worship our loving God, not as a religious exercise or ritual, but with a sincere response to the love He has already shown for us! Where else will we find the love and acceptance we so desperately need? Certainly not in some unbiblical "Love-In" or an immoral relationship. Such love can come only from the tender heart of God.

Every day, praise Him for His unconditional, perfect love. Praise Him when you wake up in the morning, thank Him as you work, and tell Him how much you love Him before you go to sleep. Respond to His limitless, ever-present love to you by expressing your heart of love to Him.

LIFE APPLICATION

EXALT YOUR GOD—Dedicate yourself in worship to our loving God through the words of the hymn, *May the Mind of Christ, My Savior:*

> May the mind of Christ my Savior, live in me from day
>   to day,
> By His love and power controlling all I do and say.
> May the Word of God dwell richly in my heart from
>   hour to hour,
> So that all may see I triumph only through His power.
> May the love of Jesus fill me, as the waters fill the sea;
> Him exalting, self-abasing—This is victory.
> May His beauty rest upon me as I seek the lost to win,
> And may they forget the channel, seeing only Him.

Praise Him for the many ways He has displayed His love in your life.

REFLECT HIS IMAGE—To help you understand love, read 1 Corinthians 13 repeatedly in as many translations as are available to you. Let the words and message sink into your mind and soul. Insert your name in place of the word "love." By faith, ask God to develop these qualities in you.

SHARE HIS MAJESTY—Is there someone in your life who needs to know how much God loves him? Perhaps a parent, spouse, or friend has not shown a healthy love to them. First John 4:18 says, "Perfect love expels all fear." Tell that person that there is someone who loves perfectly and unselfishly—our loving Creator. Look for ways to demonstrate God's love to that person.

CHAPTER 21

GOD HELPS US SPREAD HIS LOVE

O ur heavenly Father loves us, His children, in innumerable ways. Occasionally, we are able to witness a human love that is a reflection, small though it may be, of God's sacrificial and unconditional love for us.

On a cold Christmas Eve in 1952, when Korea was in the throes of civil war, one young woman struggled along a village street, obviously soon to deliver a child. She pleaded with passersby, "Help me! Please. My baby." No one paid any attention to her.

A middle-aged couple walked by. The wife pushed away the young mother and sneered, "Where's the father? Where's your American man now?" The couple laughed and went on.

The young woman almost doubled up from a contraction as she watched them go. "Please...," she begged.

She had heard of a missionary who lived in a neighboring village who might help her. Hurriedly, she began walking to that village. If only he would help her baby. Shivering and in pain, she struggled over the frozen countryside. But the night was so cold. Snow began to fall. Realizing that her time was near to deliver her baby, she took shelter under a bridge. There, alone, her baby was

221

born on Christmas Eve.

Worried about her newborn son, she took off her own clothes, wrapped them around the baby, and held him close in the warm circle of her arms.

The next day, the missionary braved the new snow to deliver Christmas packages. The sun sparkled over the countryside. As he walked along, he heard the cry of a baby. He followed the sound to a bridge. Under it, he found a young mother frozen to death, still clutching her crying newborn son. The missionary tenderly lifted the baby out of her arms.

When the baby was ten years old, his now adoptive father told him the story of his mother's death on Christmas Eve. The young boy cried, realizing the sacrifice his mother had made for him.

The next morning, the missionary rose early to find the young boy's bed empty. Seeing a fresh set of small footprints in the snow outside, he bundled up warmly in a winter coat and followed the trail. It led back to the bridge where the young mother had died.

As the missionary approached the bridge, he stopped, stunned. Kneeling in the snow was his son, naked and shivering uncontrollably. His clothes lay beside him in a small pile. Moving closer, he heard the boy say through chattering teeth: "Mother, were you this cold for me?"

That story reminds me of another mother and Son who sacrificed so much. One winter night, Jesus left his home, His glory, and the warmth of heaven to be born in a stable to an unwelcome world. Just before He was born, Mary, His mother, was not welcome in any of the cozy inns in Bethlehem. Instead, she delivered her baby in the darkness of a cold stable. The Creator of the Universe, the Perfect Judge who could destroy the world with a single word, was willing to endure this inauspicious beginning for you and me. That is unconditional love!

We who have experienced God's unconditional love are commanded to share that love with others. But how does God express His supernatural love through us? John writes, "We know how much God loves us, and we have put our trust in Him. God is love, and all who live in love live in God, and God lives in them."[1]

The secret is letting God use us as His instruments to love others. We begin that process by loving God and serving Him whole-heartedly.

GOD WANTS US TO LOVE HIM WHOLEHEARTEDLY

Jesus declared, "'You must love the Lord your God with all your heart, all your soul, and all your mind.' This is the first and greatest commandment."[2] God, in His sovereignty, has created us so we find our greatest joy and fulfillment in loving Him.

One day when I was preparing a message, my young son Zac suddenly appeared with his stack of books and sat silently beside me. I was deeply moved to think that there were dozens of places in our home where he could have gone to read. I broke the silence: "Zac, I want you to know how much it means to me that you have come to sit with me."

My heart melted to hear my son say, "Dad, that's the reason I've come. I just want to be with you."

In the same way, the great heart of God longs for fellowship with us. With incredible blessings in hand, He waits for us to open our eyes and ears and reach out in faith to receive them. Oh, how He desires to walk and talk with us as He did with Adam and Eve in the Garden of Eden. I encourage you to pour out your heart to Him; tell Him of your hurts, fears, and hopes. Read His letters of love found in the Bible. Then come into His presence through praise and worship. As you linger in His presence, His Spirit will commune with your spirit to refresh your body, soul, mind, and emotions.

GOD WANTS US TO LOVE OUR NEIGHBORS

As our intimate relationship with God deepens, we become more like His Son, Jesus Christ. As a result, we are able to love others unconditionally as God loves us. John writes, "Dear friends, since God loved us that much, we surely ought to love each other."[3] God wants us to express His supernatural, *agape* love to others. We become examples of God's love to the world as we love our neighbors through the enabling of His Holy Spirit.

I am reminded of the story of the Navajo Indian woman who had been cured of a serious ailment by a missionary doctor. She was greatly impressed by the love he manifested. "If Jesus is anything like the doctor," she said, "I can trust Him forever."

That woman did not need anyone to explain God's love to her. She saw it in action through the doctor. God wants His people to be living examples of His love to others.

GOD WANTS US TO LOVE OURSELVES

One of the great preachers and Bible teachers of our time, Charles Stanley, delivered a message at one of our staff training sessions in which he revealed that he had grown up not knowing the love of a father. He had come to faith in Christ, gone to seminary, and built a large church. One day when he was feeling burned out and at the end of his rope, he invited some trusted men to join him for a time of reflection on his life. For several hours he told them his story, how unloved he had felt as a child, how even as an adult he was not experiencing the love of God.

> GOD WANTS HIS PEOPLE TO BE LIVING EXAMPLES OF HIS LOVE TO OTHERS.

Finally, one of the men asked him to rest his head on his folded arms on the table. "Imagine God putting His arms around you while you focus on the statement, 'God loves me.'"

As Stanley did so, tears began to flow. He felt overwhelmed by the love of his heavenly Father for the first time in his life. What had been an intellectual exercise of faith in the love of God had become very personal.

Jesus implied that we are to love ourselves when He said, "Love your neighbor as much as you love yourself."[4] You do not need to be brighter, thinner, prettier, or richer in God's eyes. These are the world's standards, not God's. He loves you and accepts you as you are. You have no reason to dislike yourself when your Creator demonstrated unconditional love by forgiving you and dying for you. You are complete; you have unfathomable value and dignity as a child of God!

GOD WANTS US TO LOVE OUR ENEMIES

Jesus taught His disciples, "Love your enemies and pray for those who persecute you."[5] That is difficult, if not impossible, without the ministry of the Holy Spirit in our lives.

One man who demonstrated God's love for his enemies is Richard Wurmbrand, a Romanian pastor who was imprisoned and tortured for his faith. He lost both parents, several sisters, a brother, and children during the Nazi Holocaust. During those terrible days, he was introduced to a Romanian soldier who boasted how he had killed Jews—even those who held little children in their arms.

This man did not realize that Wurmbrand was a Jew. Since Wurmbrand is a good German name and he was a Christian pastor, the soldier assumed that Richard was not Jewish. During the soldier's boasts of cruelty against Jews, Wurmbrand did not say a word. Instead, he invited the man to his home.

The soldier accepted the invitation. When they arrived, Wurmbrand explained that his wife was sick in bed. After conversing until late at night, the Romanian pastor said, "Sir, I have to tell you something. But promise me that you will listen to me ten minutes quietly. After ten minutes, you can say whatever you like." The soldier readily agreed.

Richard Wurmbrand then said, "In the other room, my wife is sleeping. She is Jewish, and I am Jewish too. Her family, which is also my family, perished in one of the big Nazi concentration camps. You boasted that you have killed in the same concentration camp where our family was sent. So you presumably are the very murderer of my family.

"Now I propose to you an experiment. We will go into the other room and will tell my wife who you are. I can assure you my wife will not say one word of reproach, will not look angrily at you, and will smile at you as at every guest. She will consider you an honored guest. Although she is sick, she will go and prepare for you coffee and some cookies. You will be received just like everybody else. If my wife, who is only human, can do this, if she can love you like this, knowing what you have done and can forgive you, then how much more will Jesus, who is love?"[6]

The tall German soldier tore at his jacket, crying, "What have I done, what have I done? I am guilty of so much blood." This man who had never heard a prayer before knelt with the pastor and asked God for forgiveness.

Then the two men came into the room where Mrs. Wurmbrand lay. She had heard nothing about what had happened in the next room, but when her husband woke her, she did exactly as he described she would. When she heard that the soldier had repented of his sins, she fell around his neck. They both wept. Pastor Wurmbrand writes of the scene, "It was a scene of love like in heaven. That is what Jesus can do. He is love."[7]

When Christians begin to love God, they will love their enemies. The world today, as in the first century, will marvel when they see our loving attitudes and actions, "How those Christians love one another."[8]

GOD'S LOVE IMPELS US TO TELL OTHERS

Have you ever been around a grandmother who has just returned from visiting her grandchildren? She is so in love with those grandchildren that she cannot stop talking about them. You had better be prepared to look at a stack of pictures.

Have you ever been around a new Christian who is so in love with Jesus that he cannot stop talking about our Savior? So what happens over time? All too often, like the church of Ephesus recorded in the Book of Revelation, many believers lose their first love and stop talking about the God who loved us so much that He gave His Son to die in their place on the cross.

The contrast between a new Christian and a "veteran" Christian is illustrated by the story of the young man who rushed back to his apartment one night after a Billy Graham meeting. He and his roommate had lived and worked together for several years. "I must tell you something," he said to his friend. "Tonight I invited

Christ to be my Savior, and He has changed my life!"

His friend smiled and said, "Wonderful! I have been a Christian for several years, all the time hoping that you would receive Christ as your Savior."

Surprised, the new Christian said, "Ever since I've known you, I have been trying to live up to your standards, but have failed miserably. Why didn't you tell me how I could know Christ?"

Paul writes, "Christ's love compels us, because we are convinced that one died for all, and therefore all died. And He died for all, that those who live should no longer live for themselves but for Him who died for them and was raised again."[9] When we genuinely realize how much God has sacrificed for us, our love for Him will stay warm and fruitful. We will not be able to keep the Good News to ourselves. God's love *is* the Good News we share with those who have no idea what it means to be loved by Christ.

Let us continually, day to day and moment to moment, drink deeply from the wellsprings of God's love. And after you are refreshed with that living water, pour some out onto dry, thirsty people around you. I assure you that seeing others respond to God's love and forgiveness will be one of the most joyful experiences you will ever have.

LOVING BY FAITH

My prayer for you is the same as Paul prayed for the believers in Ephesus: "May your roots go down deep into the soil of God's marvelous love. And may you have the power to understand, as all God's people should, how wide, how long, how high, and how deep His love really is."[10]

You may confess, "I don't have that kind of love to share with anyone." To experience and share God's supernatural love, claim it by faith.[11]

We have the potential to love anyone God puts in our path. One of the greatest lessons I have learned in my Christian life is "how to love by faith."[12] We may think we have lost our love for our spouse, for example. Yet when we *by faith* invite God's unconditional love for an "unlovable" spouse to flow through us, we will discover a rekindled love that is alive and well. That is true as well for an "unlovable" boss, associate, or employee. Nothing breaks up the hardened ground of unforgiveness and bitterness like sincere acts and words of love.

Sometimes you and I must take the first step of restoration, by faith in love. A positive response from others may not always be immediate, but keep on loving and reaching out. There is no power on earth stronger than supernatural love.

An attorney came to Arrowhead Springs one day to complain that he just could not get along with one of his partners. They hated each other, he reported. So I suggested he tell his partner that he loved him and ask him for forgiveness for not loving him.

NOTHING BREAKS UP THE HARDENED GROUND OF UNFORGIVENESS LIKE LOVE.

"I could *never* do that," he protested. But after I explained the concept of how to love by faith, he agreed to approach his partner. He went into the office early the next morning and said to his partner: "Some time ago I became a Christian and my critical attitude toward you has changed. I've come to ask you to forgive me and to tell you that I love you."

His partner practically fell out of his chair because he was so amazed at the dramatically changed attitude of the man before him. He asked, "How can I have what you have?" The attorney led his partner to faith in Christ, and they became good friends. A few days later they came to tell me of the miracle of their reconciliation and of God's supernatural love.

Begin right now to love by faith. Make a list of everyone you do not like or have a hard time loving or those who have hurt you. Perhaps your list will include your boss, a coworker, your spouse, your children, a parent, a fellow believer, or a neighbor. Now ask the Holy Spirit to fill you with love for that person and claim by faith Christ's great love for them. Then the next time you meet them, by faith draw upon God's limitless, inexhaustible, overwhelming love for them. Through the enabling of the Holy Spirit, demonstrate your love by your actions.

Love, however, is incomplete alone; it requires action. Supporting God's great love is another of His attributes: His infinite mercy. In the next chapter, we will find out how His mercy complements His love to bring us a hope for the future and a security in His presence.

LIFE APPLICATION

WRITE IT ON YOUR HEART—Commit the following statement and verses to memory. Then as you encounter situations during this week where you need to remember that God loves you, claim these promises by faith.

- Because God is love, He is unconditionally committed to my well-being.

- 1 John 4:16—"We know how much God loves us, and we have put our trust in Him. God is love, and all who live in love live in God, and God lives in them."

- Romans 8:39—"Nothing in all creation will ever be able to separate us from the love of God that is revealed in Christ Jesus our Lord."

COUNT ON GOD—God gives a wonderful promise in Romans 8. As you read Romans 8:38,39, consider the struggles and worries in your life. Trust your compassionate God to lovingly sustain you no matter what your circumstance.

OBEY GOD—First John 4:10,11 says, "This is real love. It is not that we loved God, but that He loved us and sent His Son as a sacrifice to take away our sins. Dear friends, since God loved us that much, we surely ought to love each other." Is there someone in your life that you have difficulty loving? Do not wait until you "feel" like loving him. Love is much more than a feeling, and often we must first love them by faith. Begin by praying for that person. Then, actively reach out to them in a display of kindness. You will be surprised how quickly the "feeling" of love may follow. Obey God and determine to love even the "unlovable" today.

CHAPTER 22

GOD
IS
MERCIFUL

eadlines in recent years have exclaimed: "Horrifying Earthquake Hits Japan," "Hurricane Mitch Is Most Devastating Storm on Record," "North Texas Hit By Severe Drought; Farmers Reeling."

Why are these things happening to good people? Of course, no one can read the mind of God to find out why He allows certain disasters to occur. However, these headlines also remind us of just how gracious God is to us. For the most part, the natural world around us functions according to an orderly plan. We realize that a fraction of change in our environment could destroy all life on Earth. If the distance between the Earth and sun was changed even slightly, our atmosphere would be too cold or too hot to sustain life. Without sufficient atmosphere around the Earth, harmful rays from outer space would kill us. But God sustains this planet on which we live in a marvelous fashion so that we enjoy night and day, summer and winter, rainy seasons and dry.

Jesus stated in the Sermon on the Mount, "[God] gives His sunlight to both the evil and the good, and He sends rain on the just and on the unjust, too."[1] God provides the necessities of life for

231

every human born on this planet. Many times we take His mercy for granted—until we experience a devastating blizzard with the mercury plummeting, or when summer temperatures soar into the 100s for days on end. Then we complain about how bad things are.

Unfortunately, we rarely thank God for the thousands of days of beautiful sunshine. How often do we stop to be thankful that, year after year, the flowers bloom and our grocery store shelves are stocked with food grown in the farmers' fields? When was the last time you felt gratitude for your enjoyment of food, friendships, music, art, and so many other things?

When we think of these blessings, our thoughts eventually end up at the doorstep of mercy. God's mercy is an attribute that leads Him to show compassionate concern for His people and tenderhearted treatment of the needy.[2] Our merciful God always seeks the welfare, both temporal (life on earth) and eternal (life in heaven forever), of His children and those who have not yet accepted His love and forgiveness. Although many people show mercy to others, God is the grand master of mercy. His very nature desires to relieve us of the self-imposed misery and distress we experience because of our sin. Let me give you an allegory of a merciful judge that dramatically illustrates how amazing God's mercy is.

THE MERCIFUL JUDGE

The wretched, shackled prisoner trembled with fear as he stood before the imposing bench of the toughest, fairest judge in the district. "You have been found guilty," the judge solemnly announced. Courtroom observers held their breath, waiting for what they were sure was to come.

Without a doubt the man was guilty. The evidence was clear. The judge had no choice but to pronounce a death sentence. There were no appeals for the horrendous crime, no stays of execution allowed.

Suddenly to everyone's shock, the judge did something unprecedented in legal history. He said to the prisoner, "Justice must be served. You are guilty. You are totally unlovable. Nevertheless, I love you, in spite of yourself. And because of my love for you, I have decided to take your place. I will take your punishment for you. I will die in your place. You are a free man. You can go now." The judge's gavel pounded. The courtroom was silent.

After a stunned moment, courtroom guards unlocked the prisoner's handcuffs and legs irons, removed the judge's robe, and snapped the irons on his wrists and ankles. As the judge was led away to death row, the shocked prisoner numbly walked out of the courtroom door to freedom, tears of gratitude streaming down his cheeks.

This, of course, is an allegory about God's mercy. God is the judge. Since He is perfectly just, all His actions must serve the universal law of justice. We are like the prisoner. We all deserve the death sentence, because we are all guilty of numerous sins: "All have sinned and fall short of the glory of God."[3] In His fairness, God must judge our sin with the harshest punishment: "The wages of sin is death."[4] He cannot allow us to inhabit His perfect heaven, that place without a spot of uncleanness, a thought of wrongdoing, or a charge of guilt.

In the supreme act of mercy, God displayed divine favor and forbearance to us guilty offenders. He took our punishment upon Himself. That is what Jesus Christ did for us at Calvary: "The gift of God is eternal life in Christ Jesus our Lord."[5] By His sacrifice, all who put their trust in Him are declared "not guilty" and freed! That was true mercy and grace.

OUR GRACIOUS SAVIOR

The fact is that when we sin, we will never be excused from the penalty. As we saw earlier, because of God's holiness, sin must always be punished. All our claims that we were tricked into sin or that we did not know our action was sin gets us nowhere with God.

If that sounds cruel and unfair, here is the good news! Jesus provided a dramatic reprieve from our sentence and punishment. Jesus was beaten, tortured, and hung on a cross to die in our place to satisfy God's demand for justice. The Merciful Judge became Our Gracious Savior!

Peter explains, "[Jesus] bore our sins in His body on the tree, so that we might die to sins and live for righteousness; by His wounds you have been healed."[6] When Jesus came, His blood was spilled so we could experience God's mercy. Jesus' sacrifice is the ultimate expression of God's mercy.

Jesus Christ's sacrifice on the cross satisfied God's just nature. God, the divine Judge, showed mercy and clemency for us guilty sinners. It is the mercy of God that sees man weighed down by sin and therefore in a sorry and pitiful condition, needing divine help. At the cross, God's attributes of *both* justice and mercy found complete fulfillment—simultaneously! Is that not amazing?

GOD'S MERCY EXTENDS BEYOND OUR NEW BIRTH

God's mercy does not end with the forgiveness of our sins. As His children, He provides us an abundant life that is much more than we deserve or could ever expect. In His mercy, He provides what we need to begin growing in His Spirit. His mercy also gives us peace. He shows us compassion as we walk with Him day by day. And His mercy also means that He will discipline us as a father disciplines his child. Let us look at each of these aspects of God's mercy.

AT THE CROSS, BOTH GOD'S JUSTICE AND MERCY FOUND COMPLETE FULFILLMENT.

First, God does not forgive our sins, then just send us our own way. He has a plan for our lives that will bring us to maturity in His grace.

Scott was a teenage gang member who lived in an eastern U.S. city. At 14 years old, he killed another gang member in a street fight. He was convicted and sent to a juvenile prison. While there, he attended a Bible study led by a Christian from the region. Based on the Scripture passages he was shown, Scott recognized that God's mercy extended even to him. Though feeling terribly unworthy, he received Christ as His Savior.

While in the juvenile prison, he met regularly for Bible study to grow in his new faith. He was still in his teens when he was released, but he did not want to go back to his inner city environment. Acting with the mercy of God, the Bible study leader took Scott into the home he and his wife had established as a discipling center for young men who showed genuine commitment to Jesus Christ while in prison.

Scott spent two years in the halfway house. He made such progress—completing his high school degree and growing as a Christian young man—that he was accepted as a student at a well-known Christian college. As a student, he began sharing the love and mercy of God with other young men incarcerated in the state juvenile detention centers. He wants to minister to inner city youth who are without hope because they do not know Christ.

Ephesians 2:4 describes God as being rich in mercy. Have you experienced this in your walk with God? He has an unlimited abundance of mercy, which originates in His being. He gives His abundance of mercy to us all the days of our lives—and for eternity.

GOD'S MERCY BRINGS US PEACE

Some years ago, I was invited to speak to the inmates of one of the most infamous high-security prisons in America: the Federal Penitentiary in Atlanta, Georgia. When I arrived at the penitentiary's assembly room, several of the inmates rushed over to me, embraced me, and called me "brother." They told me they had heard my messages on tape, and had been introduced to Christ or discipled by my books. Before I spoke, several stood and gave testimony of how they had been forgiven by God through faith in Christ's death on the cross and His resurrection. One man spoke of how he had murdered five people. Another man confessed to killing three. Others had committed similar crimes. They told of how they came to the prison full of hate and fear—and then they met Jesus and were transformed.

Tears streamed down my face as I listened to these testimonies of God's forgiveness, mercy, and love. Again and again different prisoners said, "I'm glad I'm here. If I had not been sent to prison, I would not know Christ, and I would probably be dead because of my life of crime."

These prisoners—these men behind bars—had experienced the wonder of God's eternal pardon from their sins. They had received peace of heart and mind. They were experiencing purpose and meaning for their lives, even in their prison cells.

God's mercy enables us to break free from the habits of sin that have bound us. As a result, we can have peace, joy, fulfillment, and purpose. We will find the true meaning for living—serving God. We will find the true joy in life—serving others. We will find true peace and fulfillment—living in God's presence and will moment by moment.

GOD'S MERCY MEANS HE HAS COMPASSION FOR US

What astounds me as an imperfect human being is that God genuinely feels pity and compassion for us during our trials and difficulties. We have the assurance that "the LORD comforts His people and will have compassion on His afflicted ones."[7] Our loving Father does not just feel our pain, He wants to relieve our pain. He will if we will trust and obey Him.

The Gospels are filled with examples of how Jesus was moved with compassion to help those who were sick, suffering, and in need. The woman who had been ill with bleeding for many years was healed when she touched His garment. Jesus reached out His hands and healed the blind man, Bartimaeus, and the ten lepers. And the woman caught in adultery? He spoke compassionately to her and forgave her, saying, "Neither do I [condemn you]. Go and sin no more."[8] We can be sure that our merciful God is beside us through every trial we face and every pain we endure, and will help us live for His glory in every situation.

GOD'S MERCY IS EVIDENT IN HIS DISCIPLINE

If you are a parent, you know that your feelings of compassion and mercy toward your child will often be tested. At times you will have to exercise discipline. A child does not know he is loved unless his parents set up behavior boundaries and then enforce them in love and fairness.

When Vonette and I disciplined our sons, Zac and Brad, we did so in love. When one of our sons disobeyed us, we would first explain why we were punishing him, then we would follow through with the appropriate discipline. When it was all over, we would hug our son and emphasize that we disciplined him because we loved him.

One day Zac came home from kindergarten with a puzzled look on his face. With a serious tone of voice, he announced, "I don't think many of the children at school have parents who love them like you love me."

Mystified, Vonette asked, "Why do you say that, honey?"

"Because they are so disobedient," he said confidently. Zac had figured out that lovingkindness includes discipline.

The loved child understands when someone cares enough to take the time to correct wrong behavior. That is the way God is with us. When we become part of His family through our spiritual birth, He corrects and rebukes us for the things we do wrong.[9] As we listen to His Spirit and obey His Word, we become fulfilled, joyful members of His family.

GOD DISPLAYS HIS MERCY THROUGH US

The most exciting aspect of God's mercy is that we can be His example of mercy here on earth. Let me tell you a story about a beloved friend, a godly man whom I highly respect and admire.

Many years ago in Korea, Dr. Joon Gon Kim and his family were enjoying an evening together. Suddenly, an angry band of Communist guerrillas invaded their village, killing everyone in their path. In their trail of blood, the guerrillas left behind the dead bodies of Dr. Kim's wife and father. Dr. Kim was beaten and left for dead. In the cool rain of the night, he revived and fled for safety with his young daughter to the mountains. They were the sole survivors.

Can you imagine how we would feel if this happened to us? Since Dr. Kim is a man of God, he knew from Scripture that he must love his enemies and pray for those who persecute him. The Spirit of God impressed upon Dr. Kim to return to the village, seek out the Communist chief who led the guerrilla attack, and tell him that he loved him. Then he was to tell that man about God's love in Christ. Dr. Kim obeyed the impression God had given him. When he met the Communist chief, the man was dumbfounded because he had believed that the guerrillas had killed Dr. Kim. He knelt in prayer with Dr. Kim and committed his life to Christ. Within a short time, more Communists came to Christ, and Dr. Kim helped build a church for these and other Communist converts.

In 1958, Dr. Kim accepted the position as director of Korean Campus Crusade for Christ, our first international ministry. He is a living demonstration of God's mercy.[10]

As I walk in the Spirit and grow in appreciation for the mercy of God to me, I find that mercy overflows from my life into the lives of others. If I plant the seeds of God's mercy in the hearts and minds of others, they produce a harvest of love for God and repentance of sin.

GOD'S MERCY HAS AN END

Although God's mercy toward His own people extends throughout eternity, His mercy toward the unrepentant sinner does not last forever.

Before Alexander the Great would lay siege to a city, he would set up a light giving notice to those who lived within the city that if they came to him while that light was still burning, he would spare their lives. But once the light was out—no mercy was to be expected.

In very much the same way, God sets up light after light and waits year after year for sinners to come to Him so that they also may have eternal life. He does not want anyone to perish, so He is giving more time for everyone to repent.[11]

But be aware that a time is coming when there will be no more mercy. God does not want us to be destroyed by our sinfulness, so He offers us mercy, but we must be willing to accept it before we run out of time. Those who feel they can wait until later to receive God's offer of mercy can never be sure that they will have the time or opportunity to receive His mercy.

The time is so urgent to call people to repentance. We do not know who has a tomorrow, or whose hearts are soft toward God. Right now is the time to present them with God's message of mercy, to show them the mercy that God has liberally given us. As we approach a new millennium, we are reminded that our Lord Jesus may return at any moment. While we ourselves must be ready, we must warn those who have not heard of His gracious mercy or who have not heeded God's call.

In light of His mercy to us, our hearts should be filled with gratitude, praise, and worship. We should reach beyond our Christian circles of comfort and extend God's mercy to those who hate or ignore us. Author David Morris writes, "When Jesus came to earth, He changed seats with us and took on all our sin, rejection, and shame so we could see ourselves from His perspective."[12] We should

> WE SHOULD NEVER LOSE THE AWE AND APPRECIATION OF WHAT GOD HAS DONE FOR US.

never lose the awe and appreciation of what God has done for us. We once wore filthy garments stained by sin and corruption; now we are clothed in spotless robes of righteousness—all because of the mercy of God! That perspective will change the way we worship, reverence, and serve our God. We will see differently the need of the people to whom He is sending us.

LIFE APPLICATION

EXALT YOUR GOD—Meditate on the following verses and praise God for the specific ways He has demonstrated mercy in your life.

> To you, O LORD, I lift up my soul; in You I trust, O my God...No one whose hope is in You will ever be put to shame...Show me Your ways, O LORD, teach me Your paths; guide me in Your truth and teach me, for You are God my Savior, and my hope is in You all day long. Remember, O LORD, Your great mercy and love, for they are from of old. Remember not the sins of my youth and my rebellious ways; according to Your love remember me, for You are good, O LORD (Psalm 25:1–7, NIV).

> God is so rich in mercy, and He loved us so very much, that even while we were dead because of our sins, He gave us life when He raised Christ from the dead (Ephesians 2:4).

> Where is another God like You, who pardons the sins of ...His people? You cannot stay angry with Your people forever, because You delight in showing mercy (Micah 7:18).

REFLECT HIS IMAGE—The Word of God states in Micah 6:8, "O people, the LORD has already told you what is good, and this is what He requires: to do what is right, to love mercy, and to walk humbly with your God." Do you love mercy? Are you quick to forgive? Spend some time with your compassionate God and ask Him to mold you into His image to become a lover of mercy.

SHARE HIS MAJESTY—Do you have a friend who needs to hear about God's mercy? If he does not know Jesus, share with him Appendix A, "How to Know God Personally." If he is a believer, remind him that his heavenly Father is "full of compassion and mercy" (James 5:11, NIV).

CHAPTER 23

GOD EXPECTS US TO EXTEND MERCY

T hink of God's offer of mercy as a banquet to which you are invited. The table is filled with the most luscious foods: spicy appetizers, gourmet entrées steaming on heated plates, a vast array of juicy fruits, iced deserts, and cool, sweet drinks. The table is so large that it has enough room for more than the few who have come. But strangely enough, outside the door to the banquet hall stands a crowd who will not enter. They cry out, "I'm so hungry, so hungry!" You can almost hear their starved stomachs rumbling from lack of food. Yet for some reason, they will not step through the door and help themselves to the free banquet provided for them. A. W. Tozer gives this analogy when he writes:

> We may plead for mercy for a lifetime in unbelief, and at the end of our days be still no more than sadly hopeful that we shall somewhere, sometime, receive it. This is to starve to death just outside the banquet hall in which we have been warmly invited. Or we may, if we will, lay hold on the mercy of God by faith, not allow skepticism and unbelief to keep us from the feast of delicious foods prepared for us.[1]

God extended His mercy to us even before we were born, and before we acknowledged our need for His forgiveness. Without our Lord's sacrifice on the cross, we could not have a relationship with God. Now, because of Christ's willingness to die in our place, we can have a deep intimacy with the God who loves us unconditionally.

The Merciful Extend Mercy

One day Peter asked Jesus how many times he had to forgive someone. Peter thought that forgiving seven times was pretty good. "No!" Jesus replied, "seventy times seven!"[2] Then Jesus gave an illustration showing how God looks on our responsibility to forgive:

One day, a king was going over his accounts, settling old debts. He saw that one of his servants owed him millions of dollars. The king ordered the servant brought before him. When he arrived, the king demanded that the servant pay every penny. But the amount was beyond the servant's ability to pay. The king ordered the man and his family sold into slavery to pay the debt. The servant fell before the king and pleaded for mercy. The king felt pity and forgave him this tremendous debt.

That is such a wonderful picture of God's mercy. We are like the servant who could not pay the debt. But God, in His mercy, took pity on us and erased our sin debt completely.

But what did this servant do? He found a fellow servant who owed him a few thousand dollars and demanded payment. Just imagine. He came from the throne room where he had been extended so much mercy and grabbed his friend by the throat and demanded payment! The friend begged for mercy. But the servant would not forgive him and had him thrown into prison.

When the other servants saw the injustice, they went to the king and reported what had happened. The king was angry! He called in the servant and demanded to know why the man had acted so harshly toward his friend when he himself had been forgiven so much. Then the king commanded the servant be thrown into prison until he had paid every penny.

God gave His only Son to die in our place. That is mercy beyond comprehension, beyond description. How, then, can we ever refuse to give mercy to others when we have received so much mercy ourselves? What others may have done to you does not compare with what God has forgiven you. That is why God expects us to have mercy on others. To the degree that we show mercy to the poor, the wretched, and the guilty, we are like God. The lesson is clear: the merciful shall obtain mercy. And who among us is not a candidate for more of God's mercy?

OUR NEED FOR MERCY HELPS US SERVE OTHERS

Just like the unforgiving servant, sometimes the hardest place to extend mercy is the area where God has given us the most mercy —our area of weakness.

Ed DeWeese came home one afternoon to find that thieves had gone through his home. The TV, stereo equipment, and jewelry were missing—about $3,000 worth. He called his wife, Beth, at work and she rushed home. The police arrived and took a report. Because the DeWeeses had just moved in, they had not taken out homeowner's insurance. After the policemen left, they prayed, "Lord, we have no insurance and cannot afford to replace these things. Please return them to us."

That is when Ed's situation really hit him. He was an ex-offender. He had gone to jail for embezzlement—sophisticated burglary. He said to Beth, "We must first forgive."

After the thief had been arrested and released on bond, Ed asked a police officer to take him to the offender's home. When Ed met the man who had robbed him, he said, "I'm the man you ripped off. But brother, I forgive you in the name of Jesus."

Ed continued to visit the thief and gave a Bible to his little brother who had assisted in the crime. Soon, the robber told the police where the stolen things were hidden, and the officers recovered the DeWeeses's belongings. When the young man pleaded guilty to burglary, Ed testified in his behalf. He then helped the young man find a job. And Ed says, "Best of all, he and his brother did receive Christ as Savior."[3]

Our past failures can make us more sensitive to those who need mercy in the very areas in which we once needed mercy. We can minister to others in a more meaningful way because we understand and have experienced the reality of God's mercy in our area of weakness.

MERCY MEANS LETTING GO OF OLD HURTS

Corrie ten Boom encountered a situation in which her willingness to forgive was challenged. During those horrible days in 1944 in the Ravensbruck concentration camp, grim guards in blue uniforms and caps bearing the Nazi swastika stood in a line with leather crops swinging from their belts. The emaciated women dressed in prison garb worked long hours every day under the watchful eye of these guards. Corrie's sister, Betsie, died in Ravensbruck, a victim of the tortuous conditions.

In 1947, after the war, Corrie spoke to a group of Germans in a sparsely furnished Munich church basement. Her mission was to help those who were ravaged by the war. During her talk, she said, "I have a home in Holland for victims of the war. Those who have been able to forgive their former enemies have been able to rebuild their lives, no matter what the physical scars. Those, however, who have nursed their bitterness remain invalids. We, as Christians, have every reason to forgive each other, for our God richly lavishes His mercy on us—if we only ask Him."

> NO SIN IS TOO BIG TO BE THROWN INTO HIS OCEAN OF FORGIVENESS.

When she finished her talk, she was approached by a balding, heavyset man in a gray overcoat, a brown felt hat clutched between his nervous hands. Horror filled her as she realized he had been one of those guards who had abused Betsie in the camp. His name was Joseph.

Joseph thrust out his hand. "A fine message, Fraulein! How good it is to know that, as you say, all our sins are at the bottom of the sea!"

Dumbfounded, Corrie did not take his hand.

He went on, "You mentioned Ravensbruck in your talk. I was a guard there. But since that time, I have become a Christian. I know that God has forgiven me for the cruel things I did there, but I would like to hear it from your lips as well. Fraulein, will you forgive me?"

Corrie remembered how he had pushed Betsie with the butt of his gun. Corrie looked down at his outstretched hand. She whispered to herself, "Jesus, help me." Her hand slowly moved toward his. Their hands touched and she finally vigorously shook his hand. With tears in her eyes, she said, "I forgive you, brother …with all my heart."

God loves us no matter what we have done. He forgives us when we ask Him. No sin is too big to be thrown into His ocean of forgiveness. Since God richly lavishes His mercy on us, we must show mercy to one another. And that means letting go of all those old hurts caused by others.

EXTENDING MERCY HAS A COST

Often the most difficult place to show mercy is in close relationships—our family and friends. A middle-aged man sat in the pastor's office, nervously wiping perspiration from his brow with the back of his hand. "There is absolutely no way I can tell this to my wife," he said. "She would be devastated. She would never forgive me. I just cannot tell her. But I want forgiveness. I need relief from all this guilt."

In this family's case, the wife's career had soared with success, while the husband's work had plateaued. She traveled on extended business trips, gaining all kinds of recognition and earning a big salary. Meanwhile, the husband was at home keeping the family fed and attending to household chores. In a weak moment when loneliness drove his attention elsewhere, his wife's best friend began to meet his sexual and emotional needs. He was caught in an ugly trap of betrayal, with seemingly no way out.

After counseling with the pastor, the husband went home and confessed his sin to his wife. He told her exactly what had happened and why. He admitted he was very wrong and assured her that his adulterous relationship with her friend was over. Much to his surprise, she forgave him, and they started all over again. This act of mercy came at no small cost to this rejected wife, but it led to the restoration of the relationship they once had.

God will reward us when we show mercy. One of mercy's rewards is the intimacy we enjoy in our human relationships. Another reward is the intimacy we experience in our relationship with our Lord. Since mercy is of the highest priority to God, when we are merciful, we become instruments of blessing and enjoy communication with God.[4]

God's Mercy Helps Us in Our Failures

If you ask Steve about God's mercy, he can tell you that it is bottomless. He worked hard in his local church, raising four children with a wife he loved dearly. Yet he was not walking in God's Spirit. He began to have a problem—greed. Little by little, he began taking money from his job. In time, his $100,000 embezzlement was discovered, and he was taken to court. Still, Steve was not truly repentant. He did not realize his great need for God's mercy and help.

Because this was his first offense, the judge was lenient. Steve received a work-program sentence in which he had to spend his weekends doing community service. He was assigned to the sheriff's department. At first he did simple jobs like washing police cruisers, but soon police officials began trusting him with greater responsibilities. Eventually, they put him in charge of handling sales of items such as pepper spray. Over the next year, Steve began embezzling money from the sheriff's department until he had taken more than $20,000!

As you might guess, he was caught once again. But this time, the court did not have mercy on him, and he was sentenced to several years in prison. Because of a paperwork mix-up, he was sent to the state penitentiary for violent criminals. Suddenly, Steve's world collapsed. His wife divorced him and he was not able to see his children. Sitting in that prison cell surrounded by men for whom violence was a way of life, he decided to commit suicide. His birthday was coming up, and he felt as if his life was over.

His three daughters sent him a birthday letter in which they said, "Dad, all we ever wanted was you. We didn't want the money." Their words pierced Steve to his very soul. At that moment, he threw himself upon God's mercy—including his greed and his pride.

When Steve was paroled, he began rebuilding his life. At first, he felt so unworthy that he did not think he could ever serve God again. But little by little, God began to restore him and heal his hurt. Three years after his release, Steve felt God nudging him to work in the singles' ministry in his church. He approached the singles' pastor, his conviction papers in hand. "I want to be honest with you, Pastor Ron. I am a convicted felon. But if you could find any place for me to serve God, that's what I want to do."

After learning about Steve's past failures, Ron smiled and said, "Of course, we have a place for you to serve. We just won't put you in charge of any finances."

Since then, Steve has humbly served God in evangelism and church leadership ministry. In His mercy, God restored Steve gently and lovingly. He will do the same for you when you come before Him in humility. God wants us to be bold in asking Him for mercy when we need it.[5] If we are in distress, guilt-ridden, persecuted, lonely, facing disaster, experiencing the contempt of others, struggling with our weakness, or undergoing some other difficulty, God wants us to come humbly to Him in prayer seeking His help.

Remember, people all around you need to be pointed to the mercy of God. Their hearts ache for that unconditional love and complete forgiveness. As ambassadors of Christ, we know the comfort of God's mercy and can show others how to receive this unlimited gift.

GOD'S MERCY DOES NOT ELIMINATE ALL CONSEQUENCES

Isn't it wonderful to celebrate the mercy God has given us? At the same time, God will not remove all the consequences of our actions just because He is merciful. In Steve's case, his sin of embezzlement still cost him his marriage. The pain for his children was real. If he could go back and do it all over again, he would rather rely on God's strength to keep him from sin and not on God's mercy to rescue him from his wrongdoing.

When David and Bathsheba committed adultery, God forgave David after he confessed his sin. Nathan the prophet says about David's forgiveness, "The LORD has forgiven you, and you won't die for this sin. But you have given the enemies of the LORD great opportunity to despise and blaspheme Him, so your child will die."[6] But David was also restored. Later, God allowed David and Bathsheba to have another child. That child became the wisest man who ever lived: King Solomon.

God does not forgive halfway. He cleared the sin-debt against David. But God, in His wisdom, knows that if we never suffer consequences for our actions, we will not learn our lesson completely. What would unbelievers think if believers got away with all kinds of misbehavior with no consequences? What would the world say about us? That we serve God because He makes everything easy for us? Instead, our consequences can be a way to glorify God.

EXTENDING MERCY IS NOT BEING TOLERANT

People today, even many Christians, are more concerned about a need for *tolerance* than a need for *mercy*. There is a great difference! Josh McDowell, a fellow Crusade staff member and founder of the "Right from Wrong" campaign, says that tolerance and Christian love cannot coexist. Similarly, tolerance and mercy cannot coexist. The Word of God exhorts Christians to speak the truth in love.[7] Mercy rooted in love demands that a person be told if he is doing something self-destructive or harmful to others.

The problem we encounter in separating mercy and tolerance is that we live in an age where the majority of our society does not accept the idea of absolute truth. The Biblical concept of sin has been replaced by a demand for tolerance of any activity. Consequently, tolerance has replaced mercy, especially in government, schools, colleges, industry, and the media. Tolerance is demanded for almost every bizarre and perverted belief and behavior.

When tolerance reigns and absolutes are eliminated, when diversity becomes the catch-all phrase for accepting even gross sinful behavior, then people feel no need for the mercy of God. Instead, many rationalize their behavior with excuses like these:

"Even if I am unfaithful to my wife, I'm sure God will understand. After all, He knows I have needs that are not being met."

"Remember, this is my first time with drugs. I am basically a good man who looks after my wife and kids, and I know God will recognize that."

What has happened? We have tried to reduce God to our size, to our standards, and to what we feel He ought to be like. This makes us feel comfortable. Too often we want *Him* to respond like *we* would respond to sin and injustice. We want *Him* to accept *us* on our standards of behavior. Since we are tolerant and non-judgmental with other's sins, we want everyone including God to be tolerant with ours. In this way, we do not have to change our ways or feel guilty about them. "Live and let live" is the world's philosophy, but it is not God's.

God set the example. He extends mercy and maintains His standards perfectly. He made the dearest sacrifice for our forgiveness; yet He judges and disciplines people for their sin. He loves unconditionally; yet He completely understands our weaknesses and failings. That is what mercy is all about. It is not sweeping bad things under the rug (like tolerance) and looking only at the good side. Mercy sees the whole picture, maintains right from wrong, and loves with the whole heart.

Can you do that? None of us can without the help of the Holy Spirit. Through Him, we can extend strong mercy without compromising with an attitude of unbiblical tolerance toward sin. Tolerance toward wrong behavior is not love; mercy is the loving response. Let us then follow Christ's example as we receive mercy from God and in return extend mercy to all we meet.

LIFE APPLICATION

WRITE IT ON YOUR HEART—Memorize the following statement and verses. Then as you encounter situations during this week where you need God's mercy, claim these promises by faith.

- Because God is merciful, He forgives me of my sins when I sincerely confess them.
- Daniel 9:9—"The Lord our God is merciful and forgiving, even though we have rebelled against Him" (NIV).
- Hebrews 4:16—"Let us come boldly to the throne of our gracious God. There we will receive His mercy, and we will find grace to help us when we need it."

COUNT ON GOD—Are you, or is someone close to you, in desperate need of God's mercy? No matter what you have done—large or small—God's mercy is sufficient. Go to Him and repent. Confess your sin, turn from it, and open your heart to His love and forgiveness. Your God of mercy will heal and restore you.

OBEY GOD—Are you harboring resentment against someone? Did someone wrong you and now you are having difficulty forgiving him? Read over the parable of the ungrateful servant in your Bible (Matthew 18). God has forgiven every sin you ever committed and any sin you will commit in the future. God has bountifully bestowed mercy on you. How ungrateful not to forgive someone who has wronged you! Obey God and go to that person today. Forgive him and experience the joy of showing mercy.

CHAPTER 24

GOD
IS
FAITHFUL

One day in Armenia in 1988, Samuel and Danielle sent their young son, Armand, off to school. Samuel squatted before his son and looked him in the eye. "Have a good day at school, and remember, no matter what, I'll always be there for you." He hugged his young son, and the boy ran off to school.

Hours later, a powerful earthquake rocked the area. Buildings crumbled; electrical power went out everywhere; people panicked. In the midst of the pandemonium, Samuel and Danielle tried to discover what happened to their son. As the day wore on, the radio announced that casualty estimates were in the thousands. People were trapped under beams and rubble in flattened buildings— even schools were destroyed.

Kissing his wife, Samuel grabbed his coat and headed for the school yard. When he reached the area, what he saw brought tears to his eyes. Armand's school was a pile of debris. Other grief-stricken parents stood nearby, weeping.

Samuel found the place where Armand's classroom used to be and began pulling a broken beam off the pile of rubble. He picked

251

up a rock and put it to the side, then another, and another.

One of the parents looking on asked, "What are you doing?"

"Digging for my son," Samuel answered.

The man exclaimed, "You're just going to make things worse! This building is unstable," and tried to pull Samuel away from his work.

Samuel just asked, "Are you going to help me?"

The man's wife shook her head sadly, "They're dead. It's no use."

Samuel set his jaw and continued digging. As time wore on, one by one, the other parents left. Concerned, a firefighter tried to pull Samuel away from the rubble. "What are you doing?" he asked.

"Digging for my son," was the reply.

"Fires are breaking out. You're in danger. We'll take care of it."

"Will you help me?" Samuel asked without stopping his work.

The firefighter instead hurried off to a more pressing emergency, leaving Samuel still digging.

All through the night and into the next day, Samuel continued digging, his hole growing larger. Parents placed flowers and pictures of their children on the ruins. Soon, a row of photos of young, happy faces smiled up from the rubble. But Samuel just squared his shoulders and snatched up a beam. Wedging it under a stubborn boulder, he tried to pry it out of the way. Finally, the boulder gave.

A faint "Help!" came from under the rubble. Samuel stopped his work and listened. He could hear nothing. He kept digging.

The faint voice came again. "Papa?"

Samuel recognized the voice! "Armand!" He began to dig furiously. Finally, he could see his young son. "Come out, son!" he said with relief.

"No," Armand said. "Let the other kids out first, 'cause I know you'll get me."

Child after child emerged until, finally, a sputtering Armand appeared. Samuel took him in his arms.

"I told the other kids not to worry," Armand said confidently. "I told them that if you were alive, you'd save me and when you saved me, they'd be saved. You promised you'd always be there for me."

Fourteen children were saved that day because one father was faithful.[1]

How much more faithful is our heavenly Father! Whether trapped by fallen debris in an earthquake or trapped by life's hardships and struggles, we are never cut off from His love for us. As Jeremiah writes, "Because of the LORD's great love we are not consumed, for His compassions never fail. They are new every morning; great is Your faithfulness."[2]

THE ANCIENT PATRIARCHS TRUSTED GOD'S FAITHFULNESS

We commonly speak of *faithfulness* as loyal, conscientious, or true in affection or allegiance. But as you look deeper at this word, you see the root word in faithfulness is "faith." Spiritually, the word means being full of faith. Hebrews 11 defines what God means by faith: "It is the confident assurance that what we hope for is going to happen. It is the evidence of things we cannot yet see."[3] If you read this entire chapter in Hebrews, you will see a thread running through it: "By faith." Hebrews lists great deeds of faith by the ancient patriarchs.

Hebrews 11:7 mentions Noah, who "built an ark to save his family from the flood. He obeyed God, who warned him about something that had never happened before." Abraham is sometimes called the "father of the faith." Hebrews says, "It was by faith that Sarah together with Abraham was able to have a child, even though they were too old and Sarah was barren. Abraham believed that God would keep his promise."[4] Abraham believed that God would keep His commitment to provide an heir because *he considered God faithful.* In time, God did send a son, Isaac, to Abraham and Sarah. Isaac became the physical link to the Messiah, Jesus Christ.

The most serious challenge to Abraham's trust came when God asked him to sacrifice his own son. Strengthened by his experience with God's faithfulness to His promises, Abraham bound Isaac and placed him on an altar, lifting the knife to sacrifice his son to God. Abraham believed that when God said that He would provide a physical line through Isaac, God would fulfill that promise—even if it meant raising Isaac from the dead. That is when the faithful God provided the ram in the thicket as a substitute for Isaac.[5]

Isaac blessed Jacob because he believed that God would be faithful to the promise He made to Abraham that his offspring would be as numerous as the stars in the sky or the sand on the seashore. The parents of Moses hid him for three months after he was born because they were not afraid of the edict of the Pharaoh. They knew God had a special purpose for their son.

In the experience of the patriarchs, God did not exist in a vacuum. He was working in their behalf at each step of life's journey. Their faith flowered into heroic deeds because they trusted in an absolutely faithful God. Their God was faithful down to the smallest detail.

GOD'S FAITHFULNESS TO US

All of us understand a little bit of how an automobile engine functions. Pistons, fan belts, water pumps, and thousands of moving parts all whirl around within a small space, making power for us to drive our car. Each piece in the motor has a different part to play in helping the engine function as it should. If one piece gets even a fraction of an inch out of line, the engine malfunctions. At the same time, oil and coolant circulate to keep the engine running smoothly. The parts all work together harmoniously as part of the whole engine.

That is the way God's attributes function too. If you took away love, God's character would not be complete. God's love works with all other attributes, like His justice, to produce the right kind of results. We can compare God's faithfulness to the oil in the engine that keeps the internal parts running smoothly. God's faithfulness means that each attribute in His character is working at full capacity at all times. When does God's love fail? Never, because He is faithful. When is God less than holy? Never, because His character is pure and He is always faithful to who He is and what He says. Therefore, you can count on Him to keep His promises and carry out His purposes.

In fact, God's faithfulness is at the core of God's nature. He is always all-knowing, all-powerful, ever-present, holy, righteous, merciful, and loving because He is faithful to His own character. He never changes any of His attributes to accommodate someone else's wishes. Paul drew on that knowledge when he wrote to the Thessalonians that they could depend on God because "the one who calls you is faithful and He will do it."[6] The psalmist writes, "Your faithfulness continues through all generations; you established the earth, and it endures."[7]

So when you get up in the morning and the sun is shining, thank God for His faithfulness. When you look outside and find it raining, thank God for His faithfulness in watering the earth and all the plants on it. If as evening approaches lightning flashes and a thunderstorm roars, thank God for His faithfulness in producing valuable nitrogen to renew the plants and trees. Truly, God's faithfulness is new every morning and refreshes us every night.

> TRULY, GOD'S FAITHFULNESS IS NEW EVERY MORNING AND REFRESHES US EVERY NIGHT.

One experience I recall about God's faithfulness began in the early 1970s. God impressed upon me that Campus Crusade for Christ should start a university to train hundreds of thousands of Christian leaders. Specifically, I understood God to say *go purchase 5,000 acres for this school and endowment residencies.* Due to legal and zoning complications, the dream never came to reality. From a human perspective, the setback did not make sense to me, but I continued to trust God. Now, more than 25 years later, God is helping us to start the International Leadership University with extensive worldwide outreach and impact. God has been so faithful to Campus Crusade for Christ and to me.

GOD'S FAITHFULNESS IS NOT CHANGED BY MAN'S RESPONSE

We tend to put conditions on our relationships. "If you look good,

I will love you." "If you have lots of money, you can be part of my inner circle." "If you do this for me, I'll do that for you."

God's faithfulness, however, is unconditional. We can sometimes see that quality reflected in the godly examples of faithfulness among His people. Let me give you an example.

Dr. Robertson McQuilkin was the well-loved president of the highly respected Columbia International University. When his wife began to show symptoms of Alzheimer's disease, Dr. McQuilkin resigned his distinguished position to care for her. Hearing of someone who is faithful to another, like Dr. McQuilkin, lifts our spirits because this kind of sacrifice is so rare. We realize that actions like these are not normal to our human nature, but that they must come from a higher source.

God's faithfulness is so much a part of who He is that He cannot become unfaithful to anyone—whether to grateful believers or to skeptics who doubt the reality of God—despite the cost. Paul assures us, "If we are faithless, He will remain faithful, for He cannot disown Himself."[8]

God also is faithful to us when we feel we have no faith left in us. Paul writes: "What if some did not have faith? Will their lack of faith nullify God's faithfulness? Not at all! Let God be true, and every man a liar."[9] God's faithfulness is not affected by anyone's lack of faith.

GOD KEEPS HIS PROMISES

It follows then, that in His faithfulness, God *always* keeps His covenants, or promises—without fail. The psalmist declares: "He remembers His covenant forever, the word He commanded, for a thousand generations."[10] Paul writes, "No matter how many promises God has made, they are 'Yes' in Christ. And so through Him the 'Amen' [so be it] is spoken by us to the glory of God."[11]

That is why we can completely trust God's Word. The writer to the Hebrews reminds us: "Let us hold unswervingly to the hope we profess, for He who promised is faithful."[12]

One way I have seen God's faithfulness over the years is that His Word produces fruit in the lives of those who love Him. As reporter Clarence W. Hall followed American troops through Okinawa in 1945, he and his Jeep driver came upon a small town that stood out as a beautiful example of a Christian community. He reported, "The old men proudly showed us their spotless homes, their terraced fields, and their prized sugar mills." The newsman saw no jails and no drunkenness, and divorce was unknown in the town.

Why was this village so unusual? An American missionary had come thirty years earlier and led two elderly townspeople to Christ and left them with a Japanese Bible. These new believers studied the Bible and started leading their fellow villagers to the Lord Jesus.

The reporter's Jeep driver was equally amazed at the difference: "So this is what comes out of only a Bible and a couple of old guys who wanted to live like Jesus." God's faithfulness to His Word had resulted in the transformation of the whole village.

I have found God faithful to His Word on tithing and sacrificial giving. When God's Word tells me "God loves a cheerful giver,"[13] I believe it. When I read, "God is able to make all grace abound to you, so that in all things at all times, having all that you need, you will abound in every good work,"[14] I believe it—and act on it. I constantly check to make sure that our tithes are paid up-to-date. I would rather live on bread and water to save money than to get behind in paying our tithes. I also feel we should give offerings above our tithes in a spirit of gratitude, compassion, and concern. Believers who give tithes, offerings, and alms to the poor and needy have few if any financial problems. In all my years of ministry, God has always provided everything I have needed in order to do what He wanted me to do.

God never forgets a promise He has made. God is perfectly capable of standing behind His Word. God is ready and able to deliver all He has promised. But we must claim His generous promises!

EXERCISING OUR FAITH

I recently boarded a plane in Europe bound for the United States. A man I had never seen before, whose name I did not even know, boarded the same plane, entered the captain's cabin and seated himself at the controls. A short time later, the aircraft began to move, and soon—by some means that I do not understand—it left the ground. Hours later we touched down in Orlando.

Not once during our flight did it occur to me to question the man at the controls. I never even thought to ask for his pilot's license or some other identification to prove he was capable of flying that plane. I never asked him to explain to me the physical laws by which he could keep such a heavy object in the air. I have flown millions of miles to most parts of the world. On each of those flights, I have placed my faith in such a stranger, believing he was capable of taking me safely to my destination.

Every day in hundreds of similar situations, believers and non-believers alike exercise faith without even thinking twice. If we have such unquestioning faith in fellow human beings—who are not only fallible, but also deliberately sinful and even unfaithful at times—how much more should we put all our faith in God, whose character and capabilities for faithfulness are beyond question?

God is reliable. He is trustworthy. He cannot be otherwise. His faithfulness ensures that every attribute we have studied so far is available to us. He wants us to reflect His faithfulness on earth. He is the example; we are His ambassadors to the world. Yet even though we understand this fact, in our humanity, we must grow in our Christian experience. That means exercising our faith in Him daily to build our trust in God as the Faithful One. Each time He proves Himself faithful in our life, our trust will become stronger.

What can you trust God for today that you were unable to trust Him for yesterday? What circumstances do you struggle with that you can begin turning over to Him? Exercising faith is just like exercising a muscle. The more you use it, the stronger it becomes. If you have difficulty trusting God, take baby steps of faith. Then lengthen these steps in the days to come.

In the next chapter, we will discover additional ways we can become more faithful as God is faithful.

LIFE APPLICATION

EXALT YOUR GOD—Worship our faithful Creator by singing the wonderful hymn, *Great Is Thy Faithfulness.*

> Great is Thy faithfulness, O God my Father,
> There is no shadow of turning with Thee;
> Thou changest not, Thy compassions, they fail not;
> As Thou hast been Thou forever wilt be.

> Great is Thy faithfulness! Great is Thy faithfulness!
> Morning by morning new mercies I see;
> All I have needed Thy hand hath provided;
> Great is Thy faithfulness, Lord, unto me!

Praise Him for the ways He has been faithful to you personally.

REFLECT HIS IMAGE—Search your heart by answering the following questions:

- Do people consider you someone they can count on?
- When you say you will do something, do you always come through?

Go to God with your answers to these questions, and ask Him to help you become a faithful person.

SHARE HIS MAJESTY—What insights have you gained about God's faithfulness from this chapter? Share them with a friend or family member and encourage them to draw even closer to their faithful Father.

CHAPTER 25

GOD ENABLES US TO BE FAITHFUL

U nfaithfulness has become a hallmark of contemporary society. Too often, husbands and wives are unfaithful in keeping their marriage vows. Parents are frequently unfaithful in their commitment to the well-being of their children. Children tend to disobey their parents. Employees do not always serve their employers as they should, and some employers take advantage of those who work for them.

God is the only one we can completely trust because He has the integrity and flawless character that enables Him to be absolutely faithful to His Word and commitments. No one else can fulfill all promises as He does.

The Bible is filled with praises for the faithfulness of God. David writes, "Your unfailing love, O LORD, is as vast as the heavens; Your faithfulness reaches beyond the clouds."[1] Psalm 89:8 declares, "O LORD God Almighty! Where is there anyone as mighty as you, LORD? Faithfulness is your very character."

But merely understanding God's faithfulness is only part of our responsibility as Christians. God's faithfulness is the essential foundation to building faithfulness in our lives. Let me give you an analogy that will help explain this principle.

The sun is the most important body in our sky. From it we get warmth, light, and beauty. If the sun would ever burn out, we could not survive. The moon is also a familiar sight in our sky. It has its own beauty, but it does not provide us with heat or light. All the light that comes from the moon is actually a reflection from the sun.

Almost every year, you could travel to some place in the United States to see a lunar eclipse. It usually lasts an hour or two. It is caused when the Earth moves between the moon and the sun, and the Earth's shadow falls upon the moon. Because the moon generates no light of its own, when the sun's light does not strike the surface of the moon, the moon is dark. We cannot see it.

We are like the moon. In our own strength, we cannot be faithful. At best, we are inconsistent, wavering, and selfish. Even when people who do not know God personally act in a faithful manner, it is only because they are created in God's image. They are reflecting God's quality of faithfulness. But it is only believers, walking in the power of the Holy Spirit, who can become truly faithful to God, their families, and themselves. Whenever we allow any sinful act of disobedience to break our fellowship with God, we no longer reflect His faithfulness. Our lives become like that darkened moon.

God wants us to have a better understanding of His faithfulness, which will result in more intimate fellowship with Him. We know that "God, who has called you into fellowship with His Son Jesus Christ our Lord, is faithful."[2] Daily, the faithfulness of God should cause us to love Him more, study His Word, share the message of salvation with others, and pray without ceasing. Such responses draw us ever deeper into our fellowship with the Savior. As we spend more time with Him, our lives begin to reflect more of His faithfulness in how we love others and in the mercy we are able to give.

OUR FAITHFUL GOD HAS PLANNED A LIFE OF JOY FOR US

God's faithfulness enables us to live a life of joy and fruitfulness.

Years ago, a friend told me the story of Sally, a woman whose life is a vivid illustration of the bittersweet way many Christians live.

When Sally's husband, Jeb, died years before, as far as she knew, he left only enough life insurance to pay off the mortgage. Now she was almost penniless. The house was deteriorating around her. Her car had been junked long ago when she could not keep up with the repair and insurance bills. When the electric bill got too high to pay, she made do with a camping stove and candlelight. She lived this way for years: destitute, lonely, and defeated.

One day an old acquaintance remembered her childhood friend and decided to visit. Miriam was heartbroken when she saw Sally's living conditions. She decided to stay a few days to encourage her friend. As she helped straighten up the house, Miriam made a startling discovery. Tucked away in the file drawer of Jeb's old roll-top desk was a folder labeled "For Sally." Inside, Miriam found a bank savings book and a key.

Sally discovered that the key fit a safety deposit box at the bank. Her eyes widened as she lifted the metal lid. Inside were several bundles of cash totaling $32,000, a pile of stock certificates, and three folders of rare coins. In all, Sally was worth more than $883,000! She had been living in misery and despair when more money than she would ever need had been available to her all along.

Although God has promised us all the strength and help we will ever need, many of us try to "go it alone." We seem unaware of the boundless resources God has provided in the person of the Holy Spirit and His faithfulness to bring about everything He promised to do. As a result, we live like Sally—unfulfilled, fruitless, and spiritually malnourished. Frantically hurrying about in our self-imposed spiritual poverty, we never cash the checks of joy, peace, and abundance that are in our hands. No wonder we think at times that God has abandoned us.

God has not moved away from us; we have just not taken advantage of the miraculous life He has planned for us. Our faithful God has reserved for us a life of abundance and joy; we have the key of the Spirit-filled life to give us access to all that God has provided for us.

I urge you to rely on our faithful God for every part of your life—emotional, financial, and spiritual. He is faithful to give us whatever we need to enjoy every moment here on earth.

GOD IS FAITHFUL DURING TRYING CIRCUMSTANCES

We all experience hard times in our lives. These struggles with sickness, danger, financial problems, grief, or depression happen to each of us at times. But these only prompt us to cling ever tighter to God—not to turn away from Him, blaming Him for causing or allowing all our troubles. He does not promise to prevent problems from coming into our lives, but He does promise to go through them with us. Suffering and death are as much a part of living as eating and breathing, and we can rely on God to use these situations to build character and faith in our lives.

God will never fail us! Moses exhorted the people of Israel, "Understand, therefore, that the LORD your God is indeed God. He is the faithful God who keeps His covenant for a thousand generations and constantly loves those who love Him and obey His commands."[3] The more we understand this, the less room we have in our hearts for worry.

> GOD'S FAITHFULNESS IS A GREAT ENCOURAGEMENT WHEN WE FACE TEMPTATION.

I have found that as I rely on God's faithfulness and the promises in His Word, He has proved more than able to walk with me through every situation. Truly, He's been faithful to me!

In Pakistan during a time of great political upheaval, Vonette and I finished a series of meetings in Latbre and rushed to the train station. Although we did not know it, an angry crowd of thousands was marching on the station to destroy the train with cocktail bombs. The director of the railway line rushed us to our compartments and told us not to open our doors under any circumstances.

As I put on my pajamas for the night, a peace filled my heart. From my studies of God's Word, I knew the Lord was with Vonette and me and our party. I was confident God would protect us. It was not until we arrived in Karachi some 28 hours later that I discovered how guardian angels had indeed watched over us. The train before us had been burned when rioting students had lain on the track and refused to move. The train ran over them and, in retaliation, the mob burned the train and killed the officials.

Our train was next to arrive. The angry mob was prepared to do the same to us, but God miraculously went before us, and we arrived safely in Karachi to discover that martial law had been declared and all was peaceful. It was during this incredible, memorable train ride that I revised my book, *Come Help Change the World*.

Today even more than ever, I rely on God to faithfully respond to my prayers when I pray in accordance with His Word and will. David writes of this assurance, "O LORD, hear my prayer, listen to my cry for mercy; in Your faithfulness and righteousness come to my relief."[4] God does not promise to make life easy for us. But He promises to be with us in all our trying circumstances, protecting us from anything that is not in the center of His will. He will be there by our side as we walk through all the difficulties and trials that come our way.

GOD FAITHFULLY PROTECTS US FROM TEMPTATION

Paul wrote to the church in Corinth, "Remember that the temptations that come into your life are no different from what others experience. And God is faithful. He will keep the temptation from becoming so strong that you can't stand up against it. When you are tempted, He will show you a way out so that you will not give in to it."[5]

God's faithfulness is a great encouragement when we face temptation. He knows exactly the limits of what we can bear. He promises that He will not allow us to get into situations where we are overpowered by temptation.

Whenever we give in to sin, it is not because we cannot say

"no." Rather, it is because our focus is on the attractiveness of the temptation, instead of on God's faithfulness to deliver us from that situation. Scripture declares, "The Lord is faithful; He will make you strong and guard you from the evil one."[6] God limits Satan and his demons from tempting us beyond our ability to resist. If we trust and obey God, He always gives us a way out of any predicament without having to yield to sin.

Often, we are more afraid of offending individuals with their own worldly agenda than we are of offending our holy, righteous, loving God. The results can be catastrophic. But never forget—God is as loving and faithful as He is just. Every day try to live before Him in a spirit of reverential awe as a child who knows that God loves and cares for him.

> GOD GAVE US EVERYTHING WE NEED FOR OUR LIFE OF WORSHIP AND WITNESS.

GOD FORGIVES US WHEN WE ARE UNFAITHFUL

When we first trusted in Christ to forgive our sin, He did so. Not one person who has called on God in faith has been refused. He has always been—and always will be—faithful to the sinner who comes to Jesus in faith.

The Holy Spirit inspired John to write, "If we confess our sins to Him, He is faithful and just to forgive us and to cleanse us from every wrong."[7] Since John was writing to believers, we have assurance that God has also forgiven all the sins we commit after our spiritual birth as well as the ones we had piled against our account before we received Christ as our Savior. No matter when we are unfaithful to God, He will be faithful to forgive when we ask. But on our part, we must be sincere in our repentance and not abuse God's grace.

Because we are still in these bodies of flesh, we have a tendency to sin and, ultimately, to be unfaithful. Our unfaithfulness may be motivated by fear or desire. At other times, our fleshly weakness competes with our desire to do God's will. No matter the cause, how encouraging it is to remember God's promise to be faithful to us even when we fail Him!

GOD FAITHFULLY GIVES US GIFTS TO SERVE HIM

God's faithfulness continues beyond the act of giving us new life in Christ and help in times of need. Paul writes to the Corinthians:

> Therefore you do not lack any spiritual gift as you eagerly wait for our Lord Jesus Christ to be revealed. He will keep you strong to the end, so that you will be blameless on the day of our Lord Jesus Christ. God, who has called you into fellowship with His Son Jesus Christ our Lord, is faithful.[8]

Our faithful God called us into fellowship with His Son—and in that act He also committed Himself to our future. That starts with giving us everything we need for our life of worship and witness, for we "do not lack any spiritual gift." Our faithful God never gives us an assignment for which He has not prepared us and enabled us.

God leads us into work experiences and training when we are available to Him. While in his teens, a young man committed himself to serving the Lord wherever God wanted to use him. In his late teens, he began teaching a preteen Bible study class on Sunday morning and as a mission outreach Sunday afternoon. Some years later, he taught high schoolers in one church and early teens in another church. While serving the Lord in the bookstore at Moody Bible Institute, he interacted with neighborhood African-American children who came into the store. Thus he was not surprised when he was called to write Sunday school curriculum for inner city teenagers. Later he was given an opportunity to write Bible studies for preteen boys for a national magazine. The Lord prepared him for these assignments over two decades—both by giving him a gift for writing and by providing life experiences that matured him in his service for God.

God is also faithful to give us less tangible gifts when we experience suffering, such as the pain of a child turning away from the Lord, a friend rejecting us, or the death of a loved one. In these life experiences, God gives us strength, wisdom, and peace to enable us to reflect His faithfulness through the situation.

In his letters to the early Christians, Peter wrote at length about the benefit of suffering. He concludes: "So then, those who suffer according to God's will should commit themselves to their faithful Creator and continue to do good."[9] Peter recognized that it is easy to turn inward and become bitter during times of inner pain and suffering. That is why he urges us to turn upward to our faithful Creator and commit ourselves to Him and find the purpose He has for us in these situations.[10]

Paul reminds us in 1 Corinthians 1:8 that "He will keep you strong to the end, so that you will be blameless on the day of our Lord Jesus Christ" (NIV). That is the glorious promise of God to all who follow Him. He will keep us faithful to the end, so that we will be with Him in eternity.

NO BETTER WAY TO LIVE

As we have seen, it is God's plan for us to become holy and advance His kingdom, and He is faithful to bring this to pass. He will leave nothing undone to bring us to a point of maturity in our Christian growth and faith. Paul declared to the Philippians, "I am sure that God, who began the good work within you, will continue His work until it is finally finished on that day when Christ Jesus comes back again."[11]

In what area of your life is fear of failure beginning to plague you? Which of your relationships is in danger and you wonder who cares? What task do you face that you feel you cannot do? You can make it through anything—for our faithful God is there for you even when you do not feel like a hero of the faith. He is working in your life right now, even though you may not see Him at work or feel His presence. Let His faithfulness in the past fuel your faith and the power of His Holy Spirit fill your soul. Then you, too, can be a hero of the faith in whatever situation you face.

Once He has filled your heart with the joy of His faithfulness to you, He will strengthen you with His power. Then you will reflect His faithful nature to others. They will see the love of God shine through you as you relate to others. Your friends and relatives will notice the consistency of your standards in all areas of your life, opening up many opportunities to help others understand the depth of God's faithfulness. As God meets your needs, lifts you up during trying circumstances, and gives you gifts to serve Him beyond your expectations, you will be a reflection of His holy nature and never-failing love and joy.

I cannot imagine a better way to live. If we can just be more and more faithful as God is faithful, we truly will change our corner of the world for Him!

As we consider all the attributes we have studied, it leads us to a characteristic of God's nature that assures us that God will always act in the way the Bible describes. This quality enables us to come to God in an intimate way with complete confidence. This attribute is that God never changes. In our last two chapters on our Gracious Savior, we will see how God's unchanging nature brings us comfort and security.

LIFE APPLICATION

WRITE IT ON YOUR HEART—Commit the following statement and verses to memory. Then as you encounter situations during this week where you need to remember that God is faithful, claim these promises.

- Because God is faithful, I can trust Him to always keep His promises.
- 1 Peter 4:19—"If you are suffering according to God's will, keep on doing what is right, and trust yourself to the God who made you, for He will never fail you."
- 2 Timothy 2:13—"If we are unfaithful, He remains faithful, for He cannot deny Himself."

COUNT ON GOD—The Bible states, "Without wavering, let us hold tightly to the hope we say we have, for God can be trusted to keep His promise" (Hebrews 10:23). People, institutions, and even churches may fail us, but our faithful God can always be trusted. Is there a specific problem or situation that you have a hard time placing in His capable hands? Give it to Him right now. He will strengthen you and help you through any difficulty.

OBEY GOD—Are you faithful to God? Do you love Him more than anything else? Jesus says in John 14:23, "If anyone loves me, he will obey My teaching" (NIV). We demonstrate our faithfulness by our obedience. In what areas of your life are you in disobedience to God's Word? Ask God to reveal these areas to you. Start today obeying the little things you know to do. Your faithful Lord will help you obey the big things when they come along later.

CHAPTER 26

GOD
NEVER
CHANGES

About 4,500 years ago, Pharaoh Khafre carved the Sphinx from limestone bedrock. Since then, this 66-foot statue of a man's head with a lion's body has stood in the Egyptian desert. For thousands of years, it has remained unchanged.

Or has it? Actually, this monument has undergone many changes. Khafre never finished the statue in his lifetime. For about a thousand years, it was abandoned to the Egyptian sands. In 1400 B.C., Thutmose IV uncovered the statue and painted it blue, yellow, and red and erected a statue of his father in front of the Sphinx's chest. Then another great pharaoh, Ramses II, extensively reworked the Sphinx in 1279 B.C. After that, the Egyptian sands once again began filling up around the gigantic face and body. Wind began to erode what the Pharaohs had done.

As early as the 15th century A.D., an Arab historian wrote that the Sphinx's face was disfigured. In 1818, a Genoese sea captain cleared away the debris from the statue's chest and uncovered an ancient chapel in front of it. He also discovered fragments of the Sphinx's stone beard, which are now in the British Museum. In the early 1900s, a French engineer cleared the Sphinx down to its base and shored up the weathered headdress with stone. During the 1980s, large slabs were added to try to stop the erosion. Still, in 1988, part of the right shoulder fell off.

The Sphinx is eroding even faster today. During the last decade, repairs are once again being made to the ancient statue. The large slabs added in the 1980s are being replaced by more natural-looking stone. Many plans for helping save the Sphinx from greater deterioration are being suggested.[1]

The real fact of life on earth is change. Since the fall of Adam when sin was introduced, change has been a part of human life. The moment we are born, we begin to age. We grow, develop, and deteriorate. No matter what modern science does to slow down this process, it continues on without stopping. Our great monuments like the Sphinx are not really a testimony to our power to create something unchanging, but merely to our best efforts to delay the deterioration and ravages of time.

Our only hope in this life lies in one fact: God never changes. He is the constant that we can count on while everything else around us deteriorates.

The Unchanging Nature of God

One fascinating fact about many of the religions of the world is the unpredictable character of their gods. New Agers believe that everything is god and god is everything. The source of authority or "truth," they say, is what you experience. Shirley MacLaine, proponent of New Age religion, says, "My own out-of-body experience…served to validate the answers to many questions—the surest knowledge being derived from experience."[2] In other words, you may believe one thing to be true today, but then an experience tomorrow will change that truth. And what you believe to be true will not be true for me. For New Agers, truth changes.

But we learned that God's truth never changes. It is the same today as it has always been.

Buddhists believe that salvation is in karma. Kenneth Latourette, a leading church historian, explains this Buddhist belief: "Karma may be described as the sum of an individual's thoughts and actions in all his previous incarnations. In each incarnation, he modifies his karma for either good or bad…The ultimate aim is not only to improve one's karma, but to do more, namely, to escape from the endless series of changes, the appalling eternal succession of births and rebirths. This would be salvation."[3]

How different this is from God's simple, unchanging plan of salvation! With God's plan, we know where we stand, what we must do, and the result—an eternal, unalterable place in the family of God.

Animists and idol worshippers have developed their understanding of how their gods work from accumulated folklore. Their gods are so capricious that they must constantly be appeased with sacrifices and a variety of rituals so they will not change the rules of the game. But we can read God's rules in His never-changing Word.

The God of the Bible is the only unchanging Supreme Being. He has never altered one bit of His character or His purpose. That is what I love about our wonderful and marvelous God. I have known Him personally since 1944, and today He is just the same in His holiness and love, His grace and mercy as He was when I first turned my life over to Him. Theologians call this consistency and dependability God's *immutability*.

When I get up in the morning to pray, His response will not be different from when I pray to Him at bedtime. When I confront a difficult situation, I have calmness of heart because I know His unchanging Holy Spirit is present to guide me.

The Bible presents the God we worship as One who is the same from eternity to eternity. The writer of the Book of Hebrews compares the immutability of God to His changing creation: "They will perish, but You remain; they will all wear out like a garment. You will roll them up like a robe; like a garment they will be changed. But You remain the same, and Your years will never end."[4] He never changes in His essential being, never varies how He reacts to sinful man, to man's repentance, or to man's worship. Sin and unbelief always displease Him; obedience and faith always warm His heart.

GOD'S NAME INDICATES HIS UNCHANGEABLE NATURE

In the beginning of this book, we discovered God's most holy name, I AM. Through this name, God introduced the concept that He is unchangeable. He identifies Himself with that incredible statement: "I AM WHO I AM. This is what you are to say to the Israelites: 'I AM has sent me to you.'"[5] The use of the present tense in I AM means that the God who met Adam and Eve in the Garden of Eden was the same God who met Abraham and Sarah and gave them a son—and He is the same God who acts on our behalf today.

> GOD'S PURPOSES, MOTIVES, THOUGHTS, AND ACTIONS ARE FOREVER THE SAME.

God's unchanging nature applies to all of His attributes as well. We are exceedingly glad that His love, grace, and mercy are unchanging. We appreciate the fact that His holiness cannot change. Emotions or circumstances do not affect God. He "does not change like shifting shadows."[6]

The fact that we can depend on God's immutability is tremendously reassuring for us today. We must admit that at times we violate one of God's unchanging attributes, such as His holiness. But we know that when we repent, His unchanging grace brings us forgiveness and favor.[7] We can proclaim God's message of love and forgiveness without fear that God will change the rules the next day.

GOD DOES NOT GROW OR DEVELOP

When you look at a newborn baby, you realize the tremendous amount of growing and learning that little person has to do. He cannot talk, walk, or reason. His body does not have the ability to sing, scratch his back, or throw a ball. His mind cannot tell you what he is feeling or remember what a tree feels like. He must go through all the stages of maturity—toddlerhood, childhood, puberty, adulthood, middle age, old age. In each stage, he will learn many new things.

God has never had to grow or change or develop. Although Jesus did grow in His physical body, He has always known everything and been able to do everything. He laid aside His divine majesty and assumed human nature in the form of a servant.[8]

Therefore, God has never had to learn anything—He has always been omniscient. God has never had to develop talents or skills —He has always been able to do everything. He has never needed to mature—He has always been perfect in all of His attributes.

God is also not moody, like we are. When I come before Him in prayer, I do not have to worry that He has just heard prayers of someone who really made Him angry and will take His anger out on me. He does not get tired, and He is not too busy to listen to my concerns. As the faithful Father, He is always there when we need Him. He is not more loving one day because He feels good and more judgmental the next because He wakes up on the wrong side of the bed. Because God's attributes always exist in fullness and in cooperation with each other, God's purposes, motives, thoughts, and actions are forever the same.

GOD'S WORD NEVER CHANGES

If God's character does not change, then it follows that His Word does not change either. If His purposes do not change, then the instructions He gives to us do not change.

Isaiah 40:6–8 records that "people are like the grass that dies away. Their beauty fades as quickly as the beauty of flowers in a field. The grass withers, and the flowers fade beneath the breath of the LORD. And so it is with people. The grass withers, and the flowers fade, but the word of our God stands forever."

Let us take a look at how true that is. The first verse in the Bible, Genesis 1:1, reads: "In the beginning God…" In Revelation 22:13, the last book of the Bible, Jesus says, "I am the Alpha and Omega, the First and the Last, the Beginning and the End."

Salvation has never changed in God's Word. When God referred to Abraham, He said, "Abram believed the LORD, and the LORD declared him righteous because of his faith."[9] In the New

Testament centuries later, Romans 3:27,28 says, "Can we boast, then, that we have done anything to be accepted by God? No, because our acquittal is not based on our good deeds. It is based on our faith. So we are made right with God through faith and not by obeying the law."

The principles throughout the Old and New Testaments are the same. God deals with each of us in the same way, with the same love and graciousness.

IMMUTABILITY INCLUDES VARIETY

A common, misinformed picture of heaven today is of saints floating around on clouds playing harps—for eternity. Nothing disturbs their little bit of heaven, as they presumably stay right where they are—forever! Is that your picture of heaven? Does the fact that God never changes bore you?

When we speak of God's immutability, we are not speaking of a lack of variety. They are two separate things. Look at God's creation. An elephant and a mosquito both have four legs and an appendage on the front of their faces. But who would describe an elephant and a mosquito as alike? How about a mouse and a whale? They both have tails, pointed noses, and sleek bodies. But, oh, the differences!

Immutability and creativity are not the same either. Although God never changes, He is all-creative. Just think about how many different personalities He has created throughout the world. No person is just like another. How about the many different kinds of plants He has made—from a pear cactus flower to an orchid; from a giant redwood to a delicate bluebell; from moss to seaweed. There is no end to God's creativity.

What does not change are the principles and the character that underlie the variety and creativity. God's plans for us are always to conform us to the image of His Son. He changes the way He works out His plan to fit our personalities, our circumstances, and our needs.

Sometimes, however, the unchanging nature of God's work is plain to see. Do you remember the story of Paul and Silas in prison for proclaiming God's message? Their preaching and that of other Christians produced phenomenal growth during the days of the early Church. It also produced persecution for the sake of Christ, which is why Paul and Silas were in prison. While they were praying and singing hymns at midnight, a great earthquake shook the prison's foundations. All the doors flew open and the chains fell off every prisoner.

In those days, if a Roman jailer lost his prisoners, the law required a sentence of death. The Roman jailer awoke, assumed all the prisoners had run away, and was going to commit suicide. Paul shouted, "Don't do it. We're all here!" The jailer, when he saw that the prisoners had not escaped, fell on his knees before Paul and Silas and asked how he could be saved.

Paul and Silas shared the Word of God with him, and he and his entire household believed in our Lord. The next day, the city officials released Paul and Silas.

Centuries later, the pattern repeated. In the 1930s, missionaries planted the Word of God in the southwestern mountains of Ethiopia. When World War II erupted and the missionaries were forced to leave, they left a church of only 48 believers. But in five years of foreign occupation in their land, the Ethiopian church grew to 10,000!

Raymond Davis, who worked in the interior of Ethiopia, tells of a miraculous story of God's work among the Wallamo people. The Christians had been horribly persecuted for proclaiming God's message, but their congregation had grown to more than a thousand. The government forced them to tear down their precious church building, which they had built with such sacrifice of labor and materials.

Later, they dared to rebuild their church building. Consequently, several of the church leaders, including a man named Toro, were taken to the marketplace, stripped, and beaten. Then they were thrown into jail where their jailers taunted them for believing in God. Davis writes:

> Some time later, a group of the believers in prison were praying together when a terrible rain and thunderstorm came

up. Toro says he doesn't remember the lightning ever being fiercer or the thunder claps louder. While they were praying and singing, the wind blew with such terrific force that the entire iron roof of the prison was torn completely off. The torrents of rain pouring down onto the exposed mud walls made them crumble and melt. The prisoners were free!

Many of the non-Christian prisoners fled. The terrified jailers, convinced that the storm was the direct intervention of God on behalf of the Christian prisoners, came to Toro pleading that he pray to God to withhold His anger and fury —and they would be released. The jailers kept their word.[10]

Of course, not every person imprisoned for his faith is freed by an act of God, but these two incidents show that God is still at work as He was in the lives of the first-century believers. He never changes! You can count on Him!

> WE NEED GOD'S PERSPECTIVE ON THE EVENTS OF LIFE—HE SEES IT IN WAYS WE DO NOT.

PRAISING GOD FOR HIS UNCHANGING NATURE

When you fly from Chicago to Los Angeles on some airlines you will fly over one section of the Grand Canyon. If you happen to fly over it during the late afternoon sun, the canyon's shadows help you see the incredible depth and breadth of it. But the fact remains—you are seeing only a small segment of it, for it runs well over a thousand miles. Now imagine yourself circling the Earth in the Mir space station and you come over the Grand Canyon. How much of it will you see now? All of it in one glance.

When we look at life on Earth, we see only a minute sliver of it, one minuscule slice of eternity. But God sees all of eternity at once, the end from the beginning. That is why we need God's perspective on the events of life—He sees it in ways we do not. As a result He can take corrective action to keep us from wandering off course or hurting ourselves as we march through life's parade of circumstances and events.

What a great God we have! We can trust Him not to turn against us, for His love is unchanging. We can trust Him for life after death, for He is eternal. That is why the writer of Hebrews could say: "Jesus Christ is the same yesterday, today, and forever."[11]

That is the God we worship and adore—and serve unconditionally. It is the God we proclaim to the entire world without ceasing, for He is worthy not only of our worship but also our obedience to His Great Commission to go and to love.

St. John Chrysostom, a third-century church leader, wrote of His Lord and Savior:

> It is fitting and right to sing of you, to praise you, to thank you, to adore you in all places of your dominion. For you are the ineffable God, inconceivable, invisible, incomprehensible, existing forever and yet ever the same, you and your only-begotten Son and your Holy Spirit. You brought us into being out of nothingness, and when we had fallen, you raised us up again. You have not ceased doing everything to lead us to heaven and to bestow upon us your future and your only-begotten Son and your Holy Spirit. You do this for all the benefits of which we know, for those of which we are ignorant, and for those that are manifest to us and those that lie concealed.[12]

I urge you to take time to enjoy the wonder of God's attributes. As you learn more facts about His greatness, thank Him, glorify Him, and praise Him for all He means to you. Let the Holy Spirit fill your mind with His love and grace, and touch your deepest feelings with His comfort and gentleness. The more you worship and meditate on His attributes, the more you will become like Him. Worship Him through giving, serving, praising, singing, and giving thanks. That is the sure road to developing an intimate relationship with God!

LIFE APPLICATION

EXALT YOUR GOD—Worship God with the powerful words of the hymn *Immortal, Invisible.*

> Immortal, invisible, God only wise,
> In light inaccessible, hid from our eyes.
> Most blessed, most glorious, the Ancient of Days,
> Almighty, victorious, Thy great name we praise.
>
> To all, life Thou givest—to both great and small;
> In all life Thou livest, the true life of all;
> We blossom and flourish as leaves on the tree,
> And wither and perish—but naught changeth Thee.

REFLECT HIS IMAGE—By nature, we, as humans, change. We grow older, taller, thinner, or fatter, and our emotions fluctuate. But we can reflect God's unchanging nature by being people who are consistent—in our relationships and in our love for God. Examine your heart and ask God to make you a person who perseveres no matter what, a person who, as Jesus said, "stands firm to the end" (Matthew 10:22, NIV).

SHARE HIS MAJESTY—Jesus stated in Matthew 24:35, "Heaven and earth will disappear, but my words will remain forever." The Bible has encouraged and challenged individuals for thousands of years, and still speaks to us today. With whom can you share God's unchanging word? Choose a verse that has spoken to you and use it to encourage someone today.

CHAPTER 27

GOD GIVES US REST IN HIM

D o you ever wish time would stand still? Has your neighborhood changed, or a loved one grown distant or passed away? Have dear friends moved away?

One of the hardest changes for a parent is when children grow up, move away, and become independent. I remember the day that Vonette and I helped our older son, Zac, settle into his dorm room at Life Bible College in Los Angeles. Later we helped our younger son, Brad, pack his car to leave home and drive across the country to Washington, D.C. to work for Senator William Armstrong from Colorado.

Before each of our sons left home, we got down on our knees together to thank God for him and pray for his safety. When we rose, we embraced and expressed our love. Of course, as parents, we always had a few last-minute instructions. My eyes misted as I silently thanked God for each of my boys.

As Brad drove away toward Washington, D.C., Vonette and I waved valiantly. I forced a smile and stemmed my tears. *My little boy isn't little anymore*, I thought as his car disappeared around a bend. *He's on his own now.*

I treasure the heartwarming memories of Zac and Brad when they were young and in our home. Vonette and I will always love our sons, and look forward to spending time with them whenever possible. Today we still miss them as much as when they left home. As many of you know, the "empty nest" syndrome that comes when your last child leaves home is very real.

But our boys are independent adults now. They do not need us like they did when they were young. Of course, I would not wish for them to come back because they have lives, families, and ministries of their own. Some of the memories of separations are erased with our delight in visiting with our grandchildren. Yet we will never forget the emotionally difficult change we experienced when each of our sons left home.

Today, we live in a time of hyper-change. Fashions and trends change weekly; people relocate frequently; technological advances quickly make the past obsolete. A way of life that was once familiar and comfortable to us rapidly fades away. This change produces a great deal of stress. As we search for stability, we wonder if there is any permanence anymore. Is there some anchor that will hold us so we will not be swept away by the waves of change washing over society?

There are several reasons we are drawn into the undercurrents of change. For one, sin and our fallen nature promote a process of decay and deterioration. Things get progressively worse when left to themselves. You can understand that if you have ever had to maintain an old house. The water heater needs replacing; the screen door comes off its hinges; the roof leaks.

Another reason we change is because we experience pressure from others or from our circumstances. We change well-laid plans because of illness or because a family member is in crisis and needs help. An airline goes on strike so our flight is canceled. All kinds of events make us modify what we want to do.

A third reason is because of boredom. We do not want every day to be exactly the same as the last. A little spice and variety make life more enjoyable.

Also, technological achievements and other kinds of improvements stimulate change. Computers have dramatically altered the way we do things. Seldom do we mail a package of important papers. Now we can e-mail a file or fax the pages immediately. Everyone expects instant turnaround time.

But the influences that cause change in our lives have no effect on God. Let us look at several benefits we enjoy because God never changes.

GOD'S UNCHANGING NATURE PROVIDES STABILITY

A story is told of a shipwrecked sailor who clung to a rock in great danger until the tide went down. Later a friend asked him, "Didn't you shake with fear when you were hanging on the rock?"

He simply replied, "Yes, but the rock didn't."

Life and its uncertainties may shake us, but God—who is the Rock of Ages—does not move. If we cling to Him, His strength sustains us.

Since God never changes,[1] God's character is constant. Unlike us, He does not compromise or change His values. He cannot be manipulated or persuaded to go against His word. He does not have a Dr. Jekyl and Mr. Hyde personality where He will comfort us one moment and snap at us the next.

GOD'S UNCHANGING PURPOSE GIVES US ETERNAL SIGNIFICANCE

Psalm 33 states, "The LORD'S plans stand firm forever; His intentions can never be shaken."[2] God's plan existed at the beginning of creation and remains the same today. It unfolds in phases and stages, which may give us the impression of change, but His original design has always been consistent. God's purposes for us are fulfilled within the framework of time and history.

The nation of Israel is the clearest example of this truth. The Lord declared to the people of Israel, "Everything I plan will come to pass, for I do whatever I wish…I have said I would do it, and I will."[3] From the day God placed Adam and Eve in the Garden of Eden, God's hand has been leading and guiding His people.

And we are part of His plan! We share His purpose. Paul wrote to the believers in Ephesus, "For we are God's masterpiece. He has created us anew in Christ Jesus, so that we can do the good things He planned for us long ago."[4] We no longer need to feel as if we are unimportant in the cosmos. As God's people, we are His loved ones whom He has planned from the beginning to bless and to live with forever!

GOD'S UNCHANGEABLE WAYS ASSURE US OF UNWAVERING GUIDANCE

In the early 1960s, President Kennedy challenged NASA to send a man to the moon. The man in charge of that seemingly impossible assignment was a marvelous Christian and a dear friend. He told me that they had nothing to build on except the unchanging laws of God's creation. Imagine the frustration had God's laws of science, physics, and creation not been dependable. That is where the scientists started, and sure enough—the impossible mission happened on schedule!

Just as the natural laws of the universe never change, God's principles for life never change. David writes, "As for God, His way is perfect. All the LORD'S promises prove true."[5] Following His guidelines, given in Scripture, will produce fruitful lives. Not only that, He assures us that His Holy Spirit living inside us will complete what God has begun in our lives. As I look back over the events of my life, I can clearly see how God has guided me in ways that produced what He intended even when it was impossible for me to accomplish. All He required was my availability and willingness to do what He asked of me.

For example, in 1945, as a new Christian I had a dream to produce a film about the life of our Lord. I was hoping to finance the film with the profits from my business. I was long on zeal, but short on practical knowledge.

At that time, our ministry did not have the funds to produce such an ambitious project. Yet for more than 33 years, our board of directors, the staff, and I discussed the need for a film on the life of Christ which could be used as an evangelistic tool. We reviewed more than thirty films, but most of them were not scripturally accurate. We even seriously considered buying the rights to one of these films and reworking it to make it biblically accurate. But we were never able to raise the huge amount of money for the production costs. Yet I still believed that God wanted me to complete this project.

Then in 1976, I met John Heyman, a movie producer who had produced more than thirty feature-length films. I introduced John to Paul Eshelman, our U.S. Field Ministry director who later headed the *JESUS* film project. A few months later, Bunker and Carolyn Hunt, long-time friends and generous supporters of the ministry, agreed to provide financing for the film. God began to fulfill the dream that He had placed in my heart over three prior decades.

> WE ARE HIS
> LOVED ONES
> WHOM HE HAS
> PLANNED FROM
> THE BEGINNING
> TO BLESS.

Accuracy and authenticity were crucial as a team of researchers painstakingly produced a 318-page document giving the biblical, theological, historical, and archeological background of every scene as presented by the Gospel of Luke. During the filming in Israel, John Heyman demanded excellence. For example, he once stopped the cameras when he noticed a ripple-soled tennis shoe print in the dust. But excellence was what we needed to produce a film that could touch the world.

We prayed that the *JESUS* film would become a mighty evangelistic instrument to introduce millions to God. When the filming and production were completed, *JESUS* opened in America in the fall of 1979 in Warner Brothers theaters. By the end of the commercial run a year later, more than four million people had seen the film. From the beginning, however, we planned that *JESUS* would go beyond American shores. We developed a strategy to bring the film to urban centers, rural areas, islands, mountaintop villages, and countries where electricity is a rarity.

To date, more than two thousand *JESUS* film teams have been sent to remote villages and great metropolitan areas. You can imagine the excitement when a team begins to set up its equipment in places where people have never had the opportunity to view a movie, particularly in their own language.

As of April 1, 1999, *more than 2 billion people in almost 500 languages in 225 countries have viewed JESUS.* Hundreds of millions have responded with salvation decisions. God has used our thousands of staff and volunteers, almost 1,000 mission organizations, and tens of thousands of local churches of many denominations to introduce people to Jesus through this film.

God demonstrated His unchanging faithfulness when He began to work in me through a vision to fulfill His purposes.[6] Then 33 years later He brought together the resources and personnel to make the dream come true. I am sure you can point to many instances in your life where God's guidance, true to the unchanging principles of His Word, made a huge difference in your life and ministry and the lives of others. We can depend on His guidance every day of our lives if we continue to trust and obey Him.

GOD'S UNCHANGING WORD EQUIPS US WITH TIMELESS TRUTH

God does not change what He says based on opinion polls or focus groups. His words and commands are timeless. They are valid throughout all eternity. They apply to every culture, race, and nationality.

That is why the Bible has remained relevant throughout the ages and to all civilizations. What God says is always pertinent. It never becomes obsolete. His timeless truth is the surest foundation for anything we attempt.

Almost to a man, the founding fathers of our nation sought to serve and glorify Jesus Christ with their lives. One study found that of 15,000 writings by the founding fathers included in newspaper articles, pamphlets, books, monographs, and other documents, 94 percent of all quotes either directly or indirectly cited the Bible.[7] Fifty-two of the 55 framers of the Constitution were avowed biblical Christians. They were inspired by God to dedicate this new republic for His honor and glory. Even the curriculum of the institutions of higher learning used the Bible as a textbook. The efforts of our founding fathers produced miraculous results. The United States Constitution is currently the oldest operating document of any government in the world. Every other nation on earth has instituted a new form of government since our founding documents were written. The U.S. Constitution is unlike any other political instrument because the liberties it guarantees are greater than the liberties granted to the citizens of any other nation. And all this resulted in God's unchanging principles, which provided the timeless truths for our governing documents.

Abraham Lincoln, our 16th President and the man who guided our country through a civil war, stated, "I believe the Bible is the best gift God has given to man. All the good Savior gave to the world was communicated through this Book."[8]

Former President Ronald Reagan, a devout believer from his youth, declared on numerous occasions that if only the American people would "live closer to the Commandments and the Golden Rule," the problems we face would be solved.[9] As you know, the Ten Commandments and the Golden Rule are basic principles from God's Word. Tragically, we are now reaping the consequences of a society that has abandoned biblical truths. Yet as we each base our lives on His Word, we will see the joy and blessing that come from living according to God's unchanging truths.

God's Unchanging Commitment Guarantees Us Everlasting Security

Recently, I stood at the grave sites of two dear friends, and as I reflected on their lives, I realized that the most important moment we can experience is our death. When we breathe our last earthly air and take our first breath of the celestial, we transition into the presence of God! This life on earth is but a prelude to eternity. My friends had no fear of crossing over, for they knew the reality of God's unwavering faithfulness to them.

Hebrews states, "God also bound Himself with an oath, so that those who received the promise could be perfectly sure that He would never change His mind."[10] We who have given ourselves to God through the death and resurrection of Jesus Christ have received eternal life. God is committed to our redemption, our Christian walk, and our eternal destiny. God's unchanging nature assures us that we will indeed live with Him forever as He promised. God's commitment is as strong as He is constant. No one and nothing can violate His promise: "[The Holy Spirit's] presence within us is God's guarantee that He really will give us all that He promised."[11] We can bank our entire future on His unchanging character. What a sure anchor for our faith!

> GOD ALTERS
> HIS TEMPORARY
> PURPOSES IN
> RESPONSE TO
> OUR FAITH
> AND ACTIONS.

Perhaps you are thinking: *If God never changes, what is the purpose of prayer and other communication with God?* I want to caution you about using God's immutability as an excuse not to pray or to ask Him to intervene in your daily life. Although He will never change His plans, Scriptures abound that show how God alters His temporary purposes in response to our faith and actions. For example, He reverses His judgment because of sincere repentance of sinners.[12] At other times, He responds to the needs of human beings or the fervent prayer of the righteous.[13] This is one of the mysteries of God's nature. We know that God never changes, and yet He relates to us and gives us our free will. When we pray and ask Him to intervene in our lives, He does so—when it is in line with His will. He works through us as we walk and talk with Him. So I encourage you to take comfort in the fact that God never changes; but realize that when we seek His face in repentance, we can expect Him to respond to our prayers and deal with our sin.

Now that we have discovered many facets of God's character, how will our knowledge affect our lives? Intimacy with God requires changes on our part. It also means that we will give God the praise and adoration He deserves. This is where our study of

God's attributes will really bring blessings to our lives, including lasting joy, peace, fruitfulness, and confidence. In the conclusion to this book, you will find helpful suggestions on how you can cultivate a healthy fear of God and become transformed by His majesty.

LIFE APPLICATION

WRITE IT ON YOUR HEART—Commit the following statement and verses to memory. Then as you encounter situations during this week where you need to remember that God never changes, claim these promises by faith.

- Because God never changes, my future is secure and eternal.

- James 1:17—"Whatever is good and perfect comes to us from God above, who created all heaven's lights. Unlike them, He never changes or casts shifting shadows."

- Hebrews 13:8—"Jesus Christ is the same yesterday, today, and forever."

COUNT ON GOD—Paul writes in Philippians 1:6, "I am sure that God, who began the good work within you, will continue His work until it is finally finished on that day when Christ Jesus comes back again." Because God never changes, He will never change His mind, go back on His word, or leave unfinished what He has started. Every day He is molding you, maturing you, and preparing you to spend eternity with Him—and He will complete what he has begun. What promise can you claim for an area of your life where you know God is helping you change? Use your Bible concordance to find a promise and claim it for your situation.

OBEY GOD—God's standards do not vacillate based on the latest fads or opinion poll. Society's perception of right and wrong may be different from what it was just a generation ago, but this does not alter the truth. Take God's commands seriously in an area where His Word contradicts society's beliefs. Ask God to help you confirm your stance in this issue.

PART IV.

CONCLUSION

*"Oh, that they would always have
hearts like this, that they might fear
Me and obey all My commands!
If they did, they and their descendants
would prosper forever."*

DEUTERONOMY 5:29

CHAPTER 28

CULTIVATING A HEALTHY FEAR OF GOD

I grew up on my parents' ranch in Oklahoma where my father had a reputation of being one of the best ranchers in the county. Nobody could ride horses like he could. He taught my four brothers and me how to ride wild broncos. Although I learned how to feel comfortable and secure around those big horses, my father raised me to always have a healthy respect for them. I knew that if I was not careful around those powerful wild horses from Montana, I could easily be hurt or even killed if I did something foolish.

As boys growing up on a ranch, we often swam in the lakes and rivers in our county. Once, when I was about 6 or 7 years old, I ventured out into a lake far away from my brothers and friends. Suddenly, my energy gave out and I started to sink. As I went down for the third time, my older brother and one of his friends pulled me out of the water and helped me get my breath. I could have easily drowned that afternoon. Since then, I have had a respect for swimming alone in deep water.

When I was a teenager, my father and uncle taught me how to drive an automobile. I remember the thrill I experienced as I sat behind that steering wheel, stepped on the accelerator, and felt the surge of power thrust me down the country road. Once again, my parents instilled in me a healthy respect, this time for the automobile. I could have been injured or even killed if I acted foolishly behind the steering wheel of that car.

We naturally fear and respect things that have great power or that can alter our lives in the fraction of a second. We treat these things much differently than we do the ordinary objects or people in our lives.

What about God? He is the sovereign Creator and Ruler of our universe. We have glimpsed His power, holiness, and justice. How much respect should we have for Him?

In His Word, God commands us to fear Him. When the Lord was giving the children of Israel the Ten Commandments, He spoke to them from the heart of the fire on Mount Sinai. The people were greatly frightened because they understood they were in the presence of their awesome Creator God. He commanded them to fear Him.[1]

This is only one of many places throughout the Bible where God's people are instructed to fear God. But what does fearing God really mean?

When I approached one of those wild broncos, I did so with caution. I made sure the horse knew where I was and what I was going to do. When swimming in deep water, I carefully follow safe swimming rules. As I drive a car, I observe traffic laws, including speed limits. I do not recklessly hurtle down a freeway at 100 mph, because I realize that my reaction time and inability to control the car at those speeds could cause a horrible accident.

These illustrations are demonstrations of the respect and fear I have for things more powerful than I am. That is part of what it means to fear God.

WHAT DOES IT MEAN TO FEAR GOD?

God is not some hateful warlord who desires to do us harm. He is not reckless or foolish in the use of His great power and limitless abilities, so we will never become random victims of His lack of control. He is not a spooky, hideous creature who hides in the darkness to scare us when we least expect it. These are some of the reasons we normally fear someone. But that is not the kind of fear God is talking about. The psalmist records, "The LORD delights in those who fear Him, who put their hope in His unfailing love."[2] When the Scriptures tell us to fear God, it means we are to have awe, reverence, and respect for our magnificent God.

The following explanation, from *Hard Sayings of the Bible*, helps us to understand the phrase "fear the Lord":

> The term for *fear* can describe everything from dread, or being terrified, to standing in awe or having reverence. When used of the Lord, it applies to both aspects of the term, a shrinking back in recognition of the difference or holiness of God and the drawing close in awe and worship. It is an attitude of both reluctance and adoration that results in a willingness to do what God says. The fear of the Lord, then, is absolutely necessary if we are even to begin on the right foot in learning, living, or worshiping.[3]

WHY SHOULD WE FEAR GOD?

The relationship between little children and their parents may help us grasp this kind of fear. As a child, I had a loving relationship with my parents and was very close to them. Yet I was very aware that my parents were much bigger and stronger than I was. I knew that if I contradicted their rules I was powerless against them, because my parents had great authority over me. They could give or take away privileges. They expected me to behave within predefined boundaries or face the consequences.

God wants us to approach Him in the same way—with an attitude of humility, submissiveness, and a sense of respect. I believe this is one of the reasons God calls Himself our heavenly Father and us His children. We all cringe when we see tiny children sassing their parents or ignoring their requests. It is against the order of things to see children act that way. How can we behave that way toward God? We must treat Him with the greatest respect as our ultimate authority and guide.

The Word of God states, "The fear of the LORD is the beginning of wisdom, and knowledge of the Holy One is understanding."[4] Here are three reasons why we should fear God.

God Is Infinitely Superior to Us

The ancient scribes who performed the laborious task of copying the Holy Scriptures had a practice that illustrated their respect for God. When they were about to write the name of the Lord, they stopped their work and performed ceremonial washing. Then, with their clothes and body clean, they would take up a new writing utensil and carefully pen God's holy name.

What a contrast their example is to how many people treat God today. God's name has become a swear word, and even those of us who claim to serve Him often speak His name flippantly and without respect. Now that you understand more about God's character, you also understand why this is such an affront to God.

God's abilities eclipse anything we could ever think or do. He is infinitely great, and we are so small. When we stand on a beach and gaze out on the ocean, its vastness overwhelms us. Those waves can easily overpower a swimmer with their undercurrents. They can destroy houses and anything else in their path. Yet God is infinitely more powerful than all the waves in all the earth's oceans —even the super-currents generated by hurricanes and typhoons. The contrast between God's omnipotence and our impotence is beyond our ability to even imagine.

God is also infinitely perfect, and we are so imperfect. He is without any fault, without any blemish, and without any deficiency. In contrast, we have innumerable shortcomings. Compare the sight of the entire countryside covered with the purity of newly fallen snow to the slush of a tiny, dirty mud puddle. The difference between God's perfection and our imperfection is infinitely greater.

Yet with all His power and perfection, God is supremely committed to His people who are so fickle in their commitment to Him. When we consider the depth of His love for us—the magnitude of the sacrifice He has made for us, the plans and desires

He has for our eternal future—and compare that with our natural self-centered tendencies, the contrast is beyond our understanding.

Dear friend, I urge you to take a few moments to consider the immeasurable gulf between you and God. With all you now know of His superiority, does it not make you tremble at your own insignificance? At the same time, when you think of how much He loves us, tiny microscopic mites on planet Earth, does it not cause great respect for Him to well up in your heart? Keep this attitude of humble submission and respect close to you throughout your days as you serve Him.

God Has Supreme Authority Over Us

Most tyrants and dictators have been recluses who had no personal relationship with the people of their countries. God's authority over us, however, is revealed in His personal relationship to us. As we have seen, His authority comes from His three primary roles: Creator, Judge, and Savior. Let me briefly recap these areas.

As our Creator, God personally designed us and gave us life. As our Maker, He is totally justified in doing whatever He wishes with us, for He knows what is best for us.

How can we shake our fists at our Designer? How can we presume to know ourselves and run our lives better than He can? It is not possible. We are completely dependent on His omniscience and omnipresence for every moment of our being.

As Perfect Judge, God determines our eternal future. He has the authority to condemn us to eternal damnation or allow us to live in His glorious presence forever and ever, depending on our response to Him.

If we lived under the dictatorship of a supreme human ruler, we would have a clearer understanding of what it means to submit to someone greater than we are. When a dictator proclaims a law, everyone must obey without excuse or argument. If the dictator is benevolent, people prosper; if he is harsh, the people suffer. We have a God who is more than benevolent, He is perfectly just and loving. How much more should we submit to Him out of respect for His authority!

As our Redeemer, God freed us from slavery. We have been purchased with a price, and now belong to Him. First Corinthians
6:19,20 reminds us, "You do not belong to yourself, for God
bought you with a high price." He bought us with His blood and
now He has total authority over us in a beautiful love relationship.

We would deeply respect a friend who gave his most prized
possession for our welfare. Think of someone who would sell an
irreplaceable piece of jewelry that had been handed down for
generations to pay a debt you incurred and could not repay. How
would you feel about this person? Jesus paid our sin-debt with His
blood! How much more deeply should we love and respect Him!

God Blesses Those Who Reverence Him

Clearly, God is worthy of our reverence and awe simply because of
who He is. When we fear Him, the Bible promises bountiful
rewards: "The love of the LORD remains forever with those who
fear him" (Psalm 103:17); "Fear of the LORD gives life, security,
and protection from harm" (Proverbs 19:23); "Those who fear
the LORD are secure; He will be a place of refuge for their children" (Proverbs 14:26); "He will be the sure foundation for your
times, a rich store of salvation and wisdom and knowledge; the
fear of the LORD is the key to this treasure" (Isaiah 33:6, NIV).

God does not want us to be cowering slaves; we are His beloved children. On the other hand, it is wrong to treat our all-
powerful, infinite Maker as though He were our casual friend or
the "Man Upstairs." Even the Son of God revered His heavenly
Father. Jesus said, "I do nothing on My own, but speak what the
Father taught Me...For I always do those things that are pleasing
to Him."[5] God's magnificence demands respect; His position
demands honor; His holiness demands praise.

DO YOU HAVE A HEALTHY FEAR OF GOD?

Years ago, many Christians were known as God-fearing people.
What has happened to our Christian culture for us to lose that
distinction?

Over time we developed a distorted view of who God is and

lost our sense of reverence, respect, and fear of Him. Instead of seeing God as our sovereign Ruler, He is more commonly viewed as our "buddy" or "pal." Instead of recognizing Him as our awesome Creator and holy Judge, we relegate Him to the position of a peer. We have become too casual with God, even in our places of worship. In the past we referred to such places as holy sanctuaries, houses of prayer, or altars where the glory of God came down upon His people. Today, we have lost even the sense of the presence of the holy, awesome God among us when we come together to praise, worship, and learn about Him.

Fearing God arises out of a conscious commitment to give God the honor He deserves. This attitude must be cultivated in our daily lives. To do so, ask yourself the following questions:

"Do I have a reverential awe of God?" Certainly, your heart soars when you gaze up at the massive ceiling of a cathedral, at the stars on a clear night, or when you stand at the foot of a snowcapped mountain. How much more should we be overcome by a sense of wonder when considering God who created over 100 billion galaxies by merely speaking them into existence!

> WE HAVE BECOME TOO CASUAL WITH GOD, EVEN IN OUR PLACES OF WORSHIP.

Let the thought of our magnificent Creator move you to worship Him in the magnitude of who He is and how far He surpasses anything we could ever begin to imagine with our puny, finite minds. Make it a practice to take time out of each day to meditate on God's glory and to praise Him. Use your favorite worship music or commune with God in the beauty of nature. Look through the Life Applications in this book to find verses that can help you praise and worship God. Or note Scripture passages that mean a lot to you as you read your Bible, then meditate on them later.

"Do I desire to please God more than people?" If you do not, then you lower God to a human level. The world values appearance,

wealth, and position. God values a heart that is right with Him. To whose voice are you listening? If what others think is more important to you than what God thinks, what does that say about the authority and importance He has in your life?

To give God preeminence in your life, spend more time with Him. That may be as simple as talking to Him during your daily routine. Thank Him for the small blessings He gives you. For each decision, big or small, ask Him what He would have you do. Desire to please Him even in the small details of your life. As you do, your intimacy with God will grow and you will allow God to have first place in your life.

"Do I have a hatred for sin and evil?" God detests sin. The Bible says, "Don't be impressed with your own wisdom. Instead, fear the LORD and turn your back on evil. Then you will gain renewed health and vitality."[6]

What is your attitude about wickedness, sin, and evil? Do you find yourself tolerating it? Do you view it as not being so bad—especially the sin you commit?

God expects us to oppose those things that He opposes. A good rule to follow is to love what God loves and hate what God hates. Evaluate your life to see what you might be harboring that God detests. Perhaps it is a superior attitude toward people who are different. Or maybe you have a love for something, such as money, a car, or your position, that is greater than your love for God. Each of us has areas that give us trouble. Ask God to help you see the sin in your life for what it is and to help you break the patterns of evil-doing. This is a life-long process. But God will be faithful to deliver you from all sin.

Most of all, spend time in God's Word reading how Joseph, Moses, David, Daniel, Mary, Paul, and others exhibited a healthy fear of God. Remember His promise, "As high as the heavens are above the earth, so great is His love for those who fear Him."[7]

Once we begin cultivating a healthy fear of God, we will see amazing changes in our lives. God will begin doing things that we never dreamed possible. In our concluding chapter, we will discover how intimacy with God will transform our very lives!

CHAPTER 29

TRANSFORMED BY HIS MAJESTY

W hat difference are these new insights about God making in your life? God encourages us not just to listen to the Word but to follow through and do what it says.[1] Otherwise, we are like the ship's officers on the *Titanic,* who were warned by a nearby ship that icebergs had been sighted, but did nothing with the information. Because they did not act on this knowledge, the great ship struck an iceberg and sank, sending thousands to a watery grave. Truly, knowledge without action is worthless.

We are accountable to God for what we know. We must be careful to fully apply the truth He has given us and allow it to transform our lives. Only then will we experience God's best in our lives and become all God intended us to be.

The truth about God will transform your life. Paul explains the process of transformation:

> I plead with you to give your bodies to God. Let them be a living and holy sacrifice—the kind He will accept. When you think of what He has done for you, is this too much to

ask? Don't copy the behavior and customs of this world, but let God transform you into a new person by changing the way you think. Then you will know what God wants you to do, and you will know how good and pleasing and perfect His will really is."[2]

How foolish for any of us to get in the way of God as He lovingly works out His will in our lives. This chapter presents six ways to open up your heart to God and apply the truths you have learned about His majestic character to your life. You may have already begun applying them as you worked through the Life Application at the end of each chapter. The following sections will provide a more complete look at God's attributes to enable us to transform our lives.

1. Write It On Your Heart

What we hear and what we read can easily be forgotten unless we make an effort to remember. Spend time meditating on and memorizing Scripture passages that give insight into who God is and how He wants to be involved with you. Vonette and I regularly meditate on these thirteen statements related to each of the attributes presented in this book:

- Because God is a personal Spirit, I will seek intimate fellowship with Him.
- Because God is all-powerful, He can help me with anything.
- Because God is ever-present, He is always with me.
- Because God knows everything, I will go to Him with all my questions and concerns.
- Because God is sovereign, I will joyfully submit to His will.
- Because God is holy, I will devote myself to Him in purity, worship, and service.
- Because God is absolute truth, I will believe what He says and live accordingly.
- Because God is righteous, I will live by His standards.
- Because God is just, He will always treat me fairly.

- Because God is love, He is unconditionally committed to my well-being.

- Because God is merciful, He forgives me of my sins when I sincerely confess them.

- Because God is faithful, I will trust Him to always keep His promises.

- Because God never changes, my future is secure and eternal.

We had those statements printed on a laminated card that fits inside a shirt pocket or purse. We carry the cards with us wherever we go. Throughout the day as we have an opportunity, we pull out those cards and meditate on how wonderful God is.

Many times when I awaken in the middle of the night, I ponder those principles and praise God for His glorious attributes. Vonette and I often pray about these principles as we take walks together. These statements remind us of how God is at work in our current circumstances. In fact, I offered my grandchildren small awards for memorizing them. I know nothing that will help them more than a basic understanding of who God is and how they should relate to Him. You may wish to do the same with your children and grandchildren. (For more information on the *GOD: Discover the Benefits of His Attributes* card, see the end of this book).

In addition to memorizing these statements, I encourage you to select meaningful Scripture passages from previous chapters and commit them to memory. Nothing will transform your thinking more than memorizing the Word of God.

2. Exalt Your God

Make worshipping God for who He is and the great things He has done a regular part of your devotional time and your Sunday routine. Here are several ways to do this:

- Consider His marvelous attributes one at a time, thanking and praising Him for His magnificent qualities.

- Select hymns and praise songs that focus on God's attributes and honor Him by singing them to Him as an offering of worship. Some people enjoy singing the words of Scripture, making up their own tunes as they go.

- Study the many names of God in the Bible and praise Him for each one. Each name reveals a different role God exhibits among His people and reflects His glorious nature. For names of our marvelous Lord, see Appendix C.

3. Trust in God

Trusting someone means we are willing to commit our concerns to that person. What we entrust may be a secret, a struggle, some valuable asset, or even our family. Certainly by now you must realize that there is no one more trustworthy than God.

> OUR LOVING FATHER WANTS US TO ACT IN A WAY THAT IS CONSISTENT WITH WHO WE ARE.

People often fail us because they are unable to do what they said they would do. This is never the case with God. Sometimes people make promises they never intend to keep. But our God is completely honest in keeping all His promises. Perhaps a person has failed you because he or she was too busy, or only half-heartedly promised to do something. You can be assured that God is always willing to help. Someone has aptly written, "When you don't understand, when you can't see His hand, you can trust His heart." Because of His perfect attributes, you can always trust God.

Are you in a difficult situation right now? Keep your eyes focused on Him and His magnificent character qualities instead of becoming preoccupied with your circumstances. Always remember that God is bigger than any problem you may have.

The storms of life are constantly changing, but God remains the same. He is consistent and reliable. He is our anchor. Do not permit yourself to become distracted. Whatever your problems, whatever your circumstances, keep your eyes on Jesus instead of your problems. The more you grow in your relationship with

God, the easier it will be to trust Him with everything.

4. Obey God

With every command from God there is an expressed or implied promise to enable us to do what He commands us to do. God gives us commands to protect us from harm and to provide for our well-being. Every command that God gives us is consistent with His nature and a reflection of who God is. His laws are not intended to keep us from finding happiness or having a good time in life. Quite the contrary. His laws are the guardrails that keep us on the road to a happy, fulfilled, and satisfied life for all eternity.

If you are a typical Christian, your biggest problem is not that you do not know God's commands, but that, for whatever reasons, you are selectively obeying them. Surrender your will completely and irrevocably to God. Do not allow your prideful, worldly desires to create a rebellious spirit toward God. Humble yourself before Him and depend on the Holy Spirit to help you obey God completely.

5. Reflect His Image

When I think of reflecting God's image, I turn to 2 Corinthians 3:18, which says that God wants us to "be mirrors that brightly reflect the glory of the Lord. And as the Spirit of the Lord works within us, we become more and more like Him and reflect His glory even more."

God is certainly concerned with what we do, but He is even more concerned with what we are becoming. He is in the process of making us more and more like His Son. The more clearly we understand what our Triune God is like, the clearer picture we have of Jesus Christ and the character qualities God is in the process of instilling in us.

Since we are children of God, our loving Father wants us to act in a way that is consistent with who we are. As members of His royal family, when we serve Him, our actions are consistent with His glorious calling and commission on our lives.

6. Share His Majesty

Are you excited about the new things you have learned about God's magnificent nature? Do His greatness, holiness, and gracious love captivate you? Which truths have been the most life-changing to you? Now ask yourself: How can I possibly keep quiet about my new experiences with God?

Certainly you would tell others about a great book you just read, an entertaining movie you saw, or a fabulous restaurant, museum, or concert you enjoyed. How much more eager should you be to introduce people to this wonderful God who lives inside you! Look for opportunities to tell others about God's majestic qualities. Focus your thoughts on God and remain alert to what He is doing in the world around you. Do not be afraid or intimidated into silence, but speak freely to anyone who will listen about your understanding of God and what He is doing.

If someone does not know this wonderful God personally, use your conversation as a springboard to tell them how they can have a relationship with Him. Simply share with them Appendix A, "How to Know God Personally."

As you tell fellow believers what you have learned of God's attributes, they will rejoice with you. You will encourage them in their walk of faith.

AN ENCOUNTER WITH MAJESTY

It is my prayer that these insights into the magnificent character of our awesome God will become the sparks for igniting revival in your life. As His power, holiness, justice, mercy, and love become more real to you, your life will be changed forever.

The transformation of the disciples from weak, frightened followers to bold, authoritative proclaimers of the gospel was due to a promise Jesus made to reveal Himself to each one of them.[3] He also promised to give them supernatural power to preach the gospel and live overcoming lives through the gift of the Holy Spirit.[4] God wants to do the same for us today! He desires to have a close, warm, confidential, and continuing relationship with each of us—to which no human relationship can compare.

What if your life radiated the very nature of God to all around you? If you allowed God to live out His love, mercy, faithfulness, and righteousness through you, imagine what a difference it would make in your family, church, neighborhood, and work place. And what if others in your church were also impacted in this way? Just think how your church could change and what effect would this have on your community and the world at large!

There is only one word that can describe the result—revival. Revival always begins with a renewed view—a right biblical view —of God. But revival starts at the heart of the matter—our sin, disobedience, and pride.[5] Then it spreads as we hunger for God and begin to worship Him with clean hands and pure hearts.[6] This leads to renewed minds and spiritual eyes to see the awesome character and nature of our great God. The more time you spend with God, the more you will get to know His magnificent attributes and the more you will reflect the radiance of God's presence to those around you.

Will you invite God to begin a transforming work in you?

THE RADIANCE OF GOD'S PRESENCE

One of the most dramatic changes I have ever heard in a person's life happened just a few miles from Campus Crusade for Christ's headquarters in Orlando, Florida. It is the story of Jesse Blocker. Jesse had his first taste of alcohol at the age of eight. By age fourteen, he was an alcoholic. By age thirty-six, he was a hopeless drunk and drug user living on the streets. But God had another plan for Jesse's life.

One night after getting drunk at the ABC Lounge, he passed out on the railroad tracks. Several days later he awoke in the hospital with both legs missing and one arm mangled courtesy of a passing freight train. The believers at Pine Castle United Methodist Church heard about Jesse's tragic accident and began to pray for this desperate man. The church is in view of the lounge and the scene of the accident. Hospital visits availed little as Jesse let everyone know unmistakeningly about his views of God and his vow never to darken the doors of a church again. He resented these "pretty" people with their fine clothes, cars, and neat little children.

After his release from the hospital, Jesse went back to drinking. Why not? He felt his life was over—no legs, no home, no future, and no hope. He would often sit in his wheelchair at the corner of the Pine Castle UMC property holding a sign saying he would "work for food," conning anyone who came by. This pitiful sight of a man with matted long hair, disheveled clothes, and a dirty face and hands moved many churchgoers to give him a few bucks. Before most of them got home from church, Jesse had wheeled himself down to the lounge to buy just enough liquor to drown his pain one more time. Satan had Jesse bound and imprisoned in a hell on earth not too far from a fiery eternity.

One Sunday night, the Holy Spirit moved in a special way at Pine Castle. The altar was crowded with men and women crying out to God for forgiveness and revival. After several hours, one of the prayer warriors, Delores Kagi, slipped out to take a friend home. As they left the church they saw Jesse sitting at the street corner, drunk as usual with his sign collapsed over his lap. She felt led to talk to him, but instead, decided to take her friend home first. She reasoned with herself that if Jesse was still there when she returned, she would bring him into the church.

When she returned, Delores approached Jesse asking what she could do for him. He asked for a bowl of soup. She brought him the soup and stayed with him until he finished eating. Afterwards the dazed alcoholic offered no resistance when Delores wheeled him into the church and up to the altar. Those still praying at the altar gathered around Jesse and his wheelchair. After intense prayer for his salvation and deliverance, they gave Jesse a Bible and left that night with faith that God would answer their prayers for him. But Jesse continued to drink.

His family considered him not only a threat to himself, but also to others. So they petitioned a judge to order Jesse to a treatment center. The judge agreed and sent a U.S. Marshall to pick up Jesse and take him to a detoxification center for help. Because the processing took so long for those ahead of him in the line,

Jesse quietly slipped out of the building unnoticed. With a few dollars in his pocket, he headed for a liquor store, a decision that launched a thirty-day drinking binge.

Jesse became suicidal. Several days later, he and a friend were drinking on the pier at Lake Conway. Jesse tried to commit suicide by rolling himself off the pier. As he was sinking to the bottom of the lake, he said he saw the gates of hell open and felt the heat of the lake of fire. He cried out to God and said, "Dear Lord God, in the name of Jesus…" The next thing he remembered was his drinking buddy pulling him out of the murky water and struggling to get him up on the dock. Dripping wet and smelling of alcohol, he raced his wheelchair to the Pine Castle church with those scenes of hell searing his mind. The Wednesday night service was in progress as he rolled into the sanctuary and up to the altar. The church people gathered around praying and laying their hands on him as he wept his way to repentance and forgiveness.

The next morning a U.S. Marshall again picked up Jesse taking him to the Orange County Jail. While Jesse sat in his cell, God allowed him to review his entire life and relive those times of desperation when he cried out to God with all his heart. He saw that God had been there for him all those times. God began to soften Jesse's hardened heart, making it pliable like clay on a potter's wheel. There our loving Savior with His tender hands began to mold and reshape the broken life of Jesse Blocker.

> WHAT AN HONOR TO HAVE OUR ALL-POWERFUL GOD LIVE HIS GLORIOUS NATURE THROUGH YOU!

God loved Jesse so much that He arranged for Leon, an inmate and new believer, to be Jesse's cell mate. Leon began to disciple Jesse, helping him read the Gospel of John three times. The precious Word of God came alive as the Holy Spirit opened Jesse's understanding. He saw for the first time that he, Jesse Blocker, could come to know and trust the God who is all powerful, holy, and righteous, yet loving and merciful.

As Jesse progressed through nine months of detoxification, God placed a passion in his heart to reach the homeless, the alcoholic, and the addict with the good news of Jesus Christ.

Jesse began to go to his old friends on the streets and bring them back to his one-room duplex to sober up and to come to Christ. The neighbors began complaining about the drunks hanging around their homes, yet crack houses, prostitutes, and fortunetellers lived all around him. Jesse and his band of converts faced eviction.

Once again the prayer warriors at Pine Castle began to call out to God—this time with Jesse—for a place to bring the lost off the streets where they could get the help they needed. God miraculously provided a house, then another and another, until today there are five homes for men, one for women, and one for couples. The ministry also supports a children's home in a depressed neighborhood.

Jesse became the President of the Foundation for Life whose sole concern is to reach the homeless for Christ, disciple them in the Word of God during a six-month course, and see these men and women restored as godly people working again in the community. More than 300 men and women have gone through the program. What a thrill to see several rows at Pine Castle UMC filled nearly every Sunday morning and evening with men and women who were former street people. And you will always find Jesse sitting in his wheelchair at the end of a row. Recently, the church raised funds to send a busload of "Jesse's men" to a Promise Keeper's event. But the transformation does not stop with spiritual needs. The Foundation for Life helps its graduates find jobs, apartments, rented houses, furniture and appliances, medical treatment, food, and clothing. Daily you can find Jesse and praying believers of Pine Castle UMC combing the streets, woods, and prisons of Orlando sharing hope with the hopeless, deliverance with those in bondage, and provisions for the needy.

Just as the living Christ dramatically transformed Jesse's life, you, too, can find the help to change. Like Jesse, your life can then reflect God's glory shining the light of His great attributes to your world. What a privilege to have our infinite, all-powerful God live His glorious nature through you! Your life will dramatically change, and others will be drawn to our awesome God as they glimpse His glory radiating through your life.

Commit yourself right now to allowing God to transform you by His majesty!

HELPS FOR SPIRITUAL GROWTH

"Everything that was written in the past was written to teach us, so that through endurance and the encouragement of the Scriptures we might have hope."

ROMANS 15:4

APPENDIX A

HOW TO KNOW GOD PERSONALLY

Just as there are physical laws that govern the physical universe, so are there spiritual laws that govern your relationship with God.

LAW 1: *God loves you and offers a wonderful plan for your life.*

God's Love
"God so loved the world that He gave His one and only Son, that whoever believes in Him shall not perish but have eternal life" (John 3:16, NIV).

God's Plan
[Christ speaking] "I came that they might have life, and might have it abundantly" [that it might be full and meaningful] (John 10:10).

Why is it that most people are not experiencing the abundant life? Because...

LAW 2: *Man is sinful and separated from God. Therefore, he cannot know and experience God's love and plan for his life.*

Man Is Sinful
"All have sinned and fall short of the glory of God" (Romans 3:23).

Man was created to have fellowship with God; but, because of his own stubborn self-will, he chose to go his own independent way and fellowship with God was broken. This self-will, characterized by an attitude of active rebellion or passive indifference, is an evidence of what the Bible calls sin.

Man Is Separated

"The wages of sin is death" [spiritual separation from God] (Romans 6:23).

This diagram illustrates that God is holy and man is sinful. A great gulf separates the two. The arrows illustrate that man is continually trying to reach God and the abundant life through his own efforts, such as a good life, philosophy, or religion—but he inevitably fails.

The third law explains the only way to bridge this gulf...

LAW 3: *Jesus Christ is God's **only** provision for man's sin. Through Him you can know and experience God's love and plan for your life.*

He Died In Our Place

"God demonstrates His own love toward us, in that while we were yet sinners, Christ died for us" (Romans 5:8).

He Is the Only Way to God

"Jesus said to him, 'I am the way, and the truth, and the life; no one comes to the Father but through Me'" (John 14:6).

This diagram illustrates that God has bridged the gulf that separates us from Him by sending His Son, Jesus Christ, to die on the cross in our place to pay the penalty for our sins.

It is not enough just to know these three laws...

LAW 4: *We must individually **receive** Jesus Christ as Savior and Lord; then we can know and experience God's love and plan for our lives.*

We Must Receive Christ

"As many as received Him, to them He gave the right to become children of God, even to those who believe in His name" (John 1:12).

We Receive Christ Through Faith

"By grace you have been saved through faith; and that not of yourselves, it is the gift of God; not as a result of works that no one should boast" (Ephesians 2:8,9).

When We Receive Christ, We Experience a New Birth

(Read John 3:1–8.)

We Receive Christ Through Personal Invitation

[Christ speaking] "Behold, I stand at the door and knock; if anyone hears My voice and opens the door, I will come in to him" (Revelation 3:20).

Receiving Christ involves turning to God from self (repentance) and trusting Christ to come into our lives to forgive our sins and to make us what He wants us to be. Just to agree intellectually that Jesus Christ is the Son of God and that He died on the cross for our sins is not enough. Nor is it enough to have an emotional experience. We receive Jesus Christ by faith, as an act of the will.

These two circles represent two kinds of lives:

Self-Directed Life
S – Self is on the throne
† – Christ is outside the life
● – Interests are directed by self, often resulting in discord and frustration

Christ-Directed Life
† – Christ is in the life and on the throne
S – Self is yielding to Christ
● – Interests are directed by Christ, resulting in harmony with God's plan

Which circle best represents your life?

Which circle would you like to have represent your life?

The following explains how you can receive Christ:

You Can Receive Christ Right Now by Faith Through Prayer

(Prayer is talking with God)

God knows your heart and is not so concerned with your words as He is with the attitude of your heart. The following is a suggested prayer:

> *Lord Jesus, I need You. Thank You for dying on the cross for my sins. I open the door of my life and receive You as my Savior and Lord. Thank You for forgiving my sins and giving me eternal life. Take control of the throne of my life. Make me the kind of person You want me to be.*

Does this prayer express the desire of your heart? If it does, I invite you to pray this prayer right now, and Christ will come into your life, as He promised.

How to Know That Christ Is in Your Life

Did you receive Christ into your life? According to His promise in Revelation 3:20, where is Christ right now in relation to you? Christ said that He would come into your life. Would He mislead you? On what authority do you know that God has answered your prayer? (The trustworthiness of God Himself and His Word.)

The Bible Promises Eternal Life to All Who Receive Christ

"God has given us eternal life, and this life is in His Son. He who has the Son has the life; he who does not have the Son of God does not have the life" (1 John 5:11,12).

Thank God often that Christ is in your life and that He will never leave you (Hebrews 13:5). You can know on the basis of His promise that Christ lives in you and that you have eternal life from the very moment you invite Him in. He will not deceive you.

An important reminder...

Do Not Depend on Feelings

The promise of God's Word, the Bible—not our feelings—is our authority. The Christian lives by faith (trust) in the trustworthiness of God Himself and His Word. This train diagram illustrates the relationship among fact (God and His Word), faith (our trust in God and His Word), and feeling (the result of our faith and obedience). (Read John 14:21.)

 The train will run with or without the caboose. However, it would be useless to attempt to pull the train by the caboose. In the same way, as Christians we do not depend on feelings or emotions, but we place our faith (trust) in the trustworthiness of God and the promises of His Word.

Now That You Have Received Christ

The moment you received Christ by faith, as an act of the will, many things happened, including the following:

- Christ came into your life (Revelation 3:20; Colossians 1:27).
- Your sins were forgiven (Colossians 1:14).
- You became a child of God (John 1:12).
- You received eternal life (John 5:24).
- You began the great adventure for which God created you (John 10:10).

Can you think of anything more wonderful that could happen to you than receiving Christ? Would you like to thank God in prayer right now for what He has done for you? By thanking God, you demonstrate your faith.

To enjoy your new life to the fullest...

Suggestions for Christian Growth

Spiritual growth results from trusting Jesus Christ. A life of faith will enable you to trust God increasingly with every detail of your life, and to practice the following:

G *Go* to God in prayer daily (John 15:7).

R *Read* God's Word daily (Acts 17:11); begin with the Gospel of John.

O *Obey* God moment by moment (John 14:21).

W *Witness* for Christ by your life and words (Matthew 4:19; John 15:8).

T *Trust* God for every detail of your life (1 Peter 5:7).

H *Holy Spirit*—allow Him to control and empower your daily life and witness (Galatians 5:16,17; Acts 1:8; Ephesians 5:18).

Fellowship in a Good Church

God's Word instructs us not to forsake "the assembling of ourselves together" (Hebrews 10:25). If you do not belong to a church, do not wait to be invited. Take the initiative; call the pastor of a nearby church where Christ is honored and His Word is preached. Start this week, and make plans to attend regularly.

APPENDIX B

HOW TO BE FILLED WITH THE HOLY SPIRIT

Every day can be an exciting adventure for the Christian who knows the reality of being filled with the Holy Spirit and who lives constantly, moment by moment, under His gracious direction.

The Bible tells us that there are three kinds of people:

1. **Natural Man:** One who has not received Christ.

    "A natural man does not accept the things of the Spirit of God; for they are foolishness to him, and he cannot understand them, because they are spiritually appraised" (1 Corinthians 2:14, NASB).

    Self-Directed Life
    S – Self is on the throne
    † – Christ is outside the life
    ● – Interests are directed by self, often resulting in discord and frustration

2. **Spiritual Man:** One who is directed and empowered by the Holy Spirit.

    "He who is spiritual appraises all things" (1 Corinthians 2:15, NASB).

    Christ-Directed Life
    S – Christ is in the life and on the throne
    † – Self is yielding to Christ
    ● – Interests are directed by Christ, resulting in harmony with God's plan

319

3. **Carnal Man:** One who has received Christ, but who lives in defeat because he trusts in his own efforts to live the Christian life.

"I, brethren, could not speak to you as to spiritual people but as to carnal, as to babes in Christ. I fed you with milk and not with solid food; for until now you were not able to receive it, and even now you are still not able; for you are still carnal. For when there are envy, strife, and divisions among you, are you not carnal and behaving like mere men?" (1 Corinthians 3:1–3).

Self-Directed Life

S – Self is on the throne

† – Christ dethroned and not allowed to direct the life

● – Interests are directed by self, often resulting in discord and frustration

The following are four principles for living the Spirit-filled life:

1 God has provided for us an abundant and fruitful Christian life.

"Jesus said, 'I have come that they may have life, and that they may have it more abundantly'" (John 10:10, NKJ).

"The fruit of the Spirit is love, joy, peace, patience, kindness, goodness, faithfulness, gentleness, self-control; against such things there is no law" (Galatians 5:22,23).

Read John 15:5 and Acts 1:8.

The following are some personal traits of the spiritual man that result from trusting God:

- Love
- Joy
- Peace
- Patience
- Kindness
- Faithfulness
- Goodness

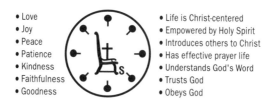

- Life is Christ-centered
- Empowered by Holy Spirit
- Introduces others to Christ
- Has effective prayer life
- Understands God's Word
- Trusts God
- Obeys God

The degree to which these traits are manifested in the life depends on the extent to which the Christian trusts the Lord with every detail of his life, and on his maturity in Christ. One who is only beginning to understand the ministry of the Holy Spirit should not be discouraged if he is not as fruitful as more mature Christians who have known and experienced this truth for a longer period.

Why is it that most Christians are not experiencing the abundant life?

2 Carnal Christians cannot experience the abundant and fruitful Christian life.

The carnal man trusts in his own efforts to live the Christian life:

- He is either uninformed about, or has forgotten, God's love, forgiveness, and power (Romans 5:8–10; Hebrews 10:1–25; 1 John 1; 2:1–3; 2 Peter 1:9).
- He has an up-and-down spiritual experience.
- He wants to do what is right, but cannot.
- He fails to draw on the power of the Holy Spirit to live the Christian life (1 Corinthians 3:1–3; Romans 7:15–24; 8:7; Galatians 5:16–18).

Some or all of the following traits may characterize the carnal man—the Christian who does not fully trust God:

- Legalistic attitude
- Impure thoughts
- Jealousy
- Guilt
- Worry
- Discouragement
- Critical spirit
- Frustration

- Aimlessness
- Fear
- Ignorance of his spiritual heritage
- Unbelief
- Disobedience
- Loss of love for God and for others
- Poor prayer life
- No desire for Bible study

(The individual who professes to be a Christian but who continues to practice sin should realize that he may not be a Christian at all, according to 1 John 2:3; 3:6–9; and Ephesians 5:5.)

The third truth gives us the only solution to this problem…

3 Jesus promised the abundant and fruitful life as the result of being filled (directed and empowered) by the Holy Spirit.

The Spirit-filled life is the Christ-directed life by which Christ lives His life in and through us in the power of the Holy Spirit (John 15).

- One becomes a Christian through the ministry of the Holy Spirit (John 3:1–8.) From the moment of spiritual birth, the Christian is indwelt by the Holy Spirit at all times (John 1:12; Colossians 2:9,10; John 14:16,17).

  All Christians are indwelt by the Holy Spirit, but not all Christians are filled (directed, controlled, and empowered) by the Holy Spirit on an ongoing basis.

- The Holy Spirit is the source of the overflowing life (John 7:37–39).

- In His last command before His ascension, Christ promised the power of the Holy Spirit to enable us to be witnesses for Him (Acts 1:1–9).

How, then, can one be filled with the Holy Spirit?

4 We are filled (directed and empowered) by the Holy Spirit by faith; then we can experience the abundant and fruitful life that Christ promised to each Christian.

You can appropriate the filling of the Holy Spirit right now if you:

- Sincerely desire to be directed and empowered by the Holy Spirit (Matthew 5:6; John 7:37–39).
- Confess your sins. By faith, thank God that He has forgiven all of your sins—past, present, and future—because Christ died for you (Colossians 2:13–15).
- Present every area of your life to God (Romans 12:1,2).
- By faith claim the fullness of the Holy Spirit, according to:

  His command: Be filled with the Spirit. "Do not get drunk on wine, which leads to debauchery. Instead, be filled with the Spirit" (Ephesians 5:18).

  His promise: He will always answer when we pray according to His will. "This is the confidence we have in approaching God: that if we ask anything according to his will, he hears us. And if we know that He hears us—whatever we ask—we know that we have what we asked of Him" (1 John 5:14,15).

How to Pray in Faith to be Filled With the Holy Spirit

We are filled with the Holy Spirit by faith alone. However, true prayer is one way of expressing your faith. The following is a suggested prayer:

> Dear Father, I need You. I acknowledge that I have been directing my own life and that, as a result, I have sinned against You. I thank You that You have forgiven my sins through Christ's death on the cross for me. I now invite Christ to again take His place on the throne of my life. Fill me with the Holy Spirit as You commanded me to be filled, and as You promised in Your Word that You would do if I asked in faith. I pray this in the name of Jesus. As an expression of my faith, I now thank You for directing my life and for filling me with the Holy Spirit.

Does this prayer express the desire of your heart? If so, bow in prayer and trust God to fill you with the Holy Spirit right now.

APPENDIX C

NAMES OF GOD

God is called by many names in the Bible. These names hold an important key to understanding the doctrine of God and His revelation to His people. The truth of God's character is focused in His names. His names express various aspects of His nature, character, and never-changing relationship to His people. Following are some of His names and their meanings.

Adonai – Lord or Master, denoting ownership. (Psalm 39:7; 54:4; 71:5; 73:28; 86:5; 86:12; 86:15; 140:7; Isaiah 6:8; Ezekiel 18:25; Luke 6:46.)

El – A generic term for God or deity. (Psalm 22; Mark 15:34.)

Elohim – The strong, faithful One; the only true God. (Genesis 1:26.)

El-Elyon – The Exalted One and all others are below Him; the Most High God. (Numbers 24:16; 2 Samuel 22:14; Psalm 18:13; Isaiah 14:12–15; Daniel 7:27.)

El-Olam – Eternal, perpetual, everlasting; the Everlasting God. (Genesis 9:16; 17:8; 21:33; Exodus 40:15; Deuteronomy 33:27; Proverbs 10:25; 45:17; Jeremiah 20:11; 31:3; Daniel 4:3; Habakkuk 3:6; John 3:16; 2 Thessalonians 1:8,9; Hebrews 5:9.)

El-Roi – To see, to perceive, understand, and know; the God who sees. (Psalm 139:1,2,7; John 5:19.)

El-Shaddai – Most powerful in strength; the Almighty God. (Genesis 17:1,2; Exodus 6:3; Job 40:2.)

Immanuel – God with us. (Matthew 1:23; Galatians 4:4,5.)

Jehovah – I AM, or self-existence; translated as Yahweh or LORD. (Exodus 3:14,15; John 4:25,26; 8:12, 8:28; 10:9,11,36; 15:1; James 1:17; Hebrews 13:8.)

Jehovah-Jireh – To have regard for the one seen, to see to his every need with provision and care; the Lord our Provider. (Genesis 22:8,14; Hebrews 22:17–19.)

Jehovah-Mekaddesh – To purify, cleanse, and sanctify unto God; the Lord who sanctifies. (Exodus 13:2; Leviticus 19:2; 20:7,8; 25:10; 1 Samuel 2:2; Psalm 103:1; Proverbs 9:10; Isaiah 6:3; John 17:17; Romans 12:1; 1 Peter 1:15,16.)

Jehovah-Nissi – A banner set up on a high place in case of invasion, assembling the people for victory; the Lord our Banner. (Exodus 14:13; 17:15,16; Deuteronomy 20:3,4; Isaiah 13:2–4,11; John 3:14; 16:33; 1 Corinthians 15:57; Ephesians 2:8,9; 6:10–12.)

Jehovah-Rohi – To tend as one cares for sheep; the Lord our Shepherd. (Isaiah 40:10,11; Ezekiel 34:11–16; Psalm 23:1,4; 139:2; John 10:11; Hebrews 13:20; 1 Peter 2:25.)

Jehovah-Rophe – Jehovah who heals; God our healer. (Numbers 12:13; Psalm 103:2,3; Jeremiah 3:22; 30:17,26; Malachi 4:2; Matthew 4:23; 11:4,5; Luke 4:18; John 5:36; Revelation 22:17.)

Jehovah-Sabaoth – An army or warriors who stand and fight against an enemy; the Lord, the captain of our salvation. (1 Samuel 1:3; Jeremiah 11:20; Zechariah 4:6.)

Jehovah-Shalom – Peace; the Lord our Peace. (Numbers 6:24–26; Judges 6:13,23,24; Isaiah 9:6; 26:2–4,12; Matthew 11:28,29; John 14:27; 16:33; Romans 5:1; 15:33; Philippians 4:5–7; Colossians 1:20.)

Jehovah-Shammah – There, in that place, therein; the Lord is there. (Exodus 33:14–16; Psalm 132:8,13,14; Isaiah 63:9; Ezekiel 43:1–7; 48:35; Matthew 28:20; John 1:14; 14:2,3; 1 Corinthians 3:16; 6:17; 2 Corinthians 6:16; Ephesians 2:19–22.)

Jehovah-Tsidkenu – Righteousness, rightness; the Lord our righteousness. (Deuteronomy 32:4; Psalm 89:14; 129:4; Jeremiah 23:5,6; 33:6–26; Daniel 9:7,8; Acts 3:14; Romans 3:20; 5:16–19; 6:11–13,18; 1 Corinthians 1:30; 2 Corinthians 5:21.)

Sources:

Nathan Stone, *Names of God* (Chicago: Moody Bible Institute, 1944).

Trent C. Butler, General Editor, *Holman Bible Dictionary* (Nashville: Holman Bible Publishers, 1991), 1004–1006.

Areon Potter, *From Darkness to Light: Demonic Oppression & the Christian* (Arvada, CO: Adonai Resources, 1994), 222–262.

END NOTES

Chapter 1

1 A. W. Tozer, *The Knowledge of the Holy* (San Francisco: HarperSanFrancisco, 1961).
2 "Karl Marx," *The New Encyclopedia Britannica*, vol. 23 (Chicago: Encyclopedia Britannica, Inc., 1978).
3 James M. Kittleson, "The Breakthrough," *Christian History*, Issue 34, 15.

Chapter 2

1 John 4:24.
2 Isaiah 41:8.
3 Exodus 33:8–11, TLB.
4 Genesis 5:24; 6:9.
5 John 15:15.
6 Numbers 23:19; Genesis 16:13; 1 Kings 8:30.
7 John 17.
8 John 10:30; Colossians 2:9.
9 Colossians 1:18.
10 Romans 8:34.
11 Romans 8:11; John 16:13.
12 John 16:8; 1 Corinthians 2:10.
13 Genesis 1:1.
14 Colossians 1:16.
15 Psalm 104:30.
16 Luke 1:35.
17 Matthew 3:16,17.
18 Acts 2:32.
19 John 10:18.
20 Romans 1:4.
21 1 Peter 1:2.
22 Hebrews 9:14.
23 John 14:15–23.

Chapter 3

1 J. B. Phillips, *Your God Is Too Small* (New York: MacMillan Publishing, 1953).
2 Exodus 3:14, NIV.
3 Psalm 145:1–7, TLB.
4 1 Timothy 1:17, KJV.
5 Revelation 1:17,18, NIV.
6 *Our Daily Bread*, June 11, 1995 (Grand Rapids, MI: RBC Ministries).
7 Isaiah 40:12,13, NASB.
8 Colossians 1:17; Hebrews 1:3.
9 John 16:13.
10 Psalm 63:1.

Chapter 4

1 Psalm 19:1–4, NIV.
2 Pam Beasant, *1000 Facts About Space* (New York: Kingfisher Books, 1992), 10,11.
3 Isaiah 40:26.
4 Psalm 33:6,9; Job 38:4.
5 Romans 1:20.
6 1 Chronicles 29:12, NIV.
7 Ephesians 1:19.
8 Isaiah 40:15.
9 Daniel 4:35, NIV.
10 John 16:11, NIV.
11 Matthew 8:28–32, NIV.
10 Isaiah 46:10.
11 Job 42:2, NIV.
14 Psalm 33:6–9.
15 Tony Evans, *Our God Is Awesome* (Chicago: Moody Press, 1994), 162.
16 Hebrews 1:3.
17 1 Chronicles 29:10,11,13.

Chapter 5

1 Isaiah 40:28,29, TLB.
2 Isaiah 40:30,31, TLB.
3 Isaiah 14:26.
4 Romans 13:1,2.

5 Psalm 66:5,7.
6 Ephesians 1:19,20.
7 Philippians 4:13, NIV.
8 Colossians 1:11, NIV.
9 Galatians 5:16.
10 2 Peter 1:3.
11 Romans 6:1–8; Ephesians 5:18.
12 1 John 5:14,15, NIV.
13 2 Corinthians 12:9.
14 Colossians 1:28,29.
15 Acts 1:8.
16 Ephesians 3:20.
17 David Jeremiah, *Knowing the God You Worship*, audio cassettes (San Diego: Turning Point, 1994).

Chapter 6

1 Jeremiah 23:23,24, NIV.
2 John 3:8.
3 1 Kings 8:27.
4 A. W. Tozer, *The Knowledge of the Holy* (San Francisco: HarperSanFrancisco, 1961), 75,76.
5 Bill Hybels, *The God You're Looking For* (Nashville: Thomas Nelson Publishers, 1997), 24.
6 Website of the U. S. Department of Energy, www.ornl.gov/hgmis/faq/faqs1.html.
7 2 Corinthians 4:6, NIV.
8 Ephesians 5:12,13.
9 Psalm 34:18.
10 In Matthew 28:18–20, Christ gave the Great Commission where He commands His followers to take His message of love and forgiveness to the entire world.
11 John 1:14,18.
12 John 14:16,17, NIV.
13 1 Corinthians 3:16,17, NIV.
14 John 14:17, NIV.
15 Brother Lawrence, *The Practice of the Presence of God* (Pittsburgh: Whitaker House, 1982), 17.
16 Lawrence, 19.

Chapter 7

1 Psalm 139:8–10, NIV.
2 Isaiah 65:24.
3 Psalm 22:1,2.
4 Psalm 22:9,23,24.
5 Corrie ten Boom with John and Elizabeth Sherrill, *The Hiding Place* (Washington Depot, CT: 1971), 197.
6 Matthew 28:20.
7 Judy Nelson, "Golden Opportunities," *Worldwide Challenge*, January/February 1999, 41.
8 Matthew 6:4, NIV.
9 Luke 6:35, NIV.
10 Hebrews 4:13.
11 Brother Lawrence, *The Practice of the Presence of God* (Pittsburgh: Whitaker House, 1982), 38.
12 Ibid., 59.
13 Psalm 32:8, NIV.
14 Isaiah 41:10, NIV.
15 Jim Cymbala, *Fresh Wind, Fresh Fire* (Grand Rapids, MI: Zondervan Publishing House, 1997), 56.
16 David Jeremiah, *Knowing the God You Worship*, audio cassettes, (San Diego: Turning Point, 1994).
17 1 Corinthians 10:13.
18 Psalm 34:18.
19 1 Peter 5:7, NIV.
20 John 15:15.
21 Hebrews 13:5, NIV.
22 Romans 8:38,39.

Chapter 8

1 "Albert Einstein," *Compton's Encyclopedia Online* v. 3.0 (The Learning Company, Inc., 1998).
2 Isaiah 40:13,14, NIV.
3 Romans 11:33.
4 "Computers," *Compton's Encyclopedia Online* v. 3.0 (The Learning Company, Inc., 1998).
5 Ibid.
6 Stephen Charnock, *The Existence and*

Attributes of God, Vol. 1 (Grand Rapids, MI: Baker Books, reprinted 1996), 409.

7   Matthew 11:27.

8   Cited by Marcus Chown in "Let There Be Light," *New Scientist* (vol. 157, February 7, 1998), 30. As quoted in Henry M. Morris, "The Stardust Trail," *Back to Genesis* (no. 121, January 1999), a.

9   Isaiah 46:9,10.

10 Isaiah 43:25,NIV.

11 1 John 1:9.

12 Psalm 33:13–15.

13 Luke 22:31,32, NIV.

14 Deuteronomy 30:3; Isaiah 11:11,12; Jeremiah 23:3,4; Zephaniah 3:20.

15 Psalm 139:1–6.

Chapter 9

1   Matthew 10:30.

2   Isaiah 49:15,16, NIV.

3   Psalm 103:14, NIV.

4   Psalm 37:23.

5   Psalm 103:14.

6   Jeremiah 17:9,10.

7   David Jeremiah, *Knowing the God You Worship*, audio cassettes (San Diego: Turning Point, 1994).

8   Sherwood Eddy, *Pathfinders of the World Missionary Crusade* (New York: Abingdon-Cokesbury, 1945), 125. As quoted in Ruth A. Tucker, *From Jerusalem to Irian Jaya* (Grand Rapids, MI: Zondervan Publishing House, 1983), 239.

9   Acts 2:23.

10 Ephesians 1:4, NIV.

11 James 1:5,6.

12 Hosea 4:6.

13 Proverbs 3:5,6.

14 1 Corinthians 10:13, NIV.

Chapter 10

1   Charles Allen and Sharada Dwivedi,

Lives of the Indian Princes (New York: Crown Publishers, Inc., 1984), 18.

2   Ibid., 211.

3   Anne Edwards, *Royal Sisters* (New York: William Morrow and Company, Inc., 1990), 257.

4   Psalm 24:8–10, NKJ.

5   Revelation 19:1,6,16.

6   Revelation 4:2–11.

7   Daniel 2:21.

8   Jeremiah 18:6.

9   Romans 9:20, NIV.

10 Stephen Charnock, *The Existence and Attributes of God* (Grand Rapids, MI: Baker Books, reprinted 1996) vol. 2, 366.

11 Job 37:6,10–13.

12 Dick Edic, "Miraculous Memory," *Keep InTouch,* Winter 1999, Campus Crusade for Christ Alumni Relations.

13 Psalm 75:7, NIV.

14 2 Kings 24:1–4.

15 Isaiah 45:13.

16 Ephesians 1:5.

17 Ephesians 1:4.

18 Acts 1:8.

19 Romans 14:17; John 18:36.

20 Matthew 6:19–21,24–34.

21 Hebrews 4:15,16.

22 Luke 23:34.

23 A. W. Tozer, *The Attributes of God* (Camp Hill, PA: Christian Publications, 1997), 181.

Chapter 11

1   Isaiah 46:10, NIV.

2   Proverbs 19:21, NIV.

3   James 4:13–16, NIV.

4   Romans 5:12–21.

5   Genesis 3:16–19.

6   Charles Stanley, "Where Our Needs Are Met," audio cassette, (Atlanta, GA: InTouch Ministries).

7   Romans 8:28.

8   1 Peter 5:7.

9   Ephesians 1:9,10.

10 Revelation 21:26–22:5.

Chapter 12

1   Quoted in Max Boot, *Out of Order* (New York: Basic Books, 1998), 176.

2   David Jeffery, "Yellowstone: The Great Fires of 1988," *National Geographic*, February 1989, 265.

3   A. W. Tozer, *The Pursuit of God* (Camp Hill, PA: Christian Publications, 1993), 37.

4   Exodus 15:11.

5   *Nelson Study Bible*, (Nashville, TN: Thomas Nelson Publishers, 1997), 2120.

6   Isaiah 6:1–4.

7   Isaiah 6:5.

8   Stephen Charnock, *The Existence and Attributes of God* (Grand Rapids, MI: Baker Books, reprinted 1996), vol. 2, 112.

9   Louis Berkof, *Systematic Theology* (Grand Rapids, MI: Wm. B. Eerdmans Publishing Co., 1941), 73.

10 Romans 7:12.

11 Jude 4, NIV.

12 Jude 5, NIV.

13 Jude 6, NIV.

14 Matthew 7:12.

15 Joshua 24:19.

16 Proverbs 9:10.

17 Beth Moore, *A Woman's Heart: God's Dwelling Place* (Nashville, TN: Lifeway Press, 1995), 161.

18 Psalm 96:9, NIV.

19 Isaiah 6:7.

Chapter 13

1   Romans 8:1–4.

2   Psalm 2:11.

3   Proverbs 9:10, NIV.

4   Psalm 5:4.

5   Hebrews 10:10,14,18–20.

6   Isaiah 59:1,2.

7   1 Timothy 6:16.

8   1 John 1:5,7.

9   John 8:12.

10 1 Peter 1:15.

11 Romans 12:1,2.

12 Exodus 20:3–5.

13 1 Peter 1:16.

14 Ephesians 5:25–27.

Chapter 14

1   Josh McDowell, *The Myths of Sex Education* (San Bernardino, CA: Here's Life Publishers, 1990), 58.

2   McDowell, 59.

3   George Grant, *Grand Illusions: The Legacy of Planned Parenthood* (Brentwood, TN: Wolgemuth & Hyatt Publishers, Inc., 1988), 30. As quoted in Josh McDowell, *The Myths of Sex Education*, 60.

4   Robert C. Noble, "There Is No Safe Sex," *Newsweek*, April 1, 1991, 9.

5   Lorraine Day, M.D., website "Are You Safe From AIDS? You May Be In for a Big Surprise" (www.drday.com/doctors.htm).

6   *Barna Report, 1997: American Witness* (Dallas, TX: Word Publishing, 1997).

7   George Barna, *What America Believes* (Ventura, CA: Regal Books, 1991), 84–85.

8   Leviticus 18:22; 20:13; Romans 1:24–28; 1 Corinthians 6:9,10; 1 Timothy 1:8–10.

9   Charles Colson, "Neale Donald Walsch: The Words…" *The Wall Street Journal*, July 9, 1997, A12.

10 Exodus 20:14.

11 Numbers 23:19, NIV.

12 Exodus 19:18.

13 Exodus 34:1.

14 John 17:17, NIV.

15 2 Timothy 3:16.

16 John 14:6.

17 John 14:16,17, NIV.

18 John 4:24.

Chapter 15

1 "Interviews from Death Row: Reporter Kathy Chiero's developing relationship with Karla," *CBN Interviews Online*, January 30, 1998, 1.

2 "New Life on Death Row: The Karla Faye Tucker Story," *CBN Interviews Online*, 1,2.

3 1 John 4:5, NIV.

4 Proverbs 12:19.

5 Psalm 119:151,152, NIV.

6 2 Timothy 3:16.

7 Hebrews 10:23, NIV.

8 John 14:3.

9 John 14:12.

10 John 14:27.

11 John 8:44.

12 John 8:12.

13 Hebrews 13:5.

14 Matthew 6:33, NIV.

15 Philippians 4:19, NIV.

16 Matthew 16:25,26.

17 1 Corinthians 6:18.

18 Hebrews 13:4.

19 Exodus 20:14.

20 Luke 12:2.

21 Galatians 6:7, NIV.

22 Ephesians 4:31, NIV.

23 Romans 12:17,19, NIV.

24 Luke 6:27.

25 Jeremiah 17:10, NIV.

26 John 8:31,32.

27 John 10:28.

28 Titus 1:2, NIV.

29 Hebrews 6:16–18.

30 Lisa Master, "Houston, We Have a Problem," *Worldwide Challenge*, July/August 1997, 24.

31 Matthew 16:24,25.

32 1 Corinthians 13:5.

33 Romans 8:15, NIV.

34 Jeremiah 29:11.

35 Ephesians 5:18.

36 1 John 5:14,15.

Chapter 16

1 Millard J. Erickson, *Concise Dictionary of Christian Theology* (Grand Rapids, MI: Baker Book House, 1986), 75.

2 Ibid., 144.

3 Psalm 145:17, NIV.

4 Psalm 71:19, NIV.

5 Psalm 97:2.

6 Jeremiah 9:24, NIV.

7 Robert J. Wagman, *The Supreme Court: A Citizen's Guide* (New York: Pharos Books, 1993), 169–171.

8 Psalm 119:137, NIV.

9 Isaiah 64:5,6.

10 Romans 4:23,24, NIV.

11 1 Thessalonians 5:23,24.

Chapter 17

1 Psalm 116:5, NIV.

2 Romans 3:22–25.

3 Ephesians 4:22–24.

4 Matthew 6:33, NIV.

5 Psalm 5:12, NIV.

6 Henry T. Blackaby and Claude V. King, *Experiencing God* (Nashville, TN: Broadman and Holman Publishers, 1994), 167.

7 Proverbs 14:34.

8 November 11, 1620. William Bradford, *The History of Plymouth Plantation 1608–1650* (Boston, MA: Massachusetts Historical Society, 1856).

9 Quoted in *The New American*, December 12, 1986, 10.

10 Henry Halley, *Halley's Bible Handbook* (Grand Rapids, MI: Zondervan, 1965), 18.

11 October 11, 1798, in his address as President to the Military. Charles Francis Adams, ed., *The Works of John Adams–Second President of the United States* (Boston: Little, Brown, & Co., 1854), 9:229.

12 1828, in the preface to his *American Dictionary of the English Language* (San

Francisco: Foundation for American Christian Education, reprinted 1967), 12.

13 September 5, 1864, addressing the Committee of Colored People from Baltimore, *Washington Chronicle.* Quoted in Stephen Abbott Northrop, D.D., *A Cloud of Witnesses* (Portland, OR: American Heritage Ministries, 1987), 285.

14 October 12, 1816, *The Correspondence and Public Papers of John Jay*, Henry P. Johnston, ed., (New York: Burt Franklin, 1970), 4:393.

15 February 29, 1892, Justice Josiah Brewer, *Church of the Holy Trinity v. United States*, 143 US 457-458, 465-471, 36L ed 226.

16 For more information on how you can get involved in the fasting and prayer movement to be an advocate for righteousness in your area, call (800) 888-FAST (3278). If you want to read more about exciting testimonies like the one about Houston, read my book *The Transforming Power of Fasting and Prayer*. Order by calling *NewLife* Publications at (800) 235-7255.

Chapter 18

1 David Protess and Rob Warden, *A Promise of Justice* (New York: Hyperion, 1998), 222.

2 Jeremiah 17:10, NIV.

3 Robert J. Wagman, *The Supreme Court: A Citizen's Guide* (New York: Pharos Books, 1993), 7,11,12,16,17.

4 Deuteronomy 32:4.

5 *Wycliffe Bible Encyclopedia* (Chicago: Moody Press) 1975, 1:981.

6 Genesis 18:25, NIV.

7 James 4:12, NIV.

8 Quoted in Max Boot, *Out of Order* (New York: Basic Books, 1998), ix.

9 Psalm 7:11, NIV.

10 Psalm 90:8,9,11.

11 1 John 1:9.

12 Ephesians 5:18.

13 1 John 5:14,15.

14 Ecclesiastes 12:14, NIV.

15 Jeremiah 12:1.

16 Galatians 6:7, NIV.

17 Deuteronomy 32:35, NIV.

18 Romans 2:5–8, NIV.

19 Revelation 20:11–15, NIV.

Chapter 19

1 Deuteronomy 32:4, NASB.

2 Judy Nelson, "The Persecuted Church," *Worldwide Challenge*, September/October 1997, 36.

3 Raleigh Washington, "I Would Not Agree to It Because It Was Not True," *Worldwide Challenge*, March/April 1992, 24.

4 Isaiah 5:1–10.

5 Luke 18:3, NIV.

6 Luke 18:5, NIV.

7 Luke 18:7,8, NIV.

8 Robert J. Wagman, *The Supreme Court: A Citizen's Guide* (New York: Pharos Books, 1993), 41.

9 March 30, 1863. James D. Richardson, *A Compilation of the Messages and Papers of the Presidents*, 1789–1897 (Published by Authority of Congress, 1899), 6:164.

10 Merril D. Patterson, ed., *Jefferson Writings* (New York: Literary Classics of the United States, Inc., 1984), 289, from Jefferson's *Notes on the State of Virginia, Query XVIII*, 1781.

11 2 Corinthians 5:10.

12 Matthew 12:36,37.

13 Colossians 3:23,24.

14 Matthew 25:21.

15 Daniel 12:3, NIV.

16 Hebrews 6:10, NIV.

17 Colossians 3:23,24, NIV.

Chapter 20

1   "1969 Woodstock Festival & Concert" (www.woodstock69.com).
2   1 John 4:8.
3   Psalm 100:5.
4   Romans 5:5.
5   Acts 14:17, NIV.
6   Dwight L. Moody, "The Love of God," *Classic Sermons on the Attributes of God*, compiled by Warren W. Wiersbe (Peabody, MA: Hendrickson Publishers), 1989, 12.
7   Luke 19:5, NIV.
8   Ephesians 1:4,5, NIV.
9   John 13:1, NIV.
10 John 13:37,38, NIV.
11 Luke 22:32.
12 Jeremiah 31:3, NIV.
13 1 John 3:1, NIV.
14 Romans 8:38,39.
15 Romans 8:28.
16 Romans 5:1,2.
17 John 14:2,3.
18 Words by Samuel Trevor Francis, 1834–1925, *O the Deep, Deep Love of Jesus*.

Chapter 21

1   1 John 4:16.
2   Matthew 22:37,38.
3   1 John 4:11.
4   Matthew 22:39, TLB.
5   Matthew 5:44, NIV.
6   Richard Wurmbrand, "Love Conquers Everything," *The Voice of the Martyrs*, March 1999, 10.
7   Ibid.
8   John 13:35.
9   2 Corinthians 5:14,15, NIV.
10 Ephesians 3:17,18.
11 Hebrews 11:6.
12 To read more about loving by faith, order my booklet *How to Love by Faith* by calling *NewLife* Publications at (800) 235-7255.

Chapter 22

1   Matthew 5:45.
2   Millard J. Erickson, *Concise Dictionary of Christian Theology* (Grand Rapids, MI: Baker Book House, 1986), 67.
3   Romans 3:23, NIV.
4   Romans 6:23, NIV.
5   Romans 6:23, NIV.
6   1 Peter 2:24, NIV.
7   Isaiah 49:13, NIV.
8   John 8:1–11.
9   Hebrews 12:6,7.
10 Micah 6:8.
11 2 Peter 3:9.
12 David Morris, *A Lifestyle of Worship* (Ventura, CA: Renew Books, 1998), 201.

Chapter 23

1   A. W. Tozer, *The Knowledge of the Holy* (San Francisco: HarperSanFrancisco, 1961), 92.
2   Matthew 18:22.
3   Adapted from Ed DeWeese, "The Right Man to Rob," *Worldwide Challenge*, January/February 1995, 5.
4   Luke 6:35,36.
5   Hebrews 4:16.
6   2 Samuel 12:13,14.
7   Ephesians 4:15.

Chapter 24

1   Jack Canfield (ed.), Mark Victor Hansen, *Chicken Soup for the Soul: 101 Stories to Open the Heart and Rekindle the Spirit* (Health Communications, 1995), 273,274.
2   Lamentations 3:22,23, NIV.
3   Hebrews 11:1.
4   Hebrews 11:11.
5   Genesis 22:13.
6   1 Thessalonians 5:24, NIV.
7   Psalm 119:90.
8   2 Timothy 2:13, NIV.
9   Romans 3:3, NIV.

10 Psalm 105:8, NIV.

11 Corinthians 1:20, NIV.

12 Hebrews 10:23, NIV.

13 2 Corinthians 9:7, NIV.

14 2 Corinthians 9:8, NIV.

Chapter 25

1 Psalm 36:5.

2 1 Corinthians 1:9, NIV.

3 Deuteronomy 7:9.

4 Psalm 143:1, NIV.

5 1 Corinthians 10:13.

6 2 Thessalonians 3:3.

7 1 John 1:9.

8 1 Corinthians 1:7,9, NIV.

9 1 Peter 4:19, NIV.

10 Romans 5:3.

11 Philippians 1:6.

Chapter 26

1 Mark Lehner, "Computer Rebuilds the Ancient Sphinx," *National Geographic*, April 1991, 32–39.

2 Shirley MacLaine, *Dancing in the Light*, 35. As quoted in Josh McDowell and Don Stewart, *Deceivers: What Cults Believe, How They Lure Their Followers* (Nashville: Thomas Nelson Publishers, 1992), 236.

3 Kenneth S. Latourette, *Introducing Buddhism* (New York: Friendship Press, 1956), 4. As quoted in Russell P. Spittler, *Cults and Isms* (Grand Rapids, MI: Baker Book House, 1962), 96.

4 Hebrews 1:11,12, NIV.

5 Exodus 3:14, NIV.

6 James 1:17, NIV.

7 1 John 1:9.

8 Philippians 2:7,8.

9 Genesis 15:6.

10 Raymond Davis, *Fire on the Mountains* (Grand Rapids, MI: Zondervan Publishing House, 1975), 135,136.

11 Hebrews 13:8.

12 "Adoring the Ineffable: Prayers from the Liturgy of St. John Chrysostom," *Christian History*, vol. XIII, No. 4, 38.

Chapter 27

1 James 1:17.

2 Psalm 33:11.

3 Isaiah 46:10,11.

4 Ephesians 2:10.

5 Psalm 18:30.

6 Philippians 2:13.

7 John Eidsmoe, *Christianity and the Constitution*, (Grand Rapids, MI: Baker Book House, 1987), 51,53.

8 Abraham Lincoln, September 5, 1864, in an address to the Committee of Colored People from Baltimore.

9 Ronald Reagan, Gales Quotations CD-ROM (Detroit, MI: Gale Research Inc., 1995).

10 Hebrews 6:17.

11 Ephesians 1:14, TLB.

12 Jonah 3:4–10.

13 Numbers 14:1–20; 2 Kings 20:1–6; Luke 18:1–8.

Chapter 28

1 Exodus 19:17,18; 20:18–20.

2 Psalm 147:11, NIV.

3 Walter C. Kaiser, Jr., et al, *Hard Sayings of the Bible* (Downers Grove, IL: Intervarsity Press, 1996), 284.

4 Proverbs 9:10, NIV.

5 John 8:28,29.

6 Proverbs 3:7,8.

7 Psalm 103:11, NIV.

Chapter 29

1 James 1:22.

2 Romans 12:1,2.

3 John 14:21, Acts 4:13.

4 John 14:15–18; Acts 1:4,5,8.

5 2 Chronicles 7:14.

6 Psalm 24:3–6.

OTHER DISCOVER GOD RESOURCES

GOD: Discover His Character
Bill Bright

"Everything about our lives is determined and influenced by our view of God," writes Bill Bright.

In his thorough but easy-to-grasp new book, *GOD: Discover His Character*, the founder and president of Campus Crusade for Christ—a man whose ministry has impacted millions of lives worldwide—shares the fruit of his personal, lifelong study of God. These wonderful truths are certain to energize your life and walk with God, just as they have his. Through these pages Dr. Bright will equip you with a biblical vision of God. So when you're confused, you can experience His truth. When you're frightened, you can know His peace. When you're sad, you can live in His joy.

Hardcover / 336p / ISBN 1-56399-121-7 / $19.99

GOD: Discover His Character Video Series
Bill Bright

In these 13 sessions, complete on three videos, Dr. Bill Bright will equip you with a biblical vision of God. Each session will fit in a one-hour format, allowing for discussion and personal application. Dr. Bright's clear teaching is illustrated by fascinating dramas and vignettes that bring home the truth of God's attributes in everyday life. This video series, with the accompanying video guide, is ideal for youth, college, and adult Sunday school classes or study groups.

Our Great Creator (Vol. I)
Dr. Bright explores God as all-powerful, ever-present, all-knowing, and sovereign—and how those attributes can give you hope and courage in life.

Video / 150 minutes / ISBN 1-56399-122-5 / $19.99

Our Perfect Judge (Vol. II)
God, your perfect Judge, is holy, true, righteous, and just, and Dr. Bright explains how those characteristics help you to live a righteous life.

Video / 120 minutes / ISBN 1-56399-123-3 / $19.99

Our Gracious Savior (Vol. III)

Dr. Bright introduces you to the God who is loving, merciful, faithful, and unchangeable, and shows how you can experience those awesome attributes every day.

Video / 120 minutes / ISBN 1-53699-124-1 / $19.99

GOD: Discover the Benefits of His Attributes
Bill Bright

God deeply desires that you know Him better. Now there is a full-color, laminated card that can help energize your life and walk with God as you get to know His character. The handy 3" × 5" size is perfect to carry in your pocket or purse, or for sharing with friends.

Card (Package of 10) / ISBN 1-56399-130-6 / $3.99

GOD: 13 Steps to Discovering His Attributes
Bill Bright

In this handy guide, the founder and president of Campus Crusade for Christ International shares the fruit of his personal, lifelong study of God. These wonderful truths regarding God's character are certain to energize your life and walk with God, just as they have his. Keep this condensed booklet in your pocket or purse to read during quiet moments, and experience God's truth and encouragement wherever you go.

Booklet / 32p / ISBN 1-56399-126-8 / $.99

RESPONSE FORM

☐ I have received Jesus Christ as my Savior and Lord as a result of reading this book.

☐ As a new Christian I want to know Christ better and experience the abundant Christian life.

☐ I want to be one of the two million people who will join Dr. Bright in forty days of prayer and fasting for revival for America, the world, and the fulfillment of the Great Commission.

☐ Please send me *free* information on staff and ministry opportunities with Campus Crusade for Christ International.

☐ Please send me *free* information about the other books, booklets, audio cassettes, and videos by Bill and Vonette Bright.

NAME (please print)

ADDRESS

CITY   STATE   ZIP

COUNTRY   E-MAIL

Please check the appropriate box(es), clip, and mail this form to:

Dr. Bill Bright
Campus Crusade for Christ
P.O. Box 620877
Orlando, FL 32862-0877 U.S.A.

You may also fax your response to (407) 826-2149, or send E-mail to newlifepubs@ccci.org. Visit our website at www.newlifepubs.com, www.discovergod.org, and www.rsm.org.

This and other fine products from *NewLife* Publications are available from your favorite bookseller or by calling **(800) 235-7255** (within U.S.) or **(407) 826-2145** (outside U.S.).